Legitimating New Religions

LEGITIMATING NEW RELIGIONS

JAMES R. LEWIS

RUTGERS UNIVERSITY PRESS
New Brunswick, New Jersey, and London

Library of Congress Cataloging-in-Publication Data
Lewis, James R.
Legitimating new religions / James R. Lewis.
p.   cm.
Includes bibliographical references and index.
ISBN 0-8135-3323-6 (hardcover : alk. paper) — ISBN 0-8135-3324-4 (pbk. :
alk. paper)
1. Cults—Psychology.   2. Psychology, Religious.   3. Authority—Religious
aspects.   I. Title.
BP603.L49   2003
200'.9'04—dc21

                                                                    2003005987

British Cataloging-in-Publication information is available from the British
Library.

The publication program of Rutgers University is supported by the Board of
Governors of Rutgers, The State University of New Jersey.

Manufactured in the United States of America

Grateful acknowledgment is made to the L. Ron Hubbard Library for permission
to reproduce the photograph of L. Ron Hubbard on page 91.

Contents

Acknowledgments

This book flows out of two decades of research and writing in the field of new religious movements. As a consequence, so many people have assisted me in so many ways, large and small, over the years that they cannot all be acknowledged without creating a separate chapter. I would, however, like to acknowledge a few of my more significant debts.

First and foremost, thanks to Sarah Lewis and Chris Arthur at the University of Wales, Lampeter, whose input was critical for whatever coherency this work might have. Sarah patiently worked with me chapter by chapter. I did not, however, follow her advice on many points, so I bear full responsibility for any remaining weaknesses.

I am grateful to the folks at the Interlibrary Loan Department at the University of Wisconsin, Stevens Point, Library for the many requests they so graciously fulfilled for me over the course of writing this book. Not the least, I would like to thank my partner and wife, Evelyn. This project was harder to finish than most, and it might never have reached completion without her support.

As someone who takes every opportunity to interact with members of the groups he studies, I have also incurred many debts to informants and officials in certain new religions. It is not possible to acknowledge all of them here. Of these, I owe the most significant debt to Mark Lurie of the Movement for Spiritual Inner Awareness, who patiently answered many questions and corrected many small errors. I am also grateful to members and leaders of Scientology, Eckankar, the Raelian Movement, and the Church Universal and Triumphant for helping me to understand their respective movements. And many thanks to Zeena Schreck and to members of the Obsidian Enlightenment and the Temple of Lylyth for their thoughtful feedback on chapter 6.

Because the present study is in many ways a culmination of almost twenty years of research and writing in the new religions field, it is thus inevitable that it draws from previously published articles. Specifically, an earlier version of chapter 4 was published as "True Lies" in the *Journal of the Society for the Study of Metaphysical Religion* (fall 2000), chapter 6 recently appeared as "Diabolical Authority" in the *Marburg Journal of Religious Studies* (2002), an earlier version of chapter 12 was published as "Sect-Bashing in the Guise of Scholarship" in the *Marburg Journal of Religious Studies* (July 2000), the initial discussion in chapter 3 is drawn from "Shamans and Prophets," which was published in the *American Indian Quarterly* (summer 1988), and chapter 9 is a reworked version of information that originally appeared in two separate articles in *Sociological Analysis:* "Reconstructing the 'Cult' Experience" (summer 1986) and "Apostates and the Legitimation of Repression" (winter 1989).

Finally, the survey research reported in chapters 9 and 10 was supported by grants from the Society for the Scientific Study of Religion and Syracuse University. Support from these sources is gratefully acknowledged.

Legitimating New Religions

INTRODUCTION

Domination [is] the probability that certain specific commands (or all commands) will be obeyed by a given group of persons. . . . [C]ustom, personal advantage, purely affectual or ideal motives of solidarity, do not form a sufficiently reliable basis for a given domination. In addition there is normally a further element, the belief in *legitimacy*.
—Max Weber, *Economy and Society*

Back when I was an undergraduate student, I remember a short discussion from a philosophy class in which we analyzed our fear of standing on the edge of a precipice. The gist of the discussion was that, although we can provide a good rationale for this dread—perhaps we will slip or perhaps a wind will come up that will cause us to trip and fall—the anxiety we feel in these situations nevertheless seems to go deeper than the fear suggested by these reasonable-sounding explanations. When the instructor finally proposed that what we really fear is that some secret part of us will prompt us to jump to our deaths, I had the uncanny feeling he was right.

Controversial new religions have been the focus of my research for the better part of two decades. With a few exceptions, I have not been a critic of such movements. Rather, my scholarship has tended to debunk popular stereotypes. I have, however, come to at least one conclusion with which anti-cultists would agree; namely, every one of us has a secret self that wants to submit to a higher authority, not unlike the secret self that wants to cast us into the abyss. It is this impulse that surfaces under the sway of charisma.

Whenever possible in the course of my field research with new religions, I have sought direct contact with the leadership. Even when surrounded by adoring devotees in highly charged environments, I have never been even remotely impressed by a leader's imputed charisma. If, as Max Weber and later analysts theorized, charisma is socially constructed rather than an inherent characteristic of charismatic leaders, then this is as it should be. Because they are outsiders to the group's social world, academic observers should be completely immune to the magnetic influence of such gurus.

There was, however, one exception to the otherwise uniform uneventfulness of my encounters. Unexpectedly, I stepped into the magical atmosphere of a religious leader's charisma and briefly experienced her as someone of more than ordinary specialness. This leader was Elizabeth Clare Prophet, the spiritual leader of Church Universal and Triumphant. What surprised me then—and what continues to unsettle me to this day—is that I never consciously regarded her as a spiritually elevated individual, much less (as she claimed) the mouthpiece for such figures as Jesus, Buddha, and others. In fact, even at the time, I felt that she was a not particularly sensitive individual with an exaggerated sense of self who over-identified with her guru persona.

Although I am reluctant to discuss it, this experience has come to constitute a kind of touchstone in my reflections on the role of charisma in new religious movements. I will thus lead into my analysis of the legitimation of new religions by describing Church Universal and Triumphant, relating the story of the events that led up to my epiphany and sharing my reflections on this experience.

FIGURE I.1. Elizabeth Clare Prophet, longtime leader of the Church Universal and Triumphant. Courtesy of Church Universal and Triumphant.

CHURCH UNIVERSAL AND TRIUMPHANT

The Church Universal and Triumphant (C.U.T.) is a second-generation splinter of the "I AM" Religious Activity. The "I AM" Activity, founded by Guy Warren Ballard and his wife, Edna W. Ballard, is a popularized form of Theosophy. Mark L. Prophet had been active in two earlier "I AM" splinter groups, the Bridge to Freedom (now the New Age Church of Truth) and the Lighthouse of Freedom. He eventually founded his own group, the Summit Lighthouse, in Washington, D.C., in 1958. In the theosophical tradition, the spiritual evolution of the planet is conceived of as being in the hands of a group of divinely illumined beings—Jesus, Gautama Buddha, and other advanced souls. In the tradition of earlier theosophical leaders, Prophet viewed himself as serving as the mouthpiece for these ascended masters. Elizabeth Clare Wulf joined the group in 1961, eventually marrying Mark Prophet. Over the course of their marriage, Elizabeth Prophet also became a messenger. After her husband's death in 1973, Elizabeth took over his role as the primary mouthpiece for the masters and as leader of the organization.

The headquarters of Summit Lighthouse moved to Colorado Springs in 1966. In 1974, Church Universal and Triumphant (C.U.T.) was incorporated, taking over ministerial and liturgical activities from Summit Lighthouse, which remained the publishing wing of the organization. During the 1970s, the work of C.U.T. expanded tremendously. After several moves within southern California, church headquarters was finally established on the Royal Teton Ranch, in Montana, just north of Yellowstone Park, in 1986. The church also established an intentional community of several thousand people in the surrounding area.

The core beliefs of Church Universal and Triumphant are held in common with other branches of the theosophical tradition. These include the notion of Ascended Masters guiding the spiritual evolution of the planet and certain basic ideas from the South Asian tradition, such as the belief in reincarnation and karma. The church views itself as part of the larger Judeo-Christian tradition, though traditional Christians would not thus classify it.

When "cults" became a public issue in the mid-1970s, Church Universal and Triumphant was not particularly prominent. The group remained a relatively minor player in the cult wars until the move to Montana. As should have been anticipated, the intrusion of a large number of exotic outsiders into a predominantly rural area evoked curiosity and antagonism.

Much of the church's subsequent negative media coverage derived from incidents clustered around its extensive fallout shelters and its preparations for the possibility of a nuclear attack against the United States. At one point in the construction, for instance, fuel was stored in several underground tanks that ruptured and spilled gas and diesel oil into the water table. Also, in 1990 members from around the world gathered in Montana because of the predicted possibility of an atomic holocaust. This story made the front page of the *New York Times* on December 15, 1990, resulting in a flood of reporters from around the world eager for sensationalist stories about a "doomsday cult."

Also, in 1989 two church members—one of whom was Elizabeth Prophet's third husband—attempted to acquire otherwise legal weapons in a nonpublic, illegal manner for storage in underground shelters, providing more fuel for the organization's negative public image as a survivalist group. The motivation for this ill-considered act was to avoid the negative media exposure that would have resulted if members had purchased guns in Montana. The plan, however, backfired and resulted in a public relations disaster. This and other incidents were the basis for later accusations that Church Universal and Triumphant was a potential Waco (Lewis 1998b).

CONTACT AND FIRST IMPRESSIONS

I became involved with Church Universal and Triumphant shortly before the media storm that broke in the wake of the Branch Davidian tragedy. This came about as the indirect result of a deprogramming case. LaVerne Macchio, a church member, was kidnapped in the middle of the night on November 20, 1991, while her four small children looked on in horror. She was released after seven days. Her deprogrammers and kidnappers were eventually indicted and charged with second-degree kidnapping.

In the fall of 1992, I was contacted by Church Universal and Triumphant and asked to testify as an expert witness in the Macchio case. A number of my scholarly articles presented data which undermined the notion that nontraditional religions exercised extraordinary forms of influence over their members. Because the kidnappers were almost certain to invoke the mind control–brainwashing accusation as part of their defense, the prosecution felt it important to have a scholar present who could effectively debunk the idea. Intrigued by the case, I tentatively agreed to participate on the condition that the church bring me and my wife to Montana for a week, put us up at their headquarters, show us everything we wished to see, and allow us to speak with anyone with whom we desired a conversation. Assured that those conditions would be met, we prepared to spend a week in the wilds of Montana.

Anti-cultists have generally regarded the many academics who criticize the cult stereotype—and who, as a consequence, have tended to defend nontraditional religions against unreasonable persecution—as naive and gullible. However, based on my own experience as well as many conversations with colleagues, I can testify that just the opposite attitude is more often case. Scholars of stigmatized religions have a secret fear that they will one day examine a controversial religious group, give it a clean bill of health, and later discover that they have defended the People's Temple, or worse. This anxiety causes them to be, if anything, *more* skeptical than the average observer and to strive even harder for methodological objectivity than they might ordinarily.

Hence, despite my decade-long involvement with alternative religions—a period in which I had found most accusations leveled against Moonies, Hare Krishnas, and so forth to be foundationless—I was still ready to entertain many of the worst charges leveled against Elizabeth Clare Prophet's Church Universal and Triumphant in the mass media. Because much of my own scholarship had been critical of the notion of "cultic mind control," I categorically rejected the idea that the church "brainwashed" its adherents. There were, however, other accusations about which I had serious doubts: Were church members gun-toting doomsday crazies, convinced that the endtime was about to be brought about via an exchange of nuclear weapons? Was Elizabeth Prophet a power-hungry megalomaniac who lived an extravagant lifestyle by exploiting her followers? Was the church an environmentally indifferent community that carelessly dumped fuel oil and raw sewage into the pristine Yellowstone River? In this critical frame of mind, my wife and I flew to Montana in October 1992.

Congruent with my experiences of most other new religions, I found the adult members of the community to be balanced, well-integrated individuals and the children bright and open. Over the course of the week, these impressions were continually reinforced. I had innumerable conversations with intelligent staff members during which we discussed "metaphysical" matters. Because of my status as an outsider studying the church, my conversation partners were often careful to distinguish personal beliefs from doctrines taught by Church Universal and Triumphant. Although the intention behind making these distinctions was to prevent me from accidentally reporting an individual belief as a church belief, these words of caution gave me an invaluable insight into the thought world of members: Although all members adhered to certain basic beliefs, these beliefs were appropriated selectively, allowing room for a wide variance of interpretation and even disagreement. This internal tolerance spoke well for an organization that claimed to receive direct, authoritative revelations from the highest spiritual sources.

There are many incidents from that visit that stand out in my mind—too many to go into here. I was, however, particularly impressed by a relatively minor incident that occurred near the beginning of our visit. While my wife and I were with the two-year-olds during a tour of the ranch's Montessori school, a young toddler walked up to me, looked me over—as if to make some kind of quick evaluation of this stranger in his classroom—turned around, backed up, and plopped himself down on my lap. While I realize that I may be reading more into this incident than it merits, I was impressed. The toddler's action indicated that he was open and trusting—not the kind of behavior one would anticipate from an abused child. He also seemed to be exercising his faculty of discrimination, as if he would not have plopped himself into the lap of just any stranger—only strangers he judged to be "okay" in some way.

The other event that stands out in my mind from the visit was my first meeting with Elizabeth Prophet. Throughout the week, my wife and I had been in many homes, particularly in the Glastonbury area, where members buy land from the church and build their own houses. Many members were quite well off and had constructed homes reflecting their financial status. During October of 1992 when I was at the ranch, Elizabeth, her husband, and one of her adult daughters were living in a small trailer on a tiny lot immediately adjacent to the headquarters complex, and this had apparently been her residence for several years. When my wife and I finally got together with Elizabeth, we found her to be a down-to-earth individual whom we could engage in very ordinary conversation and who, at the time, seemed to be very open to receiving advice.

Again I was very favorably impressed. Had her personal material comfort been uppermost in her mind, Elizabeth could have requested—and I am sure her request would have been honored—to live in better accommodations. However, rather than place undue strain on the church's resources, she was apparently willing to accept humbler circumstances. (It should be noted that she eventually *did* move into a very comfortable home.) She could also have set up our meeting so as to have established and maintained an image of herself as a ruling queen receiving emissaries from the outside world. Instead, she approached us as regular people. During this initial encounter, I did not experience Elizabeth as someone of more than ordinarily specialness.

I should also emphasize that not all of my initial impressions were positive. For example, I developed a distinct distaste for macrobiotic cooking (the only kind of food served in the ranch cafeteria) during that week. And many of the church members I observed appeared mildly unhealthy, a characteristic I attributed to the food. I was also never entirely comfortable with either the members' habit of referring to Elizabeth as "Mother," or with the peculiar rhythmic cadence of her voice whenever she was relaying "dictations" from the ascended masters. I had a similar but stronger reaction to "decreeing," the church's central spiritual practice. Said to purify and transform individuals by attuning them to divine vibrations, decrees are also supposed to bring the power of the divine to bear on earthly matters; for example,

> Let the light flow into my being,
> Let the light expand in the center of my heart,
> Let the light expand in the center of the earth,
> And let the earth be transformed into the new day!
> (Vesta, cited in Lewis 1998b)

For maximum effect, these poetic invocations are repeated as rapidly as possible. My wife and I received special permission to participate in a Sunday morning decreeing session with hundreds of members. It is almost impossible to describe what this is like to anyone who has never experienced it. My impression was that the congregation was simultaneously praying, chanting, and cheering on some kind of cosmic football team. At that moment, I could easily understand how a more skeptical observer in my shoes would have been shaking his or her head at the bizarre ritual behavior of these "brainwashed cultists." Thus while my overall experience during the trip was positive, I also walked away with some less rosy impressions.

As it happened, the kidnapping trial that originally brought me to the ranch was closed to the testimony of outside experts by the presiding judge. I had, however, found the group attractive enough that testifying in the trial was no longer my central reason for wanting to maintain contact with the church. Church Universal and Triumphant was an intrinsically interesting movement. Also, without ignoring the organization's failings, my baseline evaluation was that the leadership and the community were fundamentally *trying to do good*. I thus found myself desiring to return to Montana for a more prolonged visit. In order to accomplish this, I persuaded the church members that they would benefit by having a whole group of academics study them. Church Universal and Triumphant eventually agreed to open its doors to a group of scholars who visited the ranch in the summer of 1993 around the time of the church's major summer conference. (Lewis and Melton 1994)

THEOPHANY

For a number of reasons, we arrived at the conference after it had been underway for several days. During our October visit, my wife, Evelyn, had developed a personal connection with Elizabeth. Following the first evening program we attended, they went off together, leaving me with my academic colleagues. As I would later discover, during their private conversation Evelyn mentioned that I was heavily burdened by anxieties. I eventually caught up with them at Elizabeth's trailer. I was still exhausted from the trip and it was quite late in the evening. I recall briefly sitting in the trailer's living room with Elizabeth, her husband, and my wife, while watching television and talking about incidents from our trip.

It was in this decidedly *un*exotic, low-pressure atmosphere that I first noticed I was regarding Elizabeth somehow differently, though initially I dismissed my state of mind as the natural deference one might have for the head of any large religious organization. When we got up to leave, Elizabeth, in response to the information she had received from Evelyn, performed a quick ritual around me with a ceremonial sword designed to "cut" away troublesome thoughts. I recall feeling somehow honored that she would take the time to focus on my spiritual well-being—though I never subsequently perceived that this "mini-exorcism" had lightened my burden in any way. I also noticed that she seemed to be radiating a tangible "magnetism"—a field of force that marked her off from other people as someone special.

Unwittingly, I had subtly fallen under the spell of charisma. Even at the time, I remember thinking about what I had been taught regarding the social construction of charisma and reflecting that perhaps there were exceptions to this principle—that there might actually be some human beings who were *intrinsically* charismatic. It did not take long, however, for me to be disabused of this notion. Evelyn and I stayed on at the Royal Teton Ranch for the next month. During that time, we gathered a range of new impressions—some negative and some positive, but mostly the later. However, I had a few unsettling encounters with "Mother's" personal failings during our last couple of days on the ranch; these finally let the air out of whatever remained of my inflated sense of her importance.

What, I later asked myself, had allowed me to be drawn into the rarified atmosphere of Elizabeth's charisma, however briefly? Although my experience was profoundly personal and immediate, in hindsight it is not difficult to place in a broader perspective. Unlike some of my colleagues who never bother to actually meet the people they write about, I typically immerse myself in the religious groups I research, fully participating in their practices (when possible) and getting to know members as flesh-and-blood people. Methodologically, this kind of an approach, when properly carried out, constitutes the "participation" aspect of participant-observer research. The explicit goal of such an approach is to be able see the world as if one is a member of the subculture one is studying, to the extent that this is reasonably possible. With respect to Church Universal and Triumphant, I had met a host of likeable, intelligent people who honored Elizabeth Prophet as the mouthpiece for the greatest spiritual teachers in our planet's history. Although they never expressed any but the most muted devotional feelings in my presence, it was easy enough to sense that many were personally devoted to Elizabeth.

I had consciously allowed myself to be drawn into the church's aura, but had not realized that I would thereby come under the sway of certain group attitudes—attitudes that infiltrated my subconscious and began to shape my experiences, however subtly. These forces were at work despite my critical reservations, and despite the commonplace circumstances in which I had fallen under the sway of the power of charisma. (Perhaps the mundane circumstances actually contributed to the experience; I might have raised my defenses in a more "exalted" setting.) One does not need to invoke exotic theories of mind control to explain the social influences at work in this situation, but I found, to my surprise and dismay, that there was a gap between my abstract understanding of these social processes and my concrete experience of the same processes.

In spite of the discomfort of these memories, I am nevertheless grateful for having experienced charisma in something like the manner in which movement participants experience their leader. Within the subculture of a new religion, charismatic leaders possess a luminous, magnetic quality that followers experience as a real force. And although such leaders typically legitimate their teachings in a variety of ways, their personal aura of power is frequently the crucial element that makes everything else "work," especially in the early stages of a movement.

LEGITIMATION

In the 1950s and early 1960s, analyses of social movements tended to focus on explanations of individual participation. By the 1970s, however, attention had shifted away from a preoccupation with what might be called the "micro" level (motives of individual participants), and social scientists began to look at the "macro" level (strategies utilized by movements to accomplish their goals). One of these new perspectives gave particular attention to the human and material resources that movements attempt to tap, and hence was referred to as "resource mobilization theory" (Jenkins 1983).

An important ideological resource for emergent movements, particularly in hostile social environments, is legitimacy. New religious movements actively seek legitimacy. However, scholars of new religious movements have not bothered to analyze the actual notion of legitimation, perhaps because, for the purpose of understanding the groups we study, it appears to be a simple concept. Like many other taken-for-granted ideas, however, there are nuances in legitimacy that easily escape the casual observer. Though it is not difficult to point to concrete examples of legitimation, this concept becomes slippery as soon as one attempts to specify its meaning with precision.

The classic discussion is Max Weber's tripartite schema of traditional, rational-legal, and charismatic legitimations of authority. The dynamics (in the sense of upsetting rather than reinforcing established authority structures) of this schema are largely confined to the factor of charisma, a form of legitimation that Weber viewed as especially—though not exclusively—characteristic of new religious movements. Weber also made it clear that he was discussing ideal types, meaning that in the empirical world one would never be able to find a pure example of charismatic authority. However, no later discussions of charisma have taken the further step of explicitly examining how the other sources of legitimacy analyzed by Weber might be deployed in modified ways by charismatic leaders.

The discussion of the strategies that power elites deploy to maintain their position has consumed a small lake of scholarly ink, not to mention a small forest of trees that sacrificed their lives to the paper industry. In contrast, the analysis of the legitimation strategies deployed by new religions has not moved forward substantially since Weber. Although scholars of new religions use the term freely, no one has published a single article, much less a book, focused on this issue—despite the fact that legitimacy is a core issue for emergent religious movements. The rudimentary state of this topic means that any attempt to extend Weber's discussion in this arena must necessarily be preliminary and exploratory.

Weber's work on the legitimation of authority provides a useful starting point for understanding the legitimation strategies deployed by new religions, but it should immediately be noted that his analysis is also inadequate. For example, in contrast to what one might anticipate from the discussion of charismatic authority in Weber's *Economy and Society* (1968), one often finds new religions appealing to tradition—though the explicit nature of such appeals means that they constitute a variation from what Weber had in mind by the traditional legitimation of authority, which he viewed as largely implicit. Also, when nascent movements attempt to justify a new idea, practice, or social arrangement by attributing it to the authority of tradition, it is through a reinterpretation of the past that they are able to portray themselves as the true embodiment of tradition. Such modifications of his schema indicate that Weber did not have the last word on this issue. In fact, upon closer examination, one finds that contemporary new religions rely upon a wide range of different strategies to gain legitimacy.

One factor contributing to this diversification of strategies is the different audiences the leadership of a new religion must address. In addition to seeking legitimacy in the eyes of followers and potential converts, an emergent movement is often compelled to address the issue of how it is regarded by the larger society—particularly by governmental agencies with the power to disrupt the group. This means that a new religion has at least four different (though overlapping) areas where legitimacy is a concern: making converts, maintaining followers, shaping public opinion, and appeasing government authorities. Also, like the members of any elite (Weber 1968, 953), founders of new religions feel compelled to justify their leadership positions to themselves.

The present study proposes to advance the understanding of legitimacy by discussing a variety of ways in which new religions draw on the authority of charisma, tradition, and rationality. This will be accomplished through the notion of *legitimation strategies*. A provisional list of specific strategies will be drawn up, and a selection of these strategies will then be explicated via a series of case studies in chapters 2 through 8. The complementary idea of delegitimation will be introduced in chapter 9 and will constitute the central theme of the balance of the study.

LEGITIMATION STRATEGIES

Charisma—which, in Weber's use of the term, includes direct revelations from divinity as well as the leader's ability to provide both
mundane and supernatural benefits to followers—may be the key-
stone in a new movement's attractiveness, but charismatic leaders
typically appeal to a variety of other sources of legitimacy. For instance, as has already been mentioned, founders of new religions
often appeal to the authority of tradition. Many modern movements also appeal to the authority of reason and science. Yet another strategy is to appeal to an ancient wisdom or to a primordial
religiosity that antedates current religions.

Despite many areas of overlap, it is useful to view these various
appeals as distinct *legitimation strategies*—though it should immediately be noted that the term "strategy" in this context is *not* meant
to imply that religious founders necessarily set out to design legitimation strategies in the same way business executives develop
marketing strategies or generals develop military strategies. Rather,
in the majority of cases, a new religion's legitimation strategies
emerge more or less spontaneously out of the ongoing life of the
community. Grouping strategies according to Weber's tripartite
schema, *some* of the strategies by which new religions legitimate
their authority are as follows:

I. *Charismatic Appeals*

The "pure charisma" (in the ordinary language sense of this term)
of the leadership.

Evidence that the leader has superior spiritual and/or psychic
gifts (miracles, prophecies).

Evidence that the leader has superior insight and/or wisdom.

Evidence that, under the inspired guidance of the leader, the
group has manifested an attractive, superior community that has
benefited followers in various ways (more loving, healthier, and so
on).

An appeal to direct revelation, in the specific sense that the
leader has received a direct transmission from the sacred, however
conceived. These revelations can lead to the production of new, authoritative scriptures, to the discovery of previously unknown sacred beings and/or to the leader's self-discovery that she or he is

spiritually special. Although any sort of revelation easily leads to the claim that the leader has a unique status as a chosen emissary of the Divine, even in the absence of such revelations the leader can lay claim to a special status, from prophet to avatar.

II. *Rational Appeals*

A direct appeal to reason/rationality.

An appeal to "common sense" or ordinary experience.

An appeal to the authority of science. This particular appeal, which has been highly popular among contemporary new religions, can take a number of different forms, as will be demonstrated in later chapters.

III. *Traditional Appeals*

An appeal to tradition, often reinterpreted to legitimate innovation. Especially in Protestantism, this takes the form of an appeal to the Bible, frequently finding new meanings or new emphases that previous Christians somehow overlooked (for example, Martin Luther).

One can also appeal to the authority of traditional religious figures, attributing new teachings to them that differ from traditional doctrines.

A more ambiguous variation on this strategy is the appeal to an ancient wisdom or a primordial religiosity that antedates current religions. In certain ways this is an appeal to tradition; in other ways it represents a different kind of appeal.

This is not meant to be an exhaustive overview. Rather, this list is simply intended to indicate the variety of possibilities.

The lines of division between these legitimation strategies are often hazy and overlapping. A New Age channeler relaying teachings from "Master Jesus," for example, is simultaneously appealing to the authority of direct revelation and to the authority of a traditional religious figure. Though here merged into a single appeal, it is nevertheless analytically useful to separate them. In this specific case, it is easy to see that the channeler could claim, alternately, that he or she is receiving transmissions from, let us say, a Venusian starship captain. In this case the message would still be authoritative because of its status as a direct revelation, but not because it is coming from a traditional religious figure.

The strategies listed above are directed primarily toward a new religion's immediate audience, namely followers and potential converts. As long as the movement remains small and noncontroversial, efforts to legitimate the group rarely extend beyond this audience. When, however, a conflict arises and attracts enough outside attention to potentially disrupt the ongoing life of a religious community, new kinds of legitimation come into play.

In the context of the contemporary world, such controversies can lead to news media stories that call a nontraditional group's legitimacy into question, especially when reporters begin to describe the group as a "cult." Legal actions such as lawsuits leveled by disgruntled ex-members present both a financial challenge and, at least potentially, a challenge to a movement's legitimacy. Further, highly controversial religions are sometimes subjected to police actions for real or imagined breaches of the law. In such situations, a group can find itself placed in the position of having to defend its status as a legitimate religion. This is especially the case when the other parties in a controversy—angry former members, anticultists, hostile governments, and so forth—seek to tip the scales of power in their favor by attempting to *de*legitimate the movement.

When this happens, the religious group finds itself compelled to address the issue of legitimacy to new audiences—public opinion, law enforcement, judges, and other government officials. In both the law court and the "court of public opinion," the group tries to prove that it is a legitimate religion. Beyond trying to manage its public image and taking certain legal countermeasures, few other options are open to small religious movements.

Though closely related, the notion of a religion's societal legitimacy is somewhat different from Weber's notion of legitimacy. Weber focused on the legitimation of authority in situations where power is exercised over other people. In contrast, the legitimacy new religions seek in the public eye has more to do with social acceptance—rather like the acceptance accorded to a legitimate child (as opposed to an illegitimate child). Relations of power are still involved, of course, but the larger society's recognition of a religion as legitimate means recognizing a religion's status as a genuine religion and thus recognizing its right to exist within the society, rather than recognizing a religion's right to exercise authority over its members.

Critics of new religions seek to persuade society that such religions are illegitimate, meaning they should not be accorded the status of a religion. Many critics would also argue that certain nontraditional or unusual religions should be abolished altogether. In other words, they seek to legitimate the repression of such groups. This represents another variation on Weber's notion: The repressive authority of the government is already recognized as legitimate. So the goal of critics is not to strengthen the legitimacy of the government's police powers, but rather to prompt the government to exercise this power against new religions by convincing the public and the authorities to *reclassify* the religion in question as a pseudo-religion, or even as a criminal organization.

METHODOLOGY AND CHAPTER OUTLINE

Over the course of the following chapters, the concept of legitimacy will be explored in the context of a series of case studies of different religious groups. These case studies will elucidate the issue of legitimacy in new religions by examining how a selection of specific legitimation strategies manifests in concrete situations. Although the focus is contemporary alternative religious movements, many of the issues raised in the discussion can be extended to any religious tradition, particularly those with a historically specifiable point of origin.

I have worked in the field of new religious movements for the better part of two decades. Most of the case studies utilized in these pages have been drawn from groups I have researched in the past. One result of this approach is that I use the Movement for Spiritual Inner Awareness—a group I spent years studying and with which I am intimately familiar—as my primary example in several chapters.

My approach involves a mix of methodologies. Although my primary point of reference is sociological, I also examine legitimation from a religious studies approach that—in the tradition of theorists such as Rudolf Otto (1992), Joachim Wach (1958) and Mircea Eliade (1959)—examines the role religious experience plays in the generation of new religious forms. Additionally, in a number of different places I bring a historical perspective to bear when drawing on comparative data from new religions of earlier periods. In chapters 9 and 10, I include data collected from survey research on former members of controversial new religions (for a brief description of this research, see Appendix B). In chapter 6, I also refer to a survey of religious Satanists (for details, see Appendix A).

I had originally envisioned this book as a series of chapters, each one of which would examine a specific legitimation strategy in the context of a specific case study. When I actually got down to writing, however, it quickly became apparent that this original vision was too artificial to do justice to the complexity of the material. As a consequence, most chapters examine a mix of different legitimation strategies in the life of one or more religious groups.

The book is divided into two major sections. Part 1 surveys the range of strategies used to legitimate new religions. Part 2 examines some of the strategies deployed by critics in their efforts to delegitimate new religions. My original conception of this study was to focus on the various strategies examined in the first section. However, as I got further into it, I found that the issue of legitimacy in contemporary new religions was too closely bound up with the cult controversy to ignore or downplay the impact of this conflict—hence part 2.

After discussing the analysis of religious experience in terms of the approach to religion articulated by the Otto-Wach-Eliade tradition,[1] chapter 2 examines the prophetic consciousness of founders of new religions via a case study of John-Roger Hinkins, the founder of the Movement for Spiritual Inner Awareness. With the exception of less formally organized audience cults and client cults, the principal source of the "prophet motive" is frequently a profound religious experience which legitimates a new religious vision in the mind of the founding prophet.

Chapter 3 carries forward this discussion in the context of Native American prophet religions. In addition to their visions, these prophets drew on familiar themes from their cultural traditions to legitimate their new religious syntheses. The theoretical perspective that portrays the personal charisma of the founder as the "glue" holding together alternate views of reality is also analyzed and critiqued.

Through the legend of Jesus' journey to India, chapter 4 examines the phenomenon of the fabrication of a pseudo-tradition.

Each successive person who perpetuated the Jesus-in-India story was attracted to the legend because the Indian Jesus could be deployed to legitimate their own brand of spirituality.

The appeal to science as a legitimation strategy is the theme of chapter 5. Religious groups like Spiritualism, Christian Science, and Scientology claim they are scientific religions because they model their approach to spirituality after the *methods* of science. In contrast, a prophet such as Rael bases his "atheistic religion" in the secularist *worldview* derived from natural science.

Chapter 6 examines the variety of legitimation strategies deployed in the Satanist tradition founded by Anton LaVey. Like Rael, LaVey appealed to the authority of science in the guise of science's contribution to the secular worldview. Additionally, he appealed to human nature as viewed through the lens of Darwinism. Another legitimation strategy LaVey made use of was to amplify his personal charismatic status by creating an impressive pseudo-biography in which he portrayed himself as an extraordinary individual.

Chapter 7 considers how Heaven's Gate was able to legitimate group suicide. The thrust of the analysis in this chapter is to argue that, from the viewpoint of participants, the teachings of the group, including their final radical act, were plausible—which is a different way of saying that the teachings appeared *legitimate* to participants. The discussion also returns to one of the themes of chapter 3, namely that, rather than relying on charisma as their sole source of legitimation, prophets plant their visions in the fertile fields of pre-existing religious ideas, an approach that allows their new teachings to appear plausible to potential recruits.

Chapter 8 examines two legitimation strategies utilized by the Enlightenment, Western Unitarianism, and the Hindu reformer Ram Mohan Roy: the invocation of the authority of tradition—a tradition reinterpreted so as to legitimate innovation—and the invocation of the image of distant societies or movements, the existence of which appear to reinforce the legitimacy claims of one's own movement.

In the next set of chapters, the discussion shifts to an examination of the delegitimation strategies that characterize the cult controversy. Chapter 9 looks at anti-cult atrocity tales in terms of the common themes that current apostate narratives share with nineteenth-century anti-Catholic and anti-Mormon apostate narratives. These themes, which aim to challenge a religion's legitimacy by portraying it as a pseudo-religion, are analyzed in terms of a deep structure that is derived from the projections of the dominant society.

Chapter 10 takes a roughly comparable approach to the pseudo-disorders of "religious insanity," which supposedly characterized converts to sectarian religion in the nineteenth century, and of "information disease," a supposedly unique psychological disorder caused by prolonged exposure to cultic brainwashing. This strategy challenges a religion's legitimacy by asserting that membership in such a religion induces psychopathology.

One of the issues overlooked by prior analyses of the cult controversy is how particular new religions are drawn into the "cult wars," as well as how the delegitimating power of anti-cult ideology is used in specific conflicts involving individuals and groups who, for the most part, have no interest in the wider anti-cult crusade. Chapter 11 examines some of the conflicts through which a specific new religion—the Movement of Spiritual Inner Awareness—has been drawn into the cult controversy.

Although certain kinds of analyses of religion have been rejected by academia, older patterns of prejudicial scholarship have tended to persist in the subfield of new religious movements. As a consequence, researchers have articulated judgmental points of view that in effect call into question the legitimacy of certain new religions. Chapter 12 analyses this issue through an examination of select scholarship on Soka Gakkai International.

PART I

LEGITIMATING NEW RELIGIONS

RELIGIOUS EXPERIENCE
AND THE ORIGINS
OF RELIGION

1

Religious experience, though related to the wide context in which it appears, is spontaneous, creative, free. This must be emphasized in contrast to all forms of determinism in which religion is viewed as a function, and in contrast to all forms of relativism in which it appears wholly dependent upon environmental factors.

—Joachim Wach,
The Comparative Study of Religions

In April of 1990, I attended the Spring Renewal, a New Age gathering, at a YMCA camp on the northeast side of the island of Maui, at which participants come together to renew their spiritual lives. The basic idea behind such gatherings is not new—the same general notion informed the annual camp meetings that were a part of nineteenth-century Evangelical Protestantism—but in most other ways the activities that take place during Spring Renewal depart markedly from the camp meetings of the past century.

The workshop that had the most personal impact for me took place early in the retreat. The workshop leader began with a discussion of women's repression across the ages and led into an analysis of the tension between the sexes that has been generated as a result of the oppressor-oppressed relationship. As part of this discussion, reference was made to the idyllic, primordial goddess religion that—in this New Age "fall-from-Eden" myth—was supposed to have been the original religion of humankind (before its suppression by males and male deities).

The workshop leader's talk gradually moved from historical generalities to personal specifics, eventually asking us to reflect on how we had hurt, and been hurt by, the various romantic partners we had encountered over the years: Infrequent are the relationships that end on a note of compassion and mutual understanding; far more common are the broken relationships that leave feelings of resentment, guilt, or both. Such feelings linger as emotional burdens that keep us from fully opening to each new experience of love. In an ideal world, he went on to say, we might be able to recontact all of our old lovers and try to effect a better resolution to our broken relationships. But, even if that was logistically possible, it would be unlikely that we would be able to completely heal all of the old bitterness. Such was the gist of the discussion that led up to a group exercise, an exercise I cannot describe with any hope of doing justice to the experience.

We stood up and formed two circles, one consisting of approximately forty males and the other of about the same number of females, and were instructed to successively ask each person of the opposite sex to forgive us and to accept our love. The exercise was quite structured: We held hands and said, "I ask your forgiveness." Our partners responded by saying, "I forgive you." We then said, "I offer you my love," and our partners responded with, "I accept your love." The men first requested forgiveness of all of the women, and then the women requested forgiveness of all of the men. While we went through this exchange, we were asked to try to see the other person as someone of the opposite sex we needed to forgive (relatives as well as ex-lovers) or as someone by whom we wanted to be forgiven. As we were forming the circles, I knew that the exercise would be powerful, but I was not prepared for the intensity of the actual experience.

I tried to bring as much sincerity to each person as I could muster, though at first I had to "act out" the exercise. It was not long, however, before the experience became quite intense. After looking into the eyes of only a few women—people who really seemed to be offering me complete forgiveness—I began to drop some of my psychological barriers. I very quickly found myself genuinely asking for forgiveness for the many times that I had consciously or unconsciously hurt my romantic partners. I do not remember at what point I began weeping, but I do remember that when I reached the camp yoga instructor I let go of the last shreds of my resistance. The instructor herself was red-faced from crying, and the fullness of her sincerity allowed me to feel completely forgiven. Feelings of pain and guilt washed through me, followed by a

wave of forgiveness and love. I felt reborn. The reciprocal experience seemed less difficult. Perhaps it was because I already felt
open, or because I had already been forgiven by every female in the
room, or some combination of these. But at that point I was ready
to forgive all of womankind for every offense, real or imagined,
that its members had ever committed against me.

RELIGIOUS EXPERIENCE AND THE NATURE OF RELIGION

By reflecting on experiences such as my forgiveness exercise experience, we can understand one reason why people join new religions,
which is that many alternative religions hold out the possibility of
life-transforming experiences—experiences that, to a greater or
lesser extent, help one to drop the burden of the past and be reborn into a new and more complete life.

Many mainstream Protestant denominations—Methodists, Baptists, and Presbyterians—once offered the seeker life-transforming
experiences in the context of revivals and camp meetings. But as
these religious bodies settled down into comfortable accommodation with the surrounding secular society, they lost their intensity.
One result of this accommodation was that revivals and camp
meetings—and the accompanying intense religious experiences—
were relegated to quaint and mildly embarrassing chapters in denominational histories.

Those of us who are happily adjusted to the social-cultural
mainstream often have a difficult time understanding intense religiosity. Academics have not been exempt from this tendency. An
earlier generation of sociologists of religion, seemingly obsessed
with the issue of conversion to nonmainstream "sect" groups, gave
excessive attention to explaining why individuals become involved in such churches.

If, however, rather than dwelling on strange externals, we
change our point of focus and attempt to really look at what might
attract someone to an alternative religion, such involvement is not
really difficult to understand. Is the attraction of transformational
experiences, for example, really so hard to comprehend? What if
we actually could let go of the burden of our past and be reborn as
new people? Such transformation may or may not be attainable,
but the attractiveness of the possibility is certainly understandable.

Many nonmainstream religions—conservative Christian sects included—hold out the promise of such life-changing experiences. Religious experience is, however, only one aspect of the spiritual life, and only one of the factors that attract individuals to deeper religious involvement.

Among the many approaches to religious studies, one of the older, yet still useful, scholarly analyses was articulated by the influential historian of religion Joachim Wach (1944). The core of religion, according to Wach and others, is religious experience. Religious experience, in turn, is expressed in at least three ways:

In a community (church, ashram, etc.)

In a doctrine (theology, worldview, etc.)

In a "cultus" (ritual, gathering, etc.)

In addition to Wach, the emphasis on—and privileging of—religious experience is central to the approach of other key religious studies theorists such as Rudolf Otto and Mircea Eliade. This tradition has been heavily criticized over the past decade. Russell T. McCutcheon, for example, has caricaturized this approach as "necessitating that the scholar of religion be religious" (1999, 69). He has also attacked the notion that religious experience is *sui generis* (1997). Evaluating the merits of McCutcheon's critique would go beyond the scope of this book. For the purpose of the present analysis, it will be assumed that one need not be religious—nor need one defend the notion of religious experience as sui generis—in order to utilize this theoretical approach.

To understand Wach's analysis through a simple example, let us imagine how my experience at the Spring Renewal might become the basis for a new religious group. In the first place, it is easy to conceive of how a community might emerge out of the shared experience of the forgiveness exercise. I spent a week at the Spring Renewal. The exercise took place on the morning of the third day, if I remember correctly. Up to that point, I did not feel like I was part of the group: I was from the mainland while most of the participants were island residents. I also tended to keep a reserved distance as part of my academic persona. After the exercise, this changed dramatically. I became quite close to a number of the participants and clearly recall wishing we could just continue to live together in that YMCA camp. This feeling of community is a natural result of shared experiences, and it is relatively easy to see how these feelings might form the basis of a spiritual fellowship.

The forgiveness exercise was also such a cleansing, uplifting experience that it is not difficult to see how it might form the basis for a regular gathering—for a "ritual," in the broader sense of that word. In other words, it is easy to imagine how the people who had shared the experience might agree to meet on a regular basis and reenact the exercise in order to recapture the original experience. This would become the rough equivalent of a church service.

Finally, it is also possible to see how the experience might constitute the basis for a new theology: The teacher who led the group initially put forward a few quasi-theological notions, such as the fall-from-Eden story of the eclipse of matriarchy by evil patriarchs. If we extend this quasi-theology to the exercise, perhaps the group experience of forgiveness might become our new religion's equivalent of a salvation experience that restored our souls to pre-patriarchical paradise.

Direct religious experience is, in a certain sense, self-legitimating: It opens the door to a sacred realm and leaves experiencers transformed. Nevertheless, such encounters do not take place in a vacuum. Those who enter into the presence of the sacred might check their cultural baggage at the door (although this point is debatable), but they reclaim that baggage immediately after the flight is over.

Although experiences and ideas are intimately bound up with one another, it is nevertheless analytically useful to separate them and to note that religious experiences and religious ideology mutually impact one another. On the one hand, the experiences one has and how one interprets the significance of such experiences are determined by that person's cultural and personal background. On the other hand, a profound encounter with the sacred can compel one to rethink and reshape her or his religious ideology. This mutual dependence extends to the issue of legitimacy: Religious experiences tend to legitimate a person's religious views, whereas a person's religious background provides the intellectual resources for interpreting her or his encounter with the sacred and seeing it as a legitimate experience.

Although the sources of religions are diverse, the discipline of religious studies has traditionally given religious experience pride of place as the matrix out of which religions emerge. The sacred breaks into mundane reality in the form of a hierophany (an appearance of the sacred; the older, theological term is "theophany," an appearance of God), and, as a consequence, the new prophet goes out and founds a religion: Buddha experiences enlightenment and subsequently forms Buddhism; Mohammed encounters the Angel Gabriel and subsequently forms Islam; Guru Nanak has a vision of God and subsequently forms Sikhism; etc. (The most well known theorist in this regard is Mircea Eliade, who described this pattern in a number of different volumes—for example, Eliade 1954, 1959.)

There are, nevertheless, many problematic aspects of this scenario as a paradigm for the beginning of *all* new religions, particularly for understanding the emergence of new sects and new denominational bodies. For example, the impulse behind the formation of many new organizations is often rooted in internal political disputes and personality clashes. New *organizations* that do not differ substantially from their parent traditions represent a somewhat different phenomenon, in that they do not actually constitute new *religions*. More problematic are the new groups that emerge out of substantial doctrinal disagreements. While such conflicts rarely generate completely new religious *traditions,* the sects thus formed *are* technically new *religions*. And although a doctrinal dispute can have its roots in a deep religious experience, frequently this is not the case.

This category of exceptions was never addressed in discussions of the classic religious studies approach to the origins of religion. In the West, this method for generating new religious sects is especially—though certainly not exclusively—evident in the many new groups formed within the Protestant tradition. Thus the failure to take this pattern into account may have been at least partially the result of the older division of labor between history of religions and church history, which tacitly reserved Christianity as the exclusive "turf" of church historians.

Ever since Martin Luther articulated the doctrine of *sola scriptura* ("scripture only") as the sole principle of religious authority, variant interpretations of the Bible have been central to the legitimation of new Christian groups. Furthermore, as will be noted in the present and in future chapters, creative reinterpretations of traditional scriptures have also played a key role as legitimation strategies in some nontraditional religions. Even when new prophets reject key components of the Christian tradition, in the western cultural milieu the words of the Bible continue to bear such an aura of authority that religious innovators feel compelled to integrate them into their new spiritual syntheses in some manner.

THE PROPHET MOTIVE

Almost all religions with a historically specifiable point of origin are initially founded by a single person. In this regard, new religions are much like new businesses: new businesses are almost always the manifestation of the vision and work of a single entrepreneur. In contrast, few if any successful businesses are the outgrowth of a committee. And there are other ways in which the model of an economic entrepreneur is an appropriate lens through which to view religious prophets.

In an insightful article published over two decades ago, sociologists of religion Rodney Stark and William Bainbridge presented several paradigms for understanding the birth of religions, including one they termed the "entrepreneurial model" (Bainbridge and Stark 1979). In certain important ways, the authors suggest, the founding prophets of new religious movements are like individuals who start new companies: Relying on their experience with prior employment in a certain line of business, entrepreneurs strike out on their own with a similar business, improving or otherwise modifying the new company in some way so as to be competitive with their former employer and with other, similar companies. In a parallel fashion, new prophets have usually been active participants in other religions. As a consequence, their new spiritual syntheses inevitably bear resemblances to their original religions.

The entrepreneurial model is useful as long as one does not equate the *prophet* motive with the *profit* motive. Though a significant motivation for the leading figures of so-called "audience cults" or "client cults" (Bainbridge and Stark 1980) may be the income derived from their activities, too much self-sacrifice is required to found most other kinds of religious bodies for economic benefits to be the primary driving force.

A less obvious problem with the entrepreneurial metaphor is that a prophet does not typically sit down in her or his drawing room and consciously develop a blueprint for a new religion in the same way an entrepreneur might develop a business plan for a new company. Instead, founders of many new religions begin prophetic careers in response to hierophanies—direct encounters with the sacred. These encounters with other realms contain the seeds of new insights that in some way challenge or supersede the doctrines and practices of their "parent" religions. The new revelations are typically experienced as originating from a higher, divine authority, rather than from the personal creativity of the prophets. Such religious experiences subsequently become primary points of reference for the articulation and legitimation of new religious forms.

Although there has been a proliferation of studies on contemporary new religions within the past few decades, comparatively few religious studies scholars have chosen to focus on the process by which religious innovators arrive at their new spiritual syntheses. This state of affairs is surprising, given that the origin of religion has traditionally been a core concern of religious studies as an academic discipline. Hence it seems that religious studies scholars have consciously or unconsciously capitulated to the popular perception of new religions as not *really* religious. At the very least, it appears that contemporary new religions have been judged as not originating out of the same depth of religious consciousness as more traditional religions such as Buddhism and Islam.

The present situation has come about for a number of different reasons. In the first place, during the late 1960s and early 1970s— at precisely the same time period when some of the more exotic new religions were becoming prominent—religious studies was busy establishing itself in the university system as an academic discipline. In the United States, the threshold event opening the door for religious studies departments in state universities was a 1963 Supreme Court decision, *Abington Township School District v. Schempp.* Although the Court ruled that public schools could not engage in Bible reading, prayer, or other devotional practices, the justices went out of their way to note that the non-devotional "teaching about" rather than the "teaching of" religion was completely consistent with secular education. An unforeseen consequence of this decision was the "promotion of religious studies in institutions of higher education" (Wiebe 1999, 107). Not coincidently, the very next year the primary professional organization for the teaching of religious studies in the United States, the National Association of Biblical Instructors, changed its name to the American Academy of Religion (AAR). However, stripped of the "devotional, ethical, and cultural purposes that religious studies founders believed to be essential to their academic work . . . religious studies could not produce a set of compelling intellectual reasons for its place in the university" (Hart 1999, 202–203). Thus, despite the fact that by 1979 the American Council of Learned Societies had admitted the AAR as a member, acceptance of religious studies as a legitimate discipline within the university came slowly.

As members of a discipline generally perceived as marginal, most religion scholars were reluctant to further marginalize themselves by giving serious attention to what at the time seemed a transitory social phenomenon. One indication of the reluctance of the religious studies academy to deal seriously with new religious movements is that the first meeting of what became the New Religious Movements Group within the AAR did not take place until 1982, despite that fact that public controversy over new religions had been raging for at least ten years prior. It was not, in fact, until a series of major tragedies that took place in the 1990s—specifically, the Branch Davidian debacle, the Solar Temple suicide/ murders, the AUM Shinrikyo gas attack, and the Heaven's Gate suicides—that the field of new religious movements was truly embraced by the religious studies establishment.

As a consequence of this situation, the study of new religions was left to sociologists until relatively recently. Sociologists of religion were thus largely free to lay the foundations for the field of contemporary new religions. During the 1970s, issues raised by the cult controversy dominated social perceptions of new religions. And because social conflict is a basic issue for sociology, more and more sociologists were drawn to the study of new religions. By the time of the Jonestown tragedy in 1978—and in sharp contrast to the situation within religious studies—the field of new religious movements was already a recognized specialization within the sociology of religion.

Sociology, however, views new religions as arising out of social forces—as a discipline, sociology does not consider religious experiences as independent motivating factors for the emergence of new religious forms. In recent years, as more and more religion academics have become involved in the study of new religions, the tendency has been to build upon these foundations uncritically. Little thought has been given to considering what this phenomenon might look like when viewed in terms of some of the unique theoretical perspectives utilized in religious studies—perspectives that, as mentioned earlier in this chapter, take religious experiences seriously as powerful, independent motivating factors (Wach 1958, 36).

In the second place, many of the phenomena encountered in the metaphysical–occult–New Age subculture—the breeding ground for the majority of groups that contemporary new religions scholars study—are the conscious fabrications of their founders, transparently designed to have the broadest possible appeal in what some have referred to as the "spiritual marketplace." The entrepreneurial model is most appropriate for such popular writer-lecturers as Deepak Chopra and Lynn Andrews, and for certain therapy-oriented movements such as EST (Erhart Seminars Training). Because of the relatively high profile of such figures and movements, it is relatively easy to infer that every religious leader in this subculture is cut from the same fabric. For this reason, scholars working in the field are predisposed to view newly emergent religions as less legitimate than more traditional religions, and this usually unconscious value-judgment influences them to approach such religions with less sensitivity than they might approach more established religious bodies: The implicit assumption seems to be, Why should anyone seriously attempt to grapple with the religious consciousness of the founders of such superficial systems of spiritual teachings?

The corrective to this misperception can be found in yet another Stark and Bainbridge article, "Of Churches, Sects, and Cults" (Stark and Bainbridge 1979). In this piece, the authors distinguish between quasi-religious phenomena represented by the informal followings attracted to figures like Andrews and Chopra ("audience cults"), movements like EST ("client cults"), and more formal groups that embody characteristics of *religion* proper ("cult movements"). When observers take this distinction into account, they find that many contemporary new *religions* exhibit traits of more traditional religious bodies. It should thus be possible to understand such religions in terms of interpretive perspectives developed in the context of the study of established religions.

The present chapter undertakes such a project via the concrete example of the formation of the Church of the Movement of Spiritual Inner Awareness (MSIA), one of the many new religions to emerge out of the metaphysical-occult subculture of the early 1970s (Lewis 1998a). It will be demonstrated that, in common with other religious traditions and in contrast to the more secular motivations underlying audience cults and client cults, MSIA grows out of the religious experiences of its founder. As part of this analysis, I will further demonstrate that the common characterization of MSIA as being little more than a reworked spin-off of Eckankar falls far short of offering an adequate portrayal of this diverse religious movement. The main body of the discussion will be preceded by a brief overview of MSIA, Eckankar, and the Sant Mat tradition.

MSIA, ECKANKAR, AND THE SANT MAT TRADITION

Similar to Western Gnosticism, the North Indian Sant Mat tradition teaches that the cosmos is a multilevel emanation in which human souls are trapped, and that the spiritual aspirant needs a series of words or names keyed to each of the lower levels in order to move through them and reach the divine source. A sound current (a "river" of vibration, alternately pictured as a ray of light) from the higher levels—an emanation from the high God her/him/itself—flows down through all of the lower levels. A living guru imparts five secret names (the *simram*) to the aspirant at the time of initiation. Contemplating the sound current and the inner light (the visual aspect of the divine sound) with the master's guidance allows the individual to follow the sound back to the source from which it emanated (the Supreme Being), resulting in spiritual liberation. Those who follow the system must live according to a code of behavior that includes vegetarianism, abstinence from alcohol, and high moral character. Two and a half hours per day are to be set aside for meditation.

In contrast to the Sant Mat lineage, Eckankar is a new religious movement founded by Paul Twitchell in California in 1965. Twitchell was a spiritual seeker who was involved in a variety of different alternative religions—including Ruhani Satsang, a Sant Mat group—before starting Eckankar. He asserted that in 1956 he experienced God-realization when he was initiated by a group of spiritual masters, the Order of the Vairagi Masters. Twitchell and his organization gained widespread attention following the publication of Twitchell's biography, *In My Soul I Am Free* (1968), written by the prominent metaphysical author Brad Steiger. Building on contemporaneous popular interest in astral projection, Eckankar's early teachings emphasized "soul travel," a practice portrayed as a blend of astral projection and sound current meditation. Critics have often accused Twitchell of plagiarizing and then reworking Sant Mat teachings so as to disguise their true origins.

The Movement of Spiritual Inner Awareness is a new religion founded by John-Roger Hinkins (born Roger Hinkins), generally referred to as "J-R." (Following MSIA convention, I will regularly refer to Hinkins as John-Roger.) In 1963, while undergoing surgery for a kidney stone, he fell into a nine-day coma. Upon awakening, he found himself aware of a new spiritual personality—"John"—who had superseded or merged with his old personality. After the operation, Hinkins began to refer to himself as "John-Roger" in recognition of his transformed self. In 1971, he formally incorporated the Church of the Movement of Spiritual Inner Awareness. In 1988, he passed the spiritual leadership of MSIA on to John Morton.

There are many levels of involvement in MSIA. These include five formal initiations (the first two are done together, making four distinct initiation events), each of which indicates progressively deeper involvement in the spiritual path that is at the core of

FIGURE 1.1. John Roger Hinkins, founder of the Movement of Spiritual Inner Awareness. Courtesy of the Movement of Spiritual Inner Awareness.

MSIA's various practices. By way of contrast, Sant Mat groups such as Ruhani Satsang have only one initiation; Eckankar, on the other hand, has ten initiations.

MSIA also teaches that people have multilevel awareness and that 90 percent of a person's consciousness is in the spiritual levels; only 10 percent is in the physical world. Because the focus of MSIA is on the 90-percent level, MSIA members are free to decide how they wish to lead their lives at the 10-percent level. In practical terms, what this means is that members make their own decisions about such matters as diet, clothing, sexual preference, whom to associate with, and the like.

MSIA, ECKANKAR, AND THE METAPHYSICAL SUBCULTURE

As different immigrant populations have established their religions in the West, the religious ecology of Europe and the United States has become ever more complex, making any attempt at generalization problematic. With that caveat, we can nevertheless distinguish two major spiritual subcultures that stand out on the current religious landscape: traditionally dominant Christianity and a strand of alternative spirituality designated variously as metaphysical, metaphysical-occult, New Age, etc. Two distinct categories of bookstores that can be found in almost any large urban area are broadly emblematic of these two religious subcultures: Christian bookstores and metaphysical bookstores. There is almost no overlap in either the stock or the clientele of these retail outlets.

Though the diversity of ideas and institutions represented in metaphysical bookstores is far broader than that found in Christian bookstores, there are, nevertheless, within the metaphysical subculture broad areas of agreement that might escape the notice of the casual observer. Many of the specifics of this shared worldview arise out of the denominational traditions that came into being in the nineteenth century, particularly Theosophy, Spiritualism, and New Thought. Hence, almost all contemporary participants in the metaphysical subculture share beliefs in reincarnation, the ultimate interconnectedness of reality, the existence of other "planes" of reality inhabited by disembodied entities, the power of the mind to influence events, and so forth.

Although they might consciously distance themselves from

certain segments of it, both MSIA and Eckankar grow out of this subculture and share its basic assumptions. For this reason, the fact that both share beliefs in reincarnation and other common metaphysical ideas cannot be taken as evidence that either MSIA or Eckankar borrowed these specific ideas from each other. Once we eliminate the commonalities originating from shared roots in the metaphysical subculture, it becomes clear how different the two systems are.

For example, MSIA teaches a Christology that sets it apart from both the Sant Mat tradition and Eckankar. Specifically, MSIA gives tremendous spiritual significance to the role of the Christ—a significance that does not correspond with anything in either the Radhasoami lineage or Eckankar. MSIA further claims (1) that Jesus Christ is the head of the Church of the Movement of Spiritual Inner Awareness (Hinkins calls Jesus his "boss") and (2) that "the Traveler's work through MSIA (Soul Transcendence) is based on Jesus' work" (*Soul Transcendence* 1995, 11). Though the organization does not embrace the label "Christian," like Christianity, the movement views itself as deriving from Christ's teachings rather than from Eckankar or the Sant Mat tradition.

This assertion seems implausible unless one is familiar with the figure of Christ in Theosophy, New Thought, and the metaphysical subculture more generally. To anyone so informed, it is obvious that John-Roger has drunk deeply from the well of esoteric Christianity and that MSIA is saturated with the language and the ideology of this strand of spirituality. In fact, if one deletes the component of MSIA relating to sound current practices and soul travel ideology, what is left looks a lot like a metaphysical church.

This emphasis on Christ stands in sharp contrast to Eckankar, which sees Christianity as a lower path. When one understands that MSIA's primary sources of spiritual nourishment are the "Christian" tradition (broadly understood) and the larger metaphysical subculture, it seems odd that anyone could characterize MSIA as nothing more than an Eckankar or a Sant Mat spin-off.

This misunderstanding appears to have been created primarily by David Christopher Lane, the only scholar to have carried out substantive work on Eckankar and MSIA. Lane's principal treatment of MSIA is contained in his 1984 essay, "The JR Controversy." This piece was later incorporated into his 1994 book, *Exposing*

Cults. The essay is highly polemical. After pointing out a number of parallels—such as correspondences between Eckankar's cosmology and MSIA's cosmology—Lane dismisses John-Roger as a spiritual "plagiarist" (Lane 1994, 109).

It does not require much reflection, however, to perceive the flawed logic in Lane's line of argumentation. In the first place, it is difficult to imagine how one could possibly distinguish religious *plagiarism* from other kinds of transmissions of religious ideas and practices. For the sake of discussion, imagine a minority group in the First Baptist Church that objects to something their church is doing and decides to go off to found the Second Baptist Church. After about a month, someone from First Baptist goes to spy on Second Baptist and discovers that the new schism has "plagiarized" almost everything from the original congregation—they use the same Bible (printed by the same publishing company, without changing so much as a single word!), and, Oh my God, they even talk about the same Jesus dying for their sins! As ludicrous as this example may seem, it elucidates a fundamental error in Lane's critique.

In the second place, with respect to the discussion of Eckankar and MSIA, Lane's argument is even more off-base because of the substantial differences between Twitchell's and Hinkins's teachings. MSIA's emphasis on Christ is only the most obvious of these differences. In point of fact, the only area of overlap—excepting the commonalities inherent in the metaphysical subculture—is that both MSIA and Eckankar teach sound current meditation. Even in this area, the widespread presence of sound current traditions in North America—everyone from Kirpal Singh to Guru Maharaji has taught *surat shabd* yoga—suggests that John-Roger's ideas on this topic may have originated from a source other than Eckankar. On the other hand, Hinkins read Twitchell's writings for a couple of years, making Eckankar the most plausible source for MSIA's sound current teachings. A spiritual seeker and self-described "metaphysical tramp" during his early adulthood, John-Roger read about and participated in any number of different spiritual groups. He has been particularly forthcoming about his familiarity with Eckankar and Paul Twitchell and readily admits that there are parallels between MSIA and the Sant Mat tradition. In an email communication to this writer (7/22/98), Hinkins briefly described the period of his life during which he read Eckankar publications and participated in Eckankar events: "I was reading much information—i.e., Rosicrucians, Readers Digest, World Books, etc.—all around the same time. I went to three or four of Eckankar's conferences, and read some of their books and discourses for around two years and continued with others over a much longer period of time." Despite this participation, John-Roger was never a formal "student" of Twitchell, in the sense of being an Eckankar initiate. The assertion that Hinkins was a second-level initiate—an assertion one sometimes finds in anti-MSIA polemical literature—seems to be based upon a mistaken inference: Eckankar teaches that students engaged in the study of the group's monthly discourses will usually receive their first initiation on the inner levels (for example, in a dream) during their first year or so of study. At the end of two years, students may then request the second initiation, which involves the physical presence of an Eck minister empowered to administer a formal initiation. Hence when John-Roger says he took Eckankar's discourses for two years, "two years" is a spiritually significant cycle of time. An Eckankar insider might easily (though mistakenly) infer that Hinkins had received his second initiation.

Despite his involvement with Eckankar, John-Roger has claimed that his sound current teachings were not derived from that organization. Instead of Eckankar or Radhasoami, he asserts that MSIA stands in the lineage of Jesus, who, as the mystical traveler of his time, initiated his disciples into the sound current. Although no historian of religion would embrace such a position as historical fact, there are, as shall presently be seen, persuasive reasons to take this as a true statement of John-Roger's personal belief about the ultimate source of his own teachings.

As discussed earlier, the founders of most new religious movements differ from founders of new businesses in that they do *not* sit down in their living rooms and consciously draw up the contours of their new religious synthesis in the same way an entrepreneur draws up a business plan. This discussion thus brings us back around to the question of the nature of the prophetic consciousness. The next section will develop this issue with reference to John-Roger Hinkins.

RELIGIOUS EXPERIENCE AND THE PROPHETIC CONSCIOUSNESS

A useful counterpoint for elucidating the nature of prophetic consciousness is provided by Andrea Grace Diem in her 1995 dissertation, "Shabdism in North America: The Influence of Radhasoami on Guru Movements." Diem prefaces her work with the claim that she is following the "phenomenological method," meaning that she is engaged in a neutral, descriptive exercise. This disclaimer is, however, belied by the great bulk of her analysis of MSIA, Eckankar, and other emergent sound current groups; her analysis focuses squarely on the issue of their "dependence" on the Radhasoami tradition. In point of fact, Diem engages in a covert polemic by relying upon a simplistic version of the entrepreneurial model, naively assuming that the *prophet* motive (especially for all founders of Radhasoami-related movements in the West) is always the *profit* motive. Even a superficial perusal of her section on MSIA makes it clear that Diem's underlying interest is to have the reader walk away with a negative impression of John-Roger and the Movement of Spiritual Inner Awareness.

Nowhere is this agenda clearer than in the passages where she imputes motivations. For example, after accusing Paul Twitchell of having reduced the daily meditation time characteristic of Sant Mat lineages from two hours to two periods of twenty minutes in order to attract more students, she then notes that, like Sant Mat teachers, John-Roger Hinkins recommends two hours per day. (Diem is technically incorrect on this point: What Hinkins actually says is that fifteen minutes is adequate, but that it may take two hours to quiet the mental chatter before one can have fifteen minutes of "quality time.") This guideline—which, Diem admits, reduces the appeal of MSIA—is presumably part of John-Roger's attempt to add "lustre and authenticity to his fledgling movement" by by-passing Eckankar and linking MSIA to the larger Sant Mat tradition (Diem 1995, 174).

However, much later in her discussion, Diem characterizes MSIA, Eckankar, and related groups as organizations that have stripped Sant Mat of its "cultural moorings"—such as "strict ethical guidelines" (245)—in order "to present a streamlined, modern path intertwined with any number of fashionable religious trends which may have caught the eye of the buying public." She then flatly states that "John-Roger of MSIA is a prime example of this type" (247). In other words, according to Diem, John-Roger dropped Sant Mat moral prohibitions against such "sins" as meat-eating and homosexuality in order to increase the appeal of MSIA on the spiritual marketplace.

The problem with this analysis of Hinkins and other founders of modern spiritual groups is that Diem *invariably* portrays calculated decisions as lying behind *every* aspect of MSIA, Eckankar, etc. Such a one-sided attribution of motives is based on the unstated assumption that John-Roger and others are self-seeking charlatans. Thus, if Hinkins makes MSIA *more* rigorous by advising movement participants to meditate for two hours per day, it must be because he wants to legitimize his organization. If, on the other hand, Hinkins makes MSIA *less* rigorous by having no proscriptions against meat-eating and homosexuality, it must be because he wants to increase the appeal of his organization to the "buying public." One suspects that, had Diem known that John-Roger advised meditating only fifteen minutes per day, she would have portrayed his motivation for setting forth this guideline as wanting to broaden the appeal of MSIA. Alternately, had he proscribed meat-eating and homosexuality, the motive would have been the quest for greater legitimacy.

What about the possibility that, based on his personal religious experiences, Hinkins had concluded that two hours of spiritual exercises per day was the ideal meditation period? Or, isn't it even vaguely possible that he came to the sincere conclusion that meat-eating and homosexuality were not harmful to one's spiritual health? To uniformly attribute self-seeking motives to John-Roger is to carry out a covert polemic—a far cry from the phenomenological approach Diem claims to follow.

An important aspect of the phenomenological method as it is *properly* deployed in religious studies is that religious experiences are taken seriously. Without pronouncing judgment on the ontological status of the spiritual agencies encountered in such experiences, a disciplined effort is made to understand the consciousness of those for whom the encounter with the sacred is ultimately real and meaningful. Theorists as diverse as Joachim Wach, Rudolf Otto, Gerardus van der Leeuw, and Mircea Eliade have gone so far as to make such experiences both the starting point and the living core of religion.

With respect to John-Roger, the turning point in his spiritual life was the near-death experience (NDE) he went through during his kidney stone operation in 1963. (Many modern NDE accounts bear resemblances to a "classic shamanic initiation" [Ellwood 1992, 64], a significant category of religious experience.) The stage was set for this operation by an earlier automobile accident:

> On July the 4th of '63 in Hollywood, California, we were driving down Yucca Street. . . . We had the green light and as we came across a guy ran the light and hit us. I didn't see him coming, except barely. I was putting the seat belt on, and I'd just put it in to get ready to tighten it down and they hit us. My head went up, and there's a bar across where the window is, and I kind of hit it. It was like, "What happened?" Of course, our car was moving around. And, I got out and I couldn't walk. I was really dizzy. And, phew, I think that put me in the hospital for a week or so. . . .
>
> The car wreck had pulled my kidney loose, and had dislodged or moved a kidney stone. And the kidney stone was [causing] blood to come out. . . . On December 3rd, my kidney was taken out of my body, opened, and the stone removed. . . . For nine days, I was, they told me, unconscious. But I would open my eyes and look around and talk to them. My mother was there all the time. . . . I remember one day opening my eyes, laying on my side. . . . And she said, "Who are you?" I remember this. And a voice said, "John." And she said, "Okay. Is Roger there?" And he said, "Yeah. Would you like to speak to Roger?" She said, "Yeah." And, it was like—click click—there was Roger. . . .
>
> [Later] I went to see a couple [who] channeled. . . . They're the ones who came up with the name, "John-Roger." This consciousness came through, and I wanted to know what happened during the surgery. . . . And so I said, "Who are you? What do you do? Why are we together? What gives?" And it says, "John the Beloved." . . . and I said, "Well, if this is John, am I now John or am I Roger? Who am I in here?" And the [couple] said, "You're both." I said, "Yeah, but Roger's my first name, and [now] I have this John." They said, "John-Roger." And it fit. What I was told . . . was that I was this consciousness before, and am still this consciousness. (John-Roger interview 1/28/98)

In the wake of his coma, in other words, Hinkins experienced himself as having two distinct consciousnesses, one of which—the new self—he came to view as having been the biblical personage John the Beloved. It appears that John-Roger was told that Roger, the persona he formerly thought himself to be, was either the reincarnation of John or that the post-operation Roger was so over-shadowed by this "supernatural personality" that the two merged into one consciousness.

Given the apparent profundity of this experience in combination with the interpretation he subsequently accepted as the explanation for his expanded sense of self, it is easy to understand why Hinkins should have come to view his ministry as being in Jesus Christ's lineage: As the reincarnation—or, in some other manner, the embodiment—of one of Jesus' chief disciples, it would make perfect sense for him to assert that Jesus was his "boss" and that he based his work on Jesus' work (that is, it would be natural for him to see MSIA as a latter-day extension of Jesus' ministry). John-Roger's boss is not, however, the Jesus of conventional Christianity, but the metaphysical Jesus—the world avatar who teaches the full course of esoteric wisdom. With these points in mind, it now becomes clear how Hinkins could seriously claim that Jesus Christ initiated his disciples into the sound current: If John-Roger believes that surat shabd yoga is the most advanced "spiritual exercise" on the planet, he would necessarily have to infer that Jesus had taught such techniques to his disciples.

Although this powerful encounter with other realms was the pivotal religious experience of Hinkins's life, it would be eight years before his revelation would lead to the formation of MSIA. In the intervening years, we can infer that he reflected on this experience and others, interpreting and reinterpreting them as he came to conclusions about the nature of spiritual reality. As with all founders of new religions, at least some of the elements of the new synthesis that would become MSIA were drawn from doctrines and practices with which he was already familiar. However—to pick up on our earlier discussion—John-Roger's spiritual experiences were the touchstones around which all other components of MSIA would be organized.

In light of Hinkins's understanding of himself as being—or as having merged his consciousness with—John the Beloved, the claim that he artificially tacked on some Christian components in order to make it appear "more Western" (Diem 1995, 163) is clearly mistaken. Instead of beginning with the Sant Mat tradition and adding a Western gloss, John-Roger began with a profound experience of being Christian (esoterically understood) and then reflectively integrated the other elements of occult wisdom that he had appropriated into a metaphysical Christian base. This is also evident in his attitude toward the Bible, an attitude which, because appeals to the authority of the Bible are widespread in the metaphysical tradition as well as within the Christian mainstream, merits examination.

ROLE OF THE BIBLE

The Bible is a powerful authority in Western societies. For this reason, the metaphysical tradition relies heavily on what is referred to as a *metaphysical interpretation* of scripture, meaning that biblical passages are interpreted symbolically and metaphorically to reveal their true import. In the case of MSIA, Hinkins draws from the biblical record, although his approach to scripture is complex, simultaneously similar and dissimilar to the approach of metaphysical Christianity. Because the focus of his exegesis is a perspective informed by his religious experience, so it was possible for John-Roger to find biblical passages containing allusions to soul travel.

Also, unlike some metaphysical churches such as Unity that embrace the Bible as the touchstone of their teachings, MSIA's approach is more selective. Readings from scripture play no role in a typical MSIA gathering, and no set of Hinkins's teachings focuses specifically on the Bible. At the same time, John-Roger often cites and otherwise refers to the Bible as an authoritative text. Furthermore, MSIA members are encouraged to read and become familiar with scripture. Although the Bible is authoritative, this authority is not exclusive, as reflected in John-Roger's response to the question, Can I find the Christ in Hindu scriptures? "Yes, but it won't be spelled that way" ("Christmas Eve with John-Roger").

The aspirant is also warned against over-focusing on scripture. In one of his talks, Hinkins asserts that spiritual teachers always advise one to "seek first the Kingdom," because "If you seek first that which is written, and try to maintain that which is written, then you sacrifice the 'moving within consciousness' of God" ("The Meditation of the Christ"). Congruent with the teachings of other metaphysical churches (Judah 1967, 17–18), John-Roger tends toward a nonliteral reading of scripture (John-Roger 1994, 14–15): "The Bible sometimes does not give us specific answers to our questions, but you must understand that the Bible is coded" (24–25). How, then, does one go about decoding scripture? MSIA does not provide explicit guidelines for this task. Instead, the implicit message seems to be that one can unlock the deeper meaning of the Bible only after one has achieved a certain level of enlightenment. Furthermore, even if we had the keys for interpreting scripture, not all of the mysteries would be found there because not all of the "hidden teachings" were encoded in the Bible. Hinkins notes, for instance, that soul travel is only alluded to in scripture: "The work that we do in soul travel—transcending the physical—is alluded to in the Bible, in a few places. Let me give you two of the references. One says, 'when you're out of the body, you're with the Lord.' It's like, Why would they make a statement like that? It's like, To worship God you must worship God in the spirit (that is, the Soul)" ("What Is the Secret Center?"). The other example John-Roger mentions in this taped discussion is the familiar Pauline epistle relating the experience of a man who was "taken up" to the third heaven.

Given the Bible's state of incompleteness, one might well ask why one should bother reading it at all. Hinkins's answer is that although the Bible is not necessary for salvation, it points the way, not unlike how a water almanac points the way to water. One can shake and twist a water almanac all day and never get a single drop of water. Similarly, the Bible does not have a magical potency to save anyone. Instead, it points the way to quenching our spiritual thirst: "What is the value of the Book? The value of the Book is it points a direction. The water almanac points a way—a direction— to where water can be found. And [the Bible] points to where the Living Waters can be found. And it points it out very beautifully, very succinctly, and, believe me, I thrill anew each time that I hear it because I've validated it inside of me" ("Christmas Eve with John-Roger"). Finally, John-Roger has periodically made the observation that our present scriptures will eventually be superseded by a new bible or bibles. He has made this assertion in the context of discussions that portray the present period as being the "biblical times" of the future: "Realize that you are biblical scripture now being written and that centuries from now, the lives that are being enthroned in the spiritual records at this time will be the 'bible' of people who will say, 'If I had lived in that time, if I could have partaken of that Christ Consciousness, then I, too, could have been saintly. I, too, could have expressed eternal love'" (John-Roger 1994, 43). From this passage as well as from many of the other statements cited above, one can see that MSIA departs significantly from tradition.

At the same time, John-Roger's utilization of the Bible as an authoritative document contributes to MSIA's legitimacy.

RELIGIOUS EXPERIENCE AND THE
FORMATION OF NEW RELIGIONS

To return to our discussion of religious experience, in twentieth-
century religious studies "religious experience" is an imprecise
notion applied to any number of different kinds of experiences.
Though theoretically open-ended, the paradigmatic experience in
the back of most people's minds whenever they discuss this topic is
a major, life-transforming encounter with the Divine—an overwhelming experience of the kind that overtook Paul on the Da-
mascus Road. John-Roger's NDE falls into this category. As indicated
by studies of people who have been through close encounters with
death, NDEs are major experiences that transform lives. In the case
of Hinkins, his NDE transformed him from a metaphysical dilet-
tante into a serious spiritual seeker.

To refer back to our earlier discussion, it is precisely such trans-
formative encounters that theorists of religion have in mind when
they discuss religious experience as the source and central point of
reference for concrete religious forms. Wach, for example, analyzed
the other major components of religion as *expressions* of direct
experiences of the sacred. In other words, religious experience is
expressed in, first, doctrine (theology, mythology, ideology), second, cultus (ritual, ceremony, gathering), and, third, community
(church, ashram, etc.). In Wach's words, "Myth and doctrine com-
prise the articulation in thought of what has been experienced in
the confrontation with Ultimate Reality. *Cultus* is the acting out of
this confrontation in worship and service. Both give direction to
and 'center' the community formed by those who are united in a
particular religious experience" (Wach 1958, 121). This does not
mean that Wach viewed religions as coming into being *ex nihilo*
out of an encounter with the Divine. Rather, the components of
any new religious synthesis are typically drawn from familiar religious forms in the prophet's environment. But it is the founder's
religious experience that provides the starting point—as well as the
essential core or template—for the form this new synthesis takes.
The prophet motive, in other words, is to express, as best as one
can, the ramifications of religious experience in new religious

forms. Other, ancillary motivations may contribute to the process, but the core motive remains essentially religious.

Taking this perspective seriously, it is easy to see that any simplistic deployment of the entrepreneurial model is misleading: Probably the majority of founders of new religions do *not* create religious forms primarily with an eye to how well they will "sell" on the spiritual marketplace (the *profit* motive). Instead, religious forms typically emerge out of the consciousness of the founder for the purpose of expressing her or his religious experience and drawing other people into a community to share her or his vision (the *prophet* motive). The impulse lying behind the formation of MSIA, for example, has been described as, "I have this experience and other people want to know about it" (John Morton interview 6/9/98).

In sharp contrast to self-seeking motives implicit in the entrepreneurial metaphor, prophets not infrequently become involved in the founding of new religious communities *against their own conscious will:* Like the biblical Jonah who rebelled against the dictates that arose out of his encounter with the Divine, prophets sometimes actively resist the promptings that direct them to engage in public ministries. From various statements he has made over the years, we can infer that this was the case with John-Roger, who probably would have preferred to remain Roger Hinkins the "metaphysical tramp" rather than take on the responsibility of serving as a spiritual director.

CONCLUDING REMARKS

The focus of the present chapter was on the prophetic consciousness of founders of new religions. The thrust of the discussion was to argue that, with the exception of less formally organized audience cults, the principal source of the prophet motive is frequently a profound religious experience, and not the narrow self-seeking suggested by facile appropriations of the entrepreneurial model. It was further argued that the founder often experiences the creative impulses arising out of the encounter with the Divine as the ultimate source of her or his new spiritual synthesis. Hence any analysis that explicitly or implicitly portrays the primarily structuring impulses behind new religions as arising from the calculated decisions of the founder de facto denigrates religious experience by ignoring its role in the emergence of many new religions.

2

NATIVE AMERICAN
PROPHET RELIGIONS

John Slocum was one of the many Indians who were caught in the cross
currents of . . . troublous times. He belonged to the Squaxin band, a
small group formerly concentrated along the shores of a southern branch
of Puget Sound. During his lifetime, however, most of his homeland was
ceded to the government and his people were scattered and reduced in
numbers in their efforts to adjust to changed conditions and new demands. Not much is known of Slocum's early life. . . . By his own admission Slocum was not industrious or provident; as a young man he had a
weakness for whisky, betting on horse races, and other white man's
vices. . . .

In the fall of [1881] he fell sick and apparently died. His friends were
summoned and preparations were made for his funeral. But during the
long wake that was held and while the mourners were waiting for his cof-
fin to arrive, Slocum revived in view of his wife and others assembled
around the room in which his body lay covered with a sheet. His resurrection was in itself an awful sight, but the words that he soon began to speak
were even more wonderful. He confirmed his death and related that his
soul had left his body and gone to the judgment place of God where it had
been confronted by an angel who turned it away from the promised land.
The error of his sinful life was revealed to him, and he was instructed to
return to earth to bear witness to his transformation and to lead other
sinners into the Christian way of life.

—H. G. Barnett, *Indian Shakers*

John Slocum subsequently went on to found the Indian Shaker
Church. Like John-Roger, the touchstone event in his life was an
encounter with the sacred that took place during a near-death experience. With the exception of the explicitly Christian emphasis
of Slocum's message, the major components of this account follow
a pattern that was more or less embodied by almost every founder
of a major Native American prophet religion. The remarkable parallels among these movements, and among similar movements in
other parts of the world (Lanternari 1965), have often been noted

by scholars and have led to various theoretical formulations, such as Anthony Wallace's influential concept of revitalization movements (1956).

The first part of the present chapter will undertake to examine the founding and legitimating of Native American prophet movements in terms of a comparison between the figure of the prophet and the figure of the shaman. The analysis will demonstrate that the death-vision is one of the few universal traits of the various American Indian prophets, that the prophetic call and the shamanic call are similar in structure but dissimilar in content, and that the ability of Native American communities to accept the legitimacy of the prophet and the prophetic message is at least partially dependent on a perceived parallel between the role of the prophet and the role of the shaman.

The second part of the chapter will examine the role of the prophet's charisma in the life of a new religion. Scholars have assumed that the prophet's charisma is the "glue" that holds together the alternate view of reality represented by such movements. This perspective misconstrues the role of charisma. Although the founder's charisma may be necessary in giving life to the vision during the nascent stages of an emergent religion, the actual adoption of the religion by a human community subsequently recruits the forces of social consensus to the side of the new revelation—forces that tend to maintain the alternate vision of reality *independently* of the personal charisma of the prophet after the new religion has come into being.

SHAMANS AND PROPHETS

At first glance, all Native American new religions seem to share a certain set of characteristics. A closer investigation, however, quickly undermines any attempt to construct an elegant model of the typical prophet religion. The principal difficulty is that out of any given set of traits, each new religion has some but not all of them. For example, if we examine a few of the major prophets in terms of a half dozen major characteristics, we immediately begin to run up against irregularities (see table 2.1). What can be seen rather quickly from table 2.1—which is in no way exhaustive—is that if only these six traits are taken to constitute the typical Native American prophet religion, no single movement ever existed that was wholly typical in the sense of embodying the entire pattern. Expanding both the list of prophets and the list of characteristics only reinforces this observation. On the other hand, there is one commonality that all of the major prophets seem to have shared—namely, the "death" experience that takes place in conjunction with the original vision. Tenskwatawa's death-vision was very similar to Slocum's (Edmunds 1983). Smohalla's (Trafzer and Beach 1985) and Handsome Lake's (Wallace 1972) experiences also closely follow this pattern. For the other two prophets who appear in table 2.1, the situation is somewhat more ambiguous.

Our information about Neolin, for example, is too scanty to know whether or not his vision came during a death experience. Wovoka's vision took place during an eclipse, an occasion on which the Paiute felt that "the sun died" (Mooney 1965, 13). An individual who was with Wovoka at the time of his first vision described his perception of what was happening to the prophet: "he fell down dead, and God came and took him to heaven" (Mooney 1965, 14). This appears to be a description of the same experience the other Indian prophets encountered.

Table 2.1.   Native American Prophets

	HANDSOME LAKE	TENSK- WATAWA	WOVOKA	SMOHALLA	JOHN SLOCUM	NEOLIN
Dissolute prior to call	yes	yes	no	no	yes	?
History as a shaman	yes/no*	yes	yes	yes	no	?
Nativistic message	no	yes	yes	yes	no	yes
"Death" experience	yes	yes	yes	yes	yes	?
Return of the dead	no	no	yes	yes	no	no
Military consequences	no	yes	no/yes**	yes	no	yes

*Handsome Lake was apparently an herbalist.
**Wovoka himself advised peace, but the U.S. military massacred Ghost Dancers.

The pattern of a revelatory vision occurring during a death experience such as a death-like illness is not, of course, uniquely characteristic of American Indian prophet religions. Although shamans regularly choose or inherit their profession, many shamans are "called" to their vocation by the spirits. The called shamans often undergo initiatory sickness that brings them close to death, during which they receive their initiatory vision (Eliade 1972, 28ff). Black Elk's well-known experience exemplifies this shamanic pattern fairly faithfully (Neihardt 1961, 18–40). The parallel between the prophetic process and the shamanic process is useful as long as we keep in mind that the *content* of the revelations diverge considerably. In particular, one is struck by the strong ethical message of the prophets, a message that departs from the central concerns of shamanism. And the ethical content of the revelation is invariably present, from the earliest Native American prophet and onwards; for example, Neolin stated, "I hate you to drink as you do, until you lose your reason; I wish you not to fight one another; you take two wives, or run after other people's wives; you do wrong; I hate such conduct; you should have but one wife, and keep her until death" (cited in Wallace 1972, 117–118). One of the more interesting findings made in the course of researching this chapter was the discovery of how accurate John Grim's outline of the differences between the shaman and the prophet proved to be. Toward the end of *The Shaman* (1983, 184–185), where he compares the shaman with other religious types, Grim asserts that the prophetic revelation—and in this section he is explicitly referring to the *Hebrew* prophets—is "the revelatory message of a personal deity," unlike the shamanic message, which is a dramatization of the shaman's "personal encounter with the numinous forces in the natural world." It contains a "moral mandate," unlike the shamanic vision, which at most "may impose certain obligations of a vocational nature" on the shaman; and it "counsels the community in response to certain tensions" present at a particular historical juncture, unlike the shaman, who "does not develop a vision of historical destiny." What is striking about Grim's comparison is how accurately his contrasting characterizations describe the difference between the *Native American* prophet and the shaman, a comparison he evidently did not have in mind when he developed his classification of religious types. American Indian prophets

NATIVE AMERICAN PROPHET RELIGIONS   51

preached a strongly ethical message and perceived themselves as mouthpieces for the "high" God (for example, Neolin's "Creator" or "master of Life") who communicates a vision of historical destiny addressed to a specific historical crisis.

The remarkably close parallel between Native American prophets and Hebrew prophets suggests that at least part of the message of the Indian prophet has been shaped by contact with Western religion. Though the question of Christian versus aboriginal sources of the millenarian-eschatological themes of movements such as the Ghost Dance is open to debate (for example, Spier 1935; Aberle 1956; Walker 1969), it is difficult to avoid seeing that the tending-toward-monotheistic God and the moral emphasis of the prophet religions have been decisively shaped by contact with Christianity. This seems to be the case, for example, even in the strongly Nativistic message of Neolin. The Protestant, Evangelical influence on Neolin expresses itself in certain very noticeable ways beyond the three points of Grim's analysis, such as in his emotional preaching, his injunction to repeat a particular written prayer, his conception of heavenly and hellish realms, and his distribution to his followers of a kind of map-like scripture, "which he called 'the great Book or Writing'" (Heckenwelder 1876, 291). Thus even in what was one of the most antiwhite and reactionary Native American movements, the message and style of the prophet was deeply indebted to Protestant Christianity.

LEGITIMATING NEW VISIONS

The syncretism theme brings us to the problematic issues of how prophets go about making their innovations and, perhaps just as importantly, how they go about legitimating their innovations. In his influential "Revitalization Movements" article, Anthony Wallace describes the prophet's creativity as a "deliberate, organized, conscious effort" (1956, 265), but, while one might well applaud his eschewing of mechanical models of culture change, his characterization of the process of innovation as "deliberate" and "conscious" appears to be inaccurate. In fact, if he is asserting that prophetic visions were somehow *deliberately* created by the Native American prophets, Wallace's own study of Handsome Lake (1972) would run counter to this portrayal of religious creativity. That this is not Wallace's intention is evidenced by his observation that successful prophets truly believe that they have communicated with the deity (1956, 272). Founders of new religions must, after all, legitimate their prophetic missions to themselves.

It would seem to be more accurate, therefore, to speak of a revelation that is experienced as originating from the spirit world and that is then creatively interpreted and adapted to the culture's historical situation (Overholt 1974). This, at least, appears to be the case from what we know about Native American new religions. It would, of course, be possible to argue that the revelation is *unconsciously* created by the prophet himself, but that is another issue.

Wallace's formulation is also weak in its failure to emphasize that the new message must invoke supernatural sanctions before a culture will be inclined to accept it. Although the openness of a community to a new revelation would obviously depend on a number of different things, one important factor is the tendency of traditional Native American religions to accept the legitimacy of visions—particularly the visions of shamans—as sources of creative inspiration in general and spiritual guidance in particular. The Arapaho, for example, "derived innovation in decorative design from inspiration by spirits" (Lowie 1982, 159). Similarly, among the Mistassini Cree, "The instructions for making the decorations on the various charms and items of hunting equipment are said to be dreamed by the hunter who owns the item" (Tanner 1979, 142). Numerous other examples of visionary creativity could be cited from individual vision quests and shamanic visions.

Wallace points out the parallel between the shamanic call and the prophetic call (1956, 272), but does not explicitly make the case for the shaman as the prototype of the prophet. Had he made this link, he might have been able to show how a community's prior familiarity with, and acceptance of, the shaman and the shamanic vision could have legitimated the "office" of prophet and the innovations called for by the prophetic vision.

What is it, however, that the prophet reveals or creates? Though Wallace intends his concept to be a rich notion incorporating all of the various facets of a culture, he emphasizes the cognitive dimensions in those places where he refers to the "mazeway" as the "mental image of the society and its culture" (1956,

266). For the purposes of this study, we will pick up on this cognitive emphasis and discuss the prophet's revelation as a new story that expands or supplants a culture's previous stories and myths about the way things are.

The worldview of a traditional culture is intimately tied up with the culture's mythology—a set of stories that, to oversimplify, describe and explain the world and provide the paradigms for ritual and human action. Traditional mythologies are comprehensive in the sense that they encompass the most important concerns of any given culture. When unprecedented natural or historical events radically disturb the culture's lifestyle, the older stories become at least partially inadequate in that they fail to address the new circumstances. This situation would, to use Wallace's phrase, be a period of "mazeway stress." The appearance of Euro-Americans, and particularly the conquest of aboriginal cultures by Euro-Americans, would certainly qualify as an unprecedented event that would not (except by radical reinterpretation) be covered by traditional stories. The changed circumstances brought about by this contact are precisely what a prophet addresses, and his revelation can be understood as a new story that includes an explanation of the altered situation. It can do what older stories cannot: offer a comprehensive account of what has become the most pressing concern of the culture.

To once again see the prophet in shamanic terms, the successful prophet's role can be understood as that of a shamanic healer and shamanic storyteller writ large. In other words, prophetic visions do not just "work startling cures" (Wallace 1956, 272) for the individual prophets. Rather, they are also offered as healing stories to the culture as a whole. This way of looking at the prophet is dependent on perceiving how stories can function "therapeutically," which is when they act as a "means of finding oneself in events that might not otherwise make psychological sense at all" (Hillman 1979, 43). In terms of Grim's analysis of the shaman, we could thus say that there is a certain sense in which prophets embody or act out the new cosmology of their revelations: initially during their original death experiences, later during their recounting of the content of their visions, and more generally in their lives. In this way the prophets and their vision-story can be understood as performing a healing function for the entire culture.

THE CONQUEST SITUATION

One of the principal characteristics attributed to the religions of nonindustrialized cultures is that they are static cultural forms with no discernable history. This trait helped to legitimate the traditional division of labor between scholars who studied the "higher" religions and scholars who studied everyone else. The view that smaller, tribal traditions were—when left undisturbed by outsiders—largely unchanging persisted in the face of much disconfirming evidence. The principal resistance to acknowledging the implications of such evidence came from the West's civilized-savage ideology—an ideology that required a static, regressive counterimage (that is, primitive savages) for the West's self-congratulatory self-image as dynamic and progressive. A more contemporary view is that such religions are flexible traditions, quite capable of adapting to social and environmental changes (Walls 1987). There are, nevertheless, limits to a culture's adaptability, as when the intrusion of colonialists radically disrupts the lifestyle of a tribal society.

The religious life of a traditional culture is built around the most pressing concerns of the group, such as its economic concerns (for example, a hunting society will typically have hunting myths and rituals). Thus a conquest situation in which a defeated people's economic base is shattered and radically reoriented (for example, hunters who are forced to become farmers) can quite suddenly make irrelevant significant segments of a traditional religion. Conquest also transforms the contact situation itself into one of the more pressing concerns of the conquered group.

Such a state of affairs can lead to several different outcomes. If the intruding society is open to assimilation, one possible scenario is that the conquered group will abandon its traditions in favor of the conqueror's traditions. In the case of American Indians, Euro-American society, although professing an ideology of assimilation, was never really open to accepting Native Americans as equals. After tribal groups such as the Cherokee, for example, had adopted

Euro-American culture in the early nineteenth century, they were rewarded with forced removal to Western territories.

With the possibility of full assimilation closed off and the alternative of violent warfare suicidal—particularly after the War of 1812, the last historical juncture at which there was a reasonable chance of turning the tide of conquest—defeated tribes had few options beyond getting by as best they could within the limitations imposed by the United States government. Bare existence is not, however, enough to fulfill a human community. Lacking a spiritual vision that could imaginatively transform their situation into a condition with ultimate meaning, post-conquest life tended to be characterized by all of the traits one usually associates with demoralized social groups, such as alcoholism and a high suicide rate. Although the religions of their ancestors might still have been relevant to many aspects of life, the received tradition did not address their oppressed state. And while Christianity contains many elements that speak to oppressed peoples, it was often rejected because of its association with the conquerors.

Situations such as these constitute ideal environments for the emergence of millenarian movements. Often these revelations provide divine sanctions for new lifestyles. New religious visions also tend to address the presence of Euro-Americans in some manner. At the level of ritual, the usual effect of prophet religions was to encourage religious practices—often modified versions of traditional dances and rituals—within groups which had partially or completely abandoned community ceremonials, thus providing Native Americans with religio-social activities that helped to preserve group identity.

Generally speaking, contemporary Westerners are unaware of these prophet religions beyond the Ghost Dance of 1890 (originating with the Paiute prophet Wovoka), a movement that left a significant trace in the historical record because of the many tribes affected and because of the Ghost Dancers massacred at Wounded Knee. In addition to the movements and prophets already examined, there were numerous other Indian prophets, such as Kenekuk, Main Poc, Josiah Francis, Wodziwob, Jake Hunt, Kolaskin, Isatal, and John Wilson. One should also take into consideration the various individuals who adapted the Ghost Dances of 1870 and 1890 to the needs of particular tribal groups.

As already noted, the revelations of the prophets were often remarkably similar, especially in their emphatic moralism. The new
visions were similar on this point because the demoralized social
conditions they sought to redress were similar. It is not until one
examines the position their revelations took on the topic of the
non-Indian presence that Native American prophets begin to diverge significantly from one another. On the one hand, a prophet
like Kenekuk led the Kickapoo to adjust to the new lifestyle imposed on them by Euro-American society. As was the case with
other new religious leaders like Handsome Lake, the Kickapoo
prophet taught that men should farm in a community where farm-
ing had been regarded as women's work (Herring 1988, 36).
Prophets like Tenskwatawa, on the other hand, encouraged their
followers to reject the culture of the intruders and take up arms
against Euro-Americans (Edmunds 1983).

These divergent types of revelation correspond with the analysis of the Italian scholar of religion Lanternari (1965), who grouped
American Indian messianic movements into two major categories,
depending on their attitude toward Euro-Americans—hostile (for
example, Neolin and Tenskwatawa) or adaptive (for example,
Handsome Lake and John Slocum). These two types, to continue to
follow Lanternari's discussion, arise at two different phases of Native American history. Hostile movements arise in the first stage,
and look back to a recovery of pre-contact conditions. Adaptive
movements, which arise in the second stage, proceed to construct
new worlds of meaning that accept the contemporaneous situation, including the ongoing Euro-American presence, as a given.

These categories are useful, although, for our present purposes,
they need to be modified so as to include a third category to distinguish movements that were simultaneously hostile *and* adaptive. In other words, a war revelation such as Tenskwatawa's was
hostile without being adaptive. However, a movement like the
Ghost Dance, which Lanternari classifies as hostile, in fact led
many tribes to become more adjusted to their situation. Some of
the potentially adaptive aspects of Wovoka's teachings are evident
in certain passages of the so-called "Messiah Letter" recorded by
James Mooney, for example, "Do not refuse to work for the whites
and do not make any trouble with them" (cited in Mooney 1965,
101).

And, had it not been for the stupidity of a few key U.S. officials in the Dakotas, the only significant violence resulting from the Ghost Dance—the Wounded Knee massacre—could easily have been avoided. Thus modified, Lanternari's classification allows us to explain why a certain subset of Native American prophet movements did not survive: Simply put, movements built around war visions (that is, hostile, nonadaptive movements) were defeated on the battlefield. So that the reader can acquire a clearer sense of this phenomenon, it will be useful to outline representative movements for each of these three categories.

THE SHAWNEE PROPHET'S INDIAN ARMAGEDDON

> At first they took it for a great bird, but they soon found it to be a monstrous canoe filled with the very people who had got the knowledge which belonged to the Shawnees. After these white people had landed, they were not content with having the knowledge which belonged to the Shawnees, but they usurped their land also. They pretended, indeed, to have purchased these lands but the very goods they gave for them were more the property of the Indians than of the white people, because the knowledge which enabled them to manufacture these goods actually belonged to the Shawnees. But these things will soon end. The Master of Life is about to restore to the Shawnees their knowledge and their rights and he will trample the Long Knives under his feet. (Cited in Edmunds 1983, 38)

Such was the gist of the conversation in 1803 when a Shawnee delegation explained their vision of the immediate future to American officials. This is an apocalyptic scenario in which God (in this case, the Shawnee Master of Life) is about to intervene on the side of a people unjustly oppressed. Here we see clearly the central promise that makes apocalyptic thinking so attractive to conquered peoples: Unable to defeat their oppressors by purely military means, the tables are to be turned through the power of divine intervention.

The scenario outlined above would become the fundamental understanding underlying the first pan–American Indian religious movement. This movement, like the later and more famous Ghost Dance, originated with the visions of a single prophet among a people demoralized by the intrusion of Euro-Americans. The religious alliances forged by Tenskwatawa, the Shawnee prophet, formed the basis for the military triumphs of Tecumseh, whose activities eventually overshadowed those of Tenskwatawa, his younger brother. As a consequence, few non-specialists are aware that Tecumseh's followers were initially motivated by a religious vision of a final confrontation in which Native Americans would defeat Euro-Americans, drive them out of North America, and restore American Indians to their former glory. This emergent eschatology was based on traditional mythology and can best be approached in terms of Shawnee creation myths.

The dominant type of creation myth among the aboriginal peoples of North America is of the earth-diver variety in which a divine being (usually an animal) dives into a universal ocean of water to bring up the first particles of earth. The Shawnees, by way of contrast, are one of the few tribes possessing a creation account in which the high god (often referred to as the "Master of Life") creates the world by imposing order on a primordial chaos. Because the original chaos is watery (the Shawnee term for the primordial condition seems to be related to other kinds of words that refer to watery expanses), these two types of creation share certain points in common (Long 1963, 188). In both kinds of stories water is an ambivalent symbol simultaneously representing creative potency as well as the threat of chaos (Schutz 1975, 77).

After creation is complete, the Creator warns the first people, "Even I myself do not know how long this place where you live will survive. And the reason I do not know is this: the world will survive as long as you interpret correctly the way I created you" (cited in Schultz 1975). "Interpreting the way" means, for the Shawnee people, adhering to the "laws"—a specific body of oral literature that sets forth the proper relationships that should be followed among human beings as well as between humans and the nonhuman world—which were spoken by the Master of Life in the beginning. The Creator's words cited above indicate that wholesale abandonment of these laws would constitute abandonment of order and return to chaos.

In common with related tribal groups, Shawnee mythology includes a migration narrative in which a large body of water is crossed. This myth has traditionally been viewed by scholars as a "cultural memory" of the migration from Asia to North America. In some versions of the tale, the original people abandon a barren and inhospitable place for a better land across the ocean. But, whatever the motivation for crossing, the great expanse of water is almost always seen as a barrier that must be overcome by magical means. In at least one version, "a great wind and a deep darkness prevailed, and the Great Serpent commenced hissing in the depths of the ocean" during the crossing (Schutz 1975, 55). The "Great Serpent" referred to here is a marine monster which, like its parallels in other mythologies across the world, concretely embodies the negative, disordering aspect of the primordial waters.

After successfully negotiating the initial stage of the journey, but prior to reaching their eventual resting place, a party of warriors is drowned by a large turtle acting in the capacity of an agent for the hostile sea snake. In retaliation, Shawnee shamans slay the serpent and cut it into small pieces. Because of the snake's potency, these fragments do not decay. The tribe collects the pieces with the intention of later using them for beneficent purposes such as healing. As a manifestation of the ambivalent power of the primordial energy, the serpent's power can be used for good or for ill. Although the original motivation behind gathering together the fragments is benevolent, Shawnee witches would later base their malevolent spells on the power of bundles made from these serpent parts.

As part of their migration myth, the Shawnees eventually reached the "heart" of the new continent, an area where the Master of Life had originally intended for them to live. In historical times, the Shawnees were still wanderers who could be found living in different parts of eastern North America during different periods of time. By the middle of the eighteenth century, the great bulk of the Shawnee nation was living in Ohio. Recognizing the threat that settlers posed both to their lands and to their traditional lifestyle, the Shawnees allied themselves first with the French (during the French and Indian War) and later with the British (during the Revolution) to oppose the advances of land-hungry colonists. After the Treaty of Paris ended the Revolutionary War, the Shawnees, in league with other tribes, fought on until decisively defeated at the Battle of Fallen Timbers. They eventually (in 1795) signed the Treaty of Greenville, an unfavorable agreement in which the tribe gave up most of its homeland in exchange for some trade goods and annuities.

In the wake of defeat, some bands moved further west. Other Shawnees, under the leadership of Black Hoof, attempted to adapt to changed conditions by turning to agriculture. The majority rejected acculturation, continued to follow the hunt as best they could, and clung to memories of a romanticized past. Many tribesmen eventually slid into demoralized, dissolute lifestyles, consuming increasing amounts of alcohol and occasionally venting their frustration in acts of intratribal and intrafamilial violence.

During this period of time, Tenskwatawa, the Shawnee prophet, was a less than stunningly successful medicine man for a small village located in eastern Indiana. Tenskwatawa (literally "The Open Door") was one of three male triplets born in early 1775; his more famous brother Tecumseh was seven years older. Tenskwatawa's father died at the Battle of Point Pleasant prior to his birth, and, after his mother abandoned him while he was still a small child, he was raised by his older sister Tecumpease, her husband, Black Fish, and other Shawnee. While still a child, he lost an eye playing with a bow and arrows. Perhaps as a consequence of this unfortunate childhood, he grew up a boastful alcoholic, acquiring the derogatory nickname "Lalawethika" (noisemaker or rattle). As a young man, he took a wife and fathered several children.

In many ways, Tenskwatawa personally embodied the demoralized state of his people. In early 1805, in the wake of an epidemic of some European disease on which the healer's ministrations had little impact, he unexpectedly fell into a coma-like state that the Shawnees interpreted as death. However, before the funeral arrangements could be completed, he revived, to the amazement of his tribesmen. Considerably more amazing were the revelations he had received during his death-like trance.

Tenskwatawa believed he had been permitted to view heaven, "a rich, fertile country, abounding in game, fish, pleasant hunting grounds and fine corn fields." But he had also witnessed sinful Shawnee spirits being tortured according to the degree of their wickedness, with drunkards (one of Tenskwatawa's principal vices) being forced to swallow molten lead. Overwhelmed by the power of his vision, Tenskwatawa abandoned his old ways. More revelations followed in succeeding months, revelations that eventually added up to a coherent new vision of religion and society (Edmunds 1983, 33–34).

Although the new revelation departed from tradition on some points (for example, notions of heavenly and hellish realms were probably not indigenous), its central thrust was a Nativistic exhortation to abandon Euro-American ways for the lifestyle of earlier generations. Tenskwatawa successfully extended his religion to other tribes, particularly the Kickapoos, Winnebagos, Sacs, and Miamis. According to Thomas Jefferson's account, the Master of Life instructed Tenskwatawa "to make known to the Indians that they were created by him distinct from the whites, of different natures, for different purposes, and . . . that they must return from all the ways of the whites to the habits and opinions of their forefathers; they must not eat the flesh of hog, of bullocks, of sheep, etc., the deer and the buffalo having been created for their food; they must not make bread of wheat, but of Indian corn; they must not wear linen nor woolen, but dress like their fathers, in the skins and furs of animals; [and] they must not drink ardent spirits" (cited in Klinck 1961, 53). This revelation called tribesmen back to the lifestyle and the principles (that is, the laws of Shawnee tradition) prescribed by the Creator. As they had been warned "in the beginning," the abandonment of tradition had brought on social chaos. Although their current degradation involved the adoption of Euro-American ways, earlier deviations had been responsible for their military defeats. A nontraditional twist to the new revelation was that the forces of chaos were now identified with Euro-Americans.

In another revelation, the Master of Life went so far as to declare that the invaders from the east were "not my children, but the children of the Evil Spirit. They grew from the scum of the great Water when it was troubled by the Evil Spirit. And the froth was driven into the Woods by a strong east wind. They are numerous, but I hate them. They are unjust. They have taken away your lands, which were not made for them" (Edmunds 1983, 38).

Although the inclusion of Euro-Americans was new, in many other ways these teachings fit well into traditional understandings. The Great Serpent was the closest being the Shawnees had to a devil, so that the identification of this snake as the source of their conquerors was a reasonable association: The Great Serpent was avenging itself for the defeat it had suffered at the hands of the Shawnee people many thousands of years ago.

In a sense, the sea snake was still alive in the form of the various fragments of its flesh used as power sources in witchcraft. In fact, prior to the Creator's revelations through Tenskwatawa, some Shawnees had already been attributing their degraded state to the machinations of the Evil One through the agency of Indian sorcerers. These associations came together when Tenskwatawa and his followers began to kill witches.

The new revelation included a redemptive scenario in which Euro-Americans would be defeated and the fortunes of Native Americans restored. The promise of restored greatness had overwhelming appeal, and the prophet's message spread quickly to other tribes. Zealous converts among the Delaware (another Algonquian tribe whose mythology had many parallels to that of the Shawnee) seized fellow tribesmen suspected of witchcraft—who, predictably, turned out to be those Delaware most opposed to the new movement—and requested that Tenskwatawa journey to their village and use his supernatural power to identify witches.

The first prisoner to be condemned by the prophet was Anne Charity, a convert to Christianity who had adopted Euro-American manners and dress. She was suspended over a large campfire and tortured until she confessed that she was indeed a witch and that she had given her evil medicine bundle to her grandson. After they burned the old woman to death, the grandson was apprehended and brought before the assembly. Rightly fearing for his life, the young man admitted to having borrowed the medicine bundle, but claimed that he had returned it to his grandmother after having used it only once, for the innocuous purpose of flying through the air. The grandson was released, but his confession served to confirm the suspicions of widespread witchcraft held by the prophet and his followers. Other individuals who had converted to Christianity or who otherwise had some kind of close association with Euro-Americans were then tortured and burnt.

Though the new movement experienced its share of ups and downs, the promise of restored greatness was overwhelmingly appealing. Consequently, the religious leadership of the prophet remained strong until Tenskwatawa's prophecy of victory failed at the battle of Tippecanoe on November 7, 1811. Although from a purely military angle the battle was indecisive, Tenskwatawa's status as a leader was irreparably damaged. The hopes that Tenskwatawa's vision addressed were then transferred to the more secular efforts of his brother Tecumseh to unite the tribes in opposition to Euro-Americans.

Following the battle of the Thames in 1813, Tenskwatawa fled to Canada where he remained for a decade. He returned to the United States after agreeing to lead the remaining Shawnees out of the Midwest to Kansas. Subsequently, in and around 1828, tribal bands founded villages along the Kansas River. There the celebrated Western artist George Catlin painted a portrait of Tenskwatawa, in 1832. He died in November 1836 in what is now Kansas City.

Unlike Christian eschatology, the end-time scenario of the Shawnee was never fixed in a single written account. Rather, it was a flexible narrative that developed over time in response to new historical circumstances. Prior to Euro-American contact, the end time was a comparatively vague idea—should the Shawnee nation ever abandon the Creator's principles, the world would end. Because the world emerged out of a watery chaos, the Shawnee may have held the view that the creation would dissolve back into the waters at the end of time.

The tribe's confrontation with Euro-American colonists influenced the Shawnee to rethink and extend their mythology to cover the contact situation. The closest beings to evil entities in their tradition were witches and the marine serpent. Even before Tenskwatawa's vision, the Shawnee had begun to view Euro-Americans in terms of these negative beings: colonists were children of the Evil Spirit (the Great Serpent), and Native Americans who converted to Anglo ways were witches. In the face of this multifaceted threat, the prophet preached an Armageddon between Native Americans and Euro-Americans and, for a new millennium, a return to tradition. Though not as fully developed as the Christian version of the eschaton, this apocalyptic scenario seemed to offer a comprehensible explanation of the unhappy situation in which the Shawnee found themselves and, perhaps more importantly, it promised a happy ending.

HANDSOME LAKE, PROPHET OF ACCOMMODATION

In the same way that Tenskwatawa almost perfectly exemplifies the war prophet, the Iroquois prophet Handsome Lake exemplifies the peace prophet. The parallels between these two men are striking. Like Tenskwatawa, Handsome Lake was somewhat of a healer (a herbalist, at the very least) and an alcoholic who encountered the Creator during a death-vision. He was also given a vision of heaven and hell, and, in time, instructions for a new religious pattern that selectively revived and rejected parts of the religious tradition of the Iroquois. Like Tenskwatawa, Handsome Lake also preached a strong moral code and instituted formal confessions (his first vision in 1799 focused on the moral reclamation of the Iroquois).

Unlike the Shawnee, however, Handsome Lake did not condemn Euro-Americans as children of the Evil Spirit. The Iroquois prophet did not even condemn Christianity. Rather, Handsome Lake's visions made it clear that in the same way in which his revelations were directed to Native Americans, Christianity was an appropriate religion for Euro-Americans. During one of his spirit journeys, for instance, the Iroquois prophet met Jesus, with whom he discussed the relative success of their respective missions (Wallace 1972, 244).

Handsome Lake's teachings included all of the essential ingredients necessary to preserve the Iroquois as a people in the face of Euro-American encroachment. In addition to the points already mentioned, an important tenet of the new faith was the preservation of the tribal land base, while simultaneously maintaining peaceful relations with their non-Iroquois neighbors. In the words of Anthony Wallace, who wrote the classic study of Handsome Lake, "He told the Iroquois to adopt the white man's mode of agriculture, which included a man's working the fields (hitherto a woman's role); he advised that some learn to read and write English; he counseled them to emphasize the integrity of the married couple and its household, rather than the old maternal lineage. In sum, his code was a blueprint of a culture that would be socially and technologically more effective in the new circumstances of reservation life than the old culture could ever have been" (1972, 281). Handsome Lake's religion was so successful that it has survived to the present day.

As members of the same general culture—the cultural sphere anthropologists refer to as the Eastern Woodlands—traditional Iroquois society was not radically different from Shawnee society. In particular, the Iroquois were not less warlike than the Shawnee. They also possessed roughly similar conceptions of witchcraft. Both had suffered defeat at the hands of land-hungry Anglo-American colonials. It is even clear that both Tenskwatawa and Handsome Lake initially experienced comparable visions. Why then, one might ask, did the Shawnee prophet end up following the path of war while Handsome Lake become a prophet of accommodation?

The answer to this question is not simple. For one thing, the Shawnee prophet and the Iroquois prophet faced different historical circumstances. More significantly, for the purposes of the present discussion, the Iroquois possessed an unusual ideological resource in the form of mythologized folklore about Deganawidah (He-Who-Thinks), the legendary founder of the Iroquois confederacy. The legend of Deganawidah was based on a Huron who, scholars hypothesize, lived in the mid-fifteenth century and brought peace to the Iroquois people.

Despite a common language and culture, in Deganawidah's day the Iroquois were split into five separate and mutually warring tribes—the Mohawk, the Onondaga, the Seneca, the Oneida, and the Cayuga. Their customs of warfare were brutal, sanctioning the killing of women and children as well as ritual cannibalism. Much of the ongoing conflict involved vendettas in which warriors attacked their neighbors for no other reason than to avenge the deaths of fellow tribesmen—who in turn had to be avenged, thus perpetuating an endless cycle of violence.

Deganawidah, an outcast from his own tribe, wandered into the Iroquois killing fields preaching a message of peace—a vision of unity that would one day be called the Great Law of Peace. According to legend, one of Deganawidah's early converts was the Mohawk Hiawatha. Hiawatha's entire family, a wife and seven daughters, had been murdered by the Onondaga war chief, Ododarhoh. Out of his mind with grief, Hiawatha had degenerated into an animalistic recluse who spent his days ambushing and eating hapless travelers.

Coming upon Hiawatha's lodge in the woods, Deganawidah is said to have climbed up onto the roof and peered down the smoke hole. Hiawatha was in the midst of preparing a human carcass for dinner. At that precise moment Hiawatha glanced at Deganaw-idah's reflection in the water of the cooking pot and mistook it for his own. The reflected image was so full of purity and kindness that Hiawatha was struck by the thought, "This is not the face of a cannibal" (cited in Peterson 1990). The force of emotion evoked by this simple thought was such that his humane side was able to break through the clouds of vengeful anger that had enveloped Hiawatha ever since the brutal deaths of his family. He immediately resolved to abandon his cannibalism. In that very moment, he took his pot some distance away from his lodge and cast out its contents.

Returning, he was greeted by Deganawidah, who shared his vision of peace with Hiawatha. His heart already opened by his resolution to abandon cannibalism, and overwhelmed by the boldness of Deganawidah's vision, Hiawatha was immediately transformed into the Huron prophet's right-hand man. At the end of his discourse, Deganawidah addressed his new disciple, "My junior brother, we now shall make our laws and when all are made we shall call the organization we have formed The Great Peace. It shall be the power to abolish war and robbery between brothers and bring peace and quietness" (cited in Peterson 1990, 69). Gradually, over the course of five years of diplomacy, these two men brought the five tribes into a confederacy. The Onondaga were the last to join, after the prophet touched the heart of the evil Ododarhoh, the murderer of Hiawatha's family, and Ododarhoh declared himself Deganawidah's disciple. After firmly establishing the Great Peace among the five nations, it is said that Deganawidah disappeared, paddling westward into the setting sun. What happened to the prophet after leaving the Iroquois is unknown.

Although Handsome Lake did not claim the mantle of Deganawidah, the impact of his teachings was to renew the Iroquois people and to restore the League of the Iroquois that the Huron prophet had established centuries earlier. Hence, whether or not the five tribes viewed Handsome Lake as the Peacemaker returned, Deganawidah had bequeathed to the Iroquois people an ideological and spiritual resource that enabled them to renew themselves and renew their culture out of the despairing and demoralized conditions that faced them at the end of the eighteenth century. In particular, the Huron prophet had taught the Iroquois people the power of forgiveness and the power of peace, and it was the tradition of these teachings that enabled them to forgive Anglo-Americans and learn to live with them in peace.

WOVOKA'S PACIFIST APOCALYPSE

When I was in the other world with the Old Man, I saw all the people who have died. But they were not sad. They were happy while engaged in their old-time occupations and dancing, gambling, and playing ball. It was a pleasant land, level, without rocks or mountains, green all the time, and rich with an abundance of game and fish. Everyone was forever young.

After showing me all of heaven, God told me to go back to earth and tell his people you must be good and love one another, have no quarreling, and live in peace with the whites; that you must work, and not lie or steal; and that you must put an end to the practice of war.

If you faithfully obey your instructions from on high, you will at last be reunited with your friends in a renewed world where there would be no more death or sickness or old age. First, though, the earth must die. Indians should not be afraid, however. For it will come alive again, just like the sun died and came alive again [during the eclipse]. In the hour of tribulation, a tremendous earthquake will shake the ground. Indians must gather on high ground. A mighty flood shall follow. The water and mud will sweep the white race and all Indian skeptics away to their death. Then the dead Indian ancestors will return, as will the vanished buffalo and other game, and everything on earth will once again be an Indian paradise. (Cited in Peterson 1990, 99)

The Ghost Dance represents an intermediate category between the above two—hostile, yet adaptive. The Paiute prophet Wovoka (also called Jack Wilson, not to be confused with the peyote prophet, John Wilson), unlike either Tenskwatawa or Handsome Lake, was not dissolute. Nevertheless, like the earlier prophets, Wovoka was a healing shaman who experienced his revelation in a death-vision during which God gave him strongly ethical teachings. The usual pattern of heavenly and hellish realms was, however, missing. Instead, Wovoka received a revelation of a millennium in which the earth would be renewed and the spirits of the dead would return. The millennium would be preceded by a general catastrophe that would destroy Euro-Americans and their material culture. This would be a cosmic rather than a military-political catastrophe. Consequently, Native Americans were instructed to keep the peace and wait.

Beyond remaining at peace and following Wovoka's ethical injunctions, American Indians were instructed to periodically perform what Euro-Americans came to call the Ghost Dance; to cite an extended account from a contemporaneous Anglo-American observer of a Sioux Ghost Dance:

> [The Ghost shirts and dresses were covered with] figures of birds, bows and arrows, sun, moon, and stars, and everything they saw in nature . . . [and] a number had stuffed birds, squirrel heads, etc., tied in their long hair. The faces of all were painted red with a black half-moon on the forehead or on one cheek.
>
> One stood directly behind another, each with his hands on his neighbor's shoulders. After walking about a few times, chanting, "Father, I come," they stopped marching, but remained in the circle, and set up the most fearful, heart-piercing wails I ever heard—crying, moaning, groaning, and shrieking out their grief, and naming over their departed friends and relatives, at the same time taking up handfuls of dust at their feet, washing their hands in it, and throwing it over their heads. Finally, they raised their eyes to heaven, their hands clasped high above their heads, and stood straight and perfectly still, invoking the power of the Great Spirit to allow them to see and talk with their people who had died. . . .
>
> And now the most intense excitement began. They would go as fast as they could, their hands moving from side to side, their bodies swaying, their arms, with hands gripped tightly in their neighbors', swinging back and forth with all their might. The ground had been worked and worn by many feet, until the fine, flour-like dust lay light and loose and to the depth of two or three inches. The wind, which had increased, would sometimes take it up, enveloping the dancers and hiding them from view. In the ring were men, women, and children; the strong and the robust, the weak, consumptive, and those near to death's door. They believed those who were sick would be cured by joining in the dancing and losing consciousness. From the beginning they chanted, to a monotonous tune, the words—"Father, I come; Mother, I come; Brother, I come; Father, give us back our arrows."
>
> All of which they would repeat over and over again until first one then another would break from the ring and stagger away and fall down. . . . [N]o one ever disturbed those who fell or took any notice of them except to keep the crowd away.
>
> They kept up dancing until fully 100 persons were lying unconscious. Then they stopped and seated themselves in a circle, and as each one recovered from his trance he was brought to the center of the ring to relate his experience. (Cited in Peterson 1990, 114–115)

FIGURE 2.1. The Ghost Dance (1896). From James Mooney, *The Ghost Dance Religion and Wounded Knee* (New York: Dover Publications, 1973).

The participants who fell down into a trance received revelations, usually from departed relatives. Performing the dance would hasten the advent of the new age.

Wovoka's revelation spoke powerfully to his contemporaries, and the dance was taken up by a wide variety of different tribes, such as the Shoshoni, Arapaho, Crow, Cheyenne, Pawnee, Kiowa, Comanche, and Sioux. As one might anticipate, relatively stable tribal groups that had adjusted successfully to changed conditions were the least inclined to accept the new teaching. The widespread excitement generated by Wovoka's vision declined rapidly in the wake of the Wounded Knee massacre (December 29, 1890), so that the effective life span of the Ghost Dance as a mass movement was no more than a few years. The prophet himself died many years later, on September 20, 1932. Quite independently of the prophet, however, the Ghost Dance continued to be practiced. For example, as late as the 1950s the dance was still being performed by the Shoshonis in something like its original form (Hultkrantz 1987, 83). Perhaps the most important adaptive responses were in tribal groups that partially adopted the Ghost Dance as a medium for reviving selected aspects of their traditional religion (for example, Lesser 1933).

This discussion brings us to the issue of the unstable, ephemeral nature that has traditionally been attributed to "non-mainstream" religious movements (e.g., the discussion of "cults" in Campbell 1972). Though American Indian movements belong in a somewhat different category from groups like the Unification Church, they share the imputed characterization of being ephemeral phenomena. It is thus relevant to the larger issue at hand to question the conventional wisdom about Native American messianic movements.

To begin with, one should immediately note that no scholar with a reasonably broad knowledge of American Indian prophets would accept the attribution of instability as being a generally applicable trait. The movements initiated by Handsome Lake, Kenekuk, and John Slocum—all founded over a hundred years ago—survive to the present day. Also, certain offshoots of the Ghost Dance, such as the Maru Cult (Meighan and Riddell 1972), as well as the Native American Church, are still very much alive (LaBarre 1938).

The impression of ephemerality appears to be the result of superficial acquaintance with the Ghost Dance of 1890, the one American Indian messiah movement with which there is widespread familiarity. There is a general awareness that the Ghost Dance led to a brief period of intense millenarian expectancy among Native Americans, an expectancy that rapidly diminished in the wake of Wounded Knee. However, most people are unaware that the Ghost Dance continued to be practiced, especially in tribes where elements of the dance became blended with the group's traditional religion. Even among academics, religion scholars without a background in Native American studies often have no acquaintance with American Indian prophet religions beyond the short segment on the Ghost Dance of 1890 in *Black Elk Speaks*, a reading that reinforces the impression of prophet religions as ephemeral phenomena that flare up and then die (Neihardt 1961).

The picture presented by this narrow base of information dovetails nicely with the commonsense view of messianic movements, which is that when predicted events do not occur, participants lose faith and the movement collapses. However, as the classic study *When Prophecy Fails* demonstrated, the failure of prophecy can, in certain circumstances, have the opposite effect of actually *increasing* one's faith (Festinger, Riecken, and Schachter 1956). One might also recall that, if we accept the testimony of the synoptic gospels, Jesus predicted an imminent apocalypse that never occurred. The time frame he gave for the advent of the millennium was, "this generation will not pass away before all these things take place" (Mark 13:30). Despite this failed prophecy, the Christian Church went on to become one of the biggest success stories of all time.

The case of Christianity should also cause us to question the bit of conventional wisdom that views the death of the founding prophet as a crisis that usually leads more or less immediately to the death of the prophet's movement. This notion has almost no empirical foundation. Specifically, the evidence supplied by the history of Native American prophet religions serves to undercut the conventional wisdom on this point. If we set aside the non-adaptive visions of the war prophets, the majority of American Indian movements found in the ethnographic literature—almost all of which were initiated in the nineteenth century—either persist in some form to the present day or at least persisted well after the deaths of their founders. Beyond these ongoing success stories, we can find other demonstrations of the point that the demise of a prophet religion is rarely correlated with the founder's death.

For example, as far as can be determined, Wodziwob, the initiator of the Ghost Dance of 1870, lived well into the twentieth century, although his movement among the Paiute collapsed within a few years of its founding. There is also the very unusual case of the prophet Kolaskin, whose religion persisted not only after his death, but prior to his death it continued to exist even after the prophet himself abandoned the movement (Lanternari 1956, 119).

Beyond the ethnocentric attitude that leads one to perceive apparently eccentric visions of the world as by nature unstable, a key factor in causing academics to attribute ephemerality to messianic movements is a mistaken theoretical perspective that portrays the personal charisma of the founder as the glue holding together alternate views of reality. Such a perspective misconstrues the role of charisma. In the first place, no matter how charismatic the prophet, his or her message must somehow address the concerns of the community in a satisfactory manner if he or she is to convince more than a handful of close associates. In other words, a contagious new vision has to have more going for it than the personality of the revealer.

In the second place, although the prophet's charisma may be necessary in giving life to the vision during the nascent stages of the new movement, the actual adoption of an emergent religion by a human community recruits the forces of social consensus to the side of the new revelation—forces that tend to maintain the alternate vision of reality independently of the charisma of the founder. To think of this in terms of the micro-sociology of knowledge (Berger and Luckmann 1966), the plausibility of a particular worldview and its accompanying lifestyle is maintained by the ongoing "conversation" that takes place among the members of a particular community. If an entire community is converted to a new vision of reality, as Native American tribes frequently were, the possibility of encountering dissonance as a result of interaction with non-believing conversation partners is largely eliminated.

Because social consensus is the real glue that maintains the plausibility of any given worldview, potential sources of crisis in the life of a religious movement lie in the area of breakdowns of social consensus, not in the passing away of the founder. Thus as long as a new religion continues satisfactorily to address the concerns of the community, the prophet's death will not induce a crisis of faith.

3

JESUS IN INDIA AND THE
FORGING OF TRADITION

The librarian and two other monks approached the ladies carrying three objects. Madame Caspari recognized them as Buddhist books made of sheets of parchment sandwiched between two pieces of wood and wrapped in brocades—green and red and blue seeded with gold.

With great reverence, the librarian unwrapped one of the books and presented the parchments to Mrs. Gasque, "These books say your Jesus was here!". . .

She pondered the implications of the find. Her mind whirled, reeled as she thought of Jesus traveling, perhaps all over the world. She realized that up until that hour, Jesus had been to her, as to most Christians, a product of Palestine. He was born there; he lived and died there. Any religious training he received was a part of the Jewish tradition. To place Jesus in Tibet or in India would mean that he had studied their customs, their languages, *their religion!*

Why did Jesus feel compelled to undertake this journey, just as she had, prior to his Palestinian mission? And to what manifold purposes did our Father send him? Indeed, this casual encounter atop the world had far-reaching theological implications. Maybe the teachings of Jesus told to John substantiated in turn the teachings of Gautama or the Vedas.

—Elizabeth Clare Prophet,
The Lost Years of Jesus

What Elizabeth Caspari did not realize on that day in 1939 was that she and the other members of her party would be the last persons to claim they had actually seen this quasi-legendary manuscript. The openness of the monks to Caspari's group stands in marked contrast to their response to earlier visits by Westerners, during which the very existence of such texts had been denied. Though Caspari took innumerable photos of her journey, unfortunately her photograph of this encounter does not show the single open page clearly enough for anyone to be able to distinguish the delicate Tibetan characters in the book. And contrary to the rather dramatic retelling of the event in Prophet's book, Caspari was apparently not cognizant of the importance of her find. Not only did she not bother to take more pictures of the manuscript, but she also failed to make further inquiries.

Caspari's story is part of a century-old tradition, which asserts that Jesus journeyed to India to undertake a course in esoteric training. This tradition has been enthusiastically embraced by many contemporary Hindu religious teachers and certain Western esoteric groups. Ancient texts discovered in India in the past few centuries, as well as certain traditional Indian legends, supposedly provide evidence for this exotic view of Jesus' early education. For a large percentage of participants in the contemporary occult–metaphysical–New Age subculture, Jesus' Indian visit is a historical fact, as well established as—if not actually more real than—the events recorded in the canonical gospels. Although no mainstream religious scholar has taken this thesis seriously, this tale has been especially popular among Indian religious teachers with Western followers, from Swami Rama to Bhaktivedanta Prabhupada to Osho (Bhagwan Rajneesh).

This chapter will examine the legend of the Hemis manuscript. Although its existence was attested to by a number of different authors, it was clearly a forged document. As will be demonstrated, the story of Jesus in India is rather like the inkblot tests utilized by psychologists, in that each successive promoter of the tale anticipated discovering his own religious beliefs reflected in Jesus' teachings. When they failed to do so, they either supplied the missing components, or edited pre-existing texts to fit their preconceptions of what Jesus must have said and done. Each successive person who perpetuated this legend was attracted to it for the same reason—the Indian Jesus could be deployed to legitimate their own brand of spirituality as well as to undermine the legitimacy of the orthodox interpretation of Christian tradition.

Appealing to the authority of traditional religious figures while simultaneously attributing teachings to them that make one's own views appear the true embodiment of tradition is a legitimation strategy one often finds in new religions. Creating new documents and then claiming either that they were received by direct revelation or that they represent previously unknown but ancient texts is also common. The present analysis will examine these complementary legitimation strategies via an analysis of the Jesus-in-India tradition. This particular tradition was chosen because the legend of Jesus' trip to India is *not* an essential or core component of any existing religion, past or present. The analysis can thus be completely blunt while at the same time avoiding the impression that the aim is to undermine the legitimacy of a specific religious group. Also, the processes at work in the generation and perpetuation of the Jesus-in-India tradition are exceptionally lucid, making this particular legend an excellent case study.

THE "DISCOVERY" OF JESUS IN INDIA

There are two distinct classes of narratives about Jesus' travels in India. The first set of tales involves an early sojourn between the age of twelve, corresponding with the last canonical mention of the young Nazarene's life before his ministry in Palestine, and thirty, when his ministry began. The purpose of this visit was to acquire esoteric knowledge. The second set of tales has Jesus survive the crucifixion and then journey to India, where he lives until he passes on at a ripe old age. These two kinds of narratives are not normally presented in combination. The present discussion will focus on the first tradition, which is more developed as well as more widely accepted. The second tradition will be dealt with briefly because of its connection with the first.

The idea that Jesus studied in India began—or, at least, first received widespread attention—in 1894 when the Russian Nicolas Notovitch published *La vie inconnue du Jesus Christ* (later translated as *The Unknown Life of Jesus Christ,* 1907). The bulk of this work recounts a trip Notovitch made to Kashmir in 1887. While there, he hears of a Buddhist monastery possessing ancient texts that include an account of Jesus' visit to India as a young man. He subsequently travels to Leh in Ladakh, where he visits Hemis Monastery, at which, through an interpreter, he transcribes the most significant sections of two large books containing the story of Issa (as Jesus is called in India). This translated text is subsequently incorporated into his *Unknown Life,* under the title *The Life of Saint Issa.*

After telling the story of Israel leading up to Jesus' childhood, Notovitch's transcription relates how Jesus left home at the age of thirteen because he did not wish to marry. He first journeys to northwest India, where he encounters Jains. He then moves to the east coast of India at Juggernath, where "[Brahmin priests] taught him to read and understand the Vedas, to cure by aid of prayer, to teach, to explain the holy scriptures to the people, and to drive out evil spirits from the bodies of men, restoring unto them their sanity" (*The Life of Saint Issa* 5:4, in Notovitch 1907). He remains in eastern India for six years, visiting holy places like Benares, preaching the doctrine of the one true God against local superstitions and the doctrine of equality against the caste system. Despite the fact that he is supposedly learning much from his Hindu mentors, in his sermons he emphatically denies the authority of the Vedas and the reality of the chief divinities of the classical Hindu pantheon. Making enemies of the Hindu priests, who decide to have him murdered, he escapes to the Himalayas, where he studies the Pali sutras with Buddhists for another six years. Not one to give up old habits, however, he spends his spare time preaching against superstition, once again angering his mentors. Beyond condemning idolatry, Jesus preaches against the doctrine of reincarnation and condemns the practice of miracle working. Afterwards he visits Persia, where he enters into conflict with Zoroastrians. Finally he leaves and returns to Palestine. The story then continues on to relate the familiar events of Jesus' biblical ministry and the Passion, although retold so as to present a story strikingly at odds with the canonical narrative.

Notovitch's book was an instant hit in Europe. Despite immediately being attacked as a forgery, *The Unknown Life of Jesus Christ* prompted other writers to seek, and even to claim they had found, the same document at Hemis Monastery. The earliest of these supporting claims was made by Swami Abhedananda, a member of the Ramakrishna movement, who knew the prominent scholar Max Müller. In 1922, he went to Hemis Monastery, where he is said to have read the same book Notovitch transcribed in 1887.

Abhedananda subsequently published certain sections of it in his Bengali book, *Kashmir O Tibbate* (In Kashmir and Tibet, 1929). In 1984, these sections, along with certain parts of Abhedananda's Bengali work, were translated and appeared in Elizabeth Clare Prophet's *The Lost Years of Jesus*. The relevant passages reflect the same basic document, with the exception that Abhedananda deleted the anti-Hindu tone found in *The Unknown Life of Jesus*

Christ and made Issa's theology more congruent with Advaita Vedanta philosophy.

Later another Russian, Nicholas Roerich, also sought out the text at Hemis, but did not find the Notovitch manuscript. Nevertheless, he eventually authored and co-authored a number of books in which he cited passages he claimed were taken from other, unnamed sources dealing with Issa's trip to India. Many of these, however, appear to have been taken directly from Notovitch. He also made reference to a number of legends about Jesus that were widespread in that part of India.

In addition to *The Unknown Life of Jesus Christ,* Roerich also appears to have been influenced by Levi Dowling's *The Aquarian Gospel of Jesus Christ,* an early twentieth-century "esoteric gospel" in which Jesus is portrayed as studying in Asia as well as in a number of Western mystery schools. Though the latter author's account of Jesus' India visit was clearly indebted to Notovitch, Dowling, unlike the others, claimed to have copied the *Aquarian Gospel* directly from the Akashic Records (a familiar concept in occult lore)—a purely spiritual record of events on earth that, according to Dowling, he accessed via clairvoyance—rather than from physical manuscripts secreted away in isolated monasteries.

Beyond Elisabeth Caspari's account mentioned at the beginning of the present chapter, these are the principal sources of what we might call the younger Jesus-in-India tradition. How plausible is this tradition? The central difficulty with this story is, of course, that the manuscript, if it ever existed, was never accessible to more than a few outsiders. Furthermore, the current status of these hypothetical texts is that they were supposedly moved to another monastery further into Tibet, where they were apparently seized and presumably destroyed by the Chinese.

With respect to the actual story related in the text, there are simply too many improbabilities for Notovitch's original narrative to be literally true. However, even if we allow for the possibility that Notovitch embellished his narrative to make it more engaging, the manuscript cannot fail to strike even sympathetic readers as spurious. Many items of historical information are anachronistic; others are simply false. For example, the Juggernath temple in eastern India, which appears to have been Jesus' destination after he left the

Jains, was built over a thousand years following Jesus' death. One should also note that the designation "Issa" for Jesus comes from the Qu'ran, composed some six centuries after Jesus' time. Other incorrect items of data include the assertion that the Buddhists are monotheists, "worshiping the one and sublime Brahma" (Notovitch 1907, VI:2).

More importantly, the narrative fails to support the very thesis it sets out to demonstrate, namely, that Jesus received his training among the masters of the East. Particularly in Notovitch's version of the story, Jesus does little but attack Indian beliefs and practices, denouncing Hinduism and Buddhism as false and idolatrous. In short, we are forced to conclude not only that the hypothetical manuscript supposedly examined by Notovitch does not tell us anything about the historical Jesus, but, further, that *The Life of Saint Issa* must have been written by someone from the West, almost certainly by the author of *The Unknown Life of Jesus Christ* himself. Before attempting to understand Notovitch's forgery and the motives of subsequent, unconnected individuals who bore false witness to the existence of *The Life of Saint Issa*, we should briefly examine what might be called the older Jesus-in-India tradition.

Around the end of the nineteenth century, a somewhat different narrative about Jesus in India emerged. Although there are different versions, they all tell the story of how Jesus survived the crucifixion and subsequently moved to India. In one version, Jesus becomes famous in India under the name Yuz-Assaf. Eventually, Jesus settles in Srinagar in Kashmir and dies at 120 years of age. This story of Jesus apparently originated in an 1899 book by Mirza Ghulam Ahmad, *Masih Hindustan Mein* (later published in English under the title *Jesus in India*). Ahmad relates how he came across a grave on Khan Yar Street in Srinagar, described as a prophet's grave. When he finds that this prophet was named Yuz-Assaf, Ahmad leaps to the conclusion that this must be Jesus' grave. Following his discovery, he infers a number of other things, such as that the Kashmiri people are part of the ten lost tribes who Jesus sought out in his old age. He also discovers Mary's grave not far away. Ahmad seems to have been the first person to claim to have found Jesus' grave in Srinagar.

What is relevant in these claims for the younger Jesus-in-India tradition is that Notovitch, who passed through Srinagar during his 1887 trip, never mentions anything about the later Jesus-in-India tradition. This indicates that, far from being an ancient legend, the story of Jesus' life and burial in Kashmir originated after Notovitch's time. And in the same way that narratives about Jesus' old age and death in India started with Ahmad, narratives about Jesus traveling to India as a young man began with Notovitch. Not only is there no hint of such a trip in any of the documents that have survived from the early Christian era, but, down through the centuries, no one ever seriously proposed a connection between India and Jesus prior to Notovitch.

THE ORIGINAL FORGERY

Though we can safely conclude that *The Life of Saint Issa* is a forgery, we should remember that the history of religion contains innumerable examples of such forged documents—including examples from such mainstream religions as Christianity and Buddhism—before we judge Notovitch too harshly. Many of the principal scriptures of Mahayana Buddhism, for instance, claim to have been authored by the historical Buddha, despite the fact that they did not appear until many centuries after his death.

It is also generally accepted that some of the epistles supposedly authored by Paul were simply forged. In both of these cases, the respective authors' strategy was to draw on the prestige of a great religious figure to legitimate particular doctrines and associated practices. In *The Gnostic Gospels,* for example, Elaine Pagels notes that a number of the pseudo-Pauline letters pick up on and amplify the antifeminist tenor of Paul's own views, presumably to legitimate the repression of uppity women in their congregations; for example, I Timothy 2:11–12: "Let a woman learn in silence with all submissiveness. I permit no woman to teach or to have authority over men; she is to keep silent" (cited in Pagels 1989, 630). An extension of this strategy is to forge a narrative in which an authoritative figure is reported as advocating a particular ideology.

In addition to associating documents with important people—either as authors or as spokespersons—texts are also forged that claim to be very ancient. The goal of both approaches is to legitimate whatever ideas are being propagated by the document. Appealing to a pure, uncorrupted, original truth that antedates current religions is frequently employed by founders of new religions. The attractiveness of this strategy is based on a deep pattern in the human psyche that tends to regard ancient origins as particularly sacred. This pattern and its implications for religion have been exhaustively explored by historians of religion such as Mircea Eliade.

Gerald Gardner, the founder of the relatively recent (mid-twentieth century) religion of Neopagan Witchcraft (commonly referred to as the "Craft" by insiders), is a useful example of someone who forged a number of important documents that he later claimed to be very old. For example, in the context of an argument over how a witch "coven" should be run and how witches should comport themselves in public, Gardner devised a set of "Craft Laws" that legitimated his personal ideas on these matters. Rather than crediting authorship to himself, he composed the document in archaic, King James–style English and claimed that the laws were very ancient. These Craft Laws became one of the founding documents of the Neopagan movement. For our present discussion, what is significant about this incident is that Gardner felt no need to name a particular person as the author of his forgery; merely ascribing ancient origins was enough to legitimate it (Lewis 1999, 345–352). In both of these cases, we are probably safe in inferring that the unknown author of I Timothy as well as Gerald Gardner believed in the truth of most if not all of the ideas they were expressing, but felt a need to support their position with an appeal to a greater authority.

Notovitch drew on both of these sources of legitimacy—an authoritative historical figure (Jesus) and ancient origins. Assuming Notovitch put his own views in the mouth of Jesus, it appears that he accepted some form of Deism. From Jesus' nonvirgin birth to his non-resurrection to his message of moralism, anti-priestcraft, and anti-miracle-working, *The Life of Saint Issa* expresses a thoroughly Deist theology. There are, however, a few unique twists. The majority of chapter 12 (12:9–21), for example, is devoted to extolling the nobility of women in their roles as wives and mothers, and encouraging men to support and protect the opposite sex; for example, "Respect woman, for she is the mother of the universe, and all the truth of divine creation lies in her. She is the basis of all that is good and beautiful, as she is also the germ of life and death. On her depends the whole existence of man, for she is his natural and moral support" (12:10–11). Also, in a complete reversal from the canonical story, Pilate is intent on executing Jesus, while the priests and elders of Israel defend him. When Jesus is finally brought before Pilate and tried, the priests and elders—changing places with the canonical Pilate—even wash their hands of the matter, saying, "We are innocent of the death of this just man" (13:25). This reassignment of guilt is interesting because it corresponds with the consensus of modern scholarship, which is that Roman authorities, not Jewish authorities, were responsible for the execution of Jesus.

Though we know too little about Notovitch's life to be able to say what motivated him to devote so much space (relatively speaking) to a discourse in praise of women, we do know enough about his background to be able to surmise why he rewrote the trial of Jesus. Though at least nominally a member of the Russian Orthodox Church, Notovitch's background was Jewish, strongly suggesting a very personal motive for turning the ancient Romans into "Christ killers," rather than blaming the Jewish people. Also, given the passion with which Notovitch's Jesus expresses himself, we are probably justified in inferring that, for the most part at least, Notovitch truly believed in the ideas contained in the text of his fabrication—true lies, if you will.

That being said, however, we should not completely factor out the role played by pecuniary motives. Notovitch was a professional writer. He undoubtedly expected that *The Unknown Life of Jesus Christ* would sell well, if not become an international bestseller: "At least eight editions were published in France in 1894 [the year it first appeared], and three separate English translations appeared in the United States. Another English translation was published in London the following year. It was also translated into German, Spanish, Swedish, and Italian" (Prophet 1984, 20). Thus although Notovitch probably hoped to popularize the views expressed in *The Unknown Life of Jesus Christ,* he was also consciously engaged in the construction of a forgery from which he anticipated financial rewards.

RE-FORGING THE STORY

The strongest objection that can be raised against the charge that *The Life of Saint Issa* was a forgery is that other witnesses claimed either to have seen the manuscript or to have recovered similar documents that resembled *The Life of Saint Issa.* Swami Abhedananda made the former claim; Nicolas Roerich made the latter. These men, otherwise viewed as honorable, however, had their own reasons for perpetuating Notovitch's bogus story. Their motives can best be inferred from the modifications and additions they made to Notovitch's text.

As noted earlier, Abhedananda reproduced somewhat modified passages from *The Life of Saint Issa* in his 1929 Bengali work, *In Kashmir and Tibet*. The differences are revealing: Notovitch's Issa is "taught" by the Brahmins (5:4), and, some time later, he warns the people that they should "Listen not to the Vedas, for their truth is counterfeit" (5:26). In sharp contrast, Abhedananda's Issa becomes a "disciple" of the Brahmins, eventually "reading, learning and expounding the Vedas" (5:4). The Swami is also more charitable toward the Jains. Notovitch's Issa rejects their invitation to stay with them because they represent a false religion, "[T]he devotees of the god Jaine prayed him to dwell among them. But he left the erring worshippers of Jaine and went to Juggernaut" (5:2–3). Abhedananda's Issa, however, turns down their invitation from a desire to remain out of the public spotlight: "And they asked him to stay in their temples. But he did not accept their invitation, because he did not want any attention from others at that time" (5:3). These are not minor differences that can be summarily dismissed. Abhedananda's Jesus is simply not Notovitch's iconoclastic prophet, railing against the perversities of the heathen. Rather, as Ramakrishna (the founder of the Swami's movement) taught, Abhedananda's Jesus was a Hindu avatar.

There are three principal ways of accounting for this discrepancy. First, there was a text at Hemis Monastery that Notovitch recorded correctly but which Abhedananda changed to suit his own views. Second, there was a text that Abhedananda recorded correctly but which Notovitch changed to suit his own views. Or third, there never was a real book at Hemis, but Abhedananda played along with forgery—albeit with some profound modifications of Notovitch's text—for his own purposes. If we take the third option as the most likely one, what might the Swami's motives have been?

For all of Abhedananda's life, the British ruled South Asia and treated Indians as second-class citizens. Furthermore, though English administrators were ambivalent about Western missionary activity in the subcontinent, few regarded indigenous religious traditions as anything more than barbaric superstitions. But what if the founder of the conquerors' own faith had spent the larger part of his life in the Indian subcontinent, studying at the feet of Hindu and Buddhist sages? Perhaps Jesus himself even preached some form of Indian wisdom after his return to Palestine, though most traces of such teachings disappeared or were destroyed by the early church. The appeal of this idea to a subject people would be tremendous. If true, it would imply that Indian civilization is the foundation for Western civilization—or, at least, the foundation of the Western religious tradition.

Abhedananda's initial interest in the story of Jesus' Indian sojourn probably derived from this attraction. After examining a copy of *The Unknown Life of Jesus Christ*, however, the Swami would have been appalled by many of the teachings of Notovitch's Jesus. At that point (to grant him the benefit of the doubt), maybe Abhedananda concluded the story was real, but that Notovitch had reinterpreted it according to Western prejudices. The Swami would then have gone to Hemis in search of the original manuscript, only to find that it was missing or to encounter monks denying it was ever there. Disappointed, perhaps Abhedananda then decided to go back over *The Life of Saint Issa* and rewrite it to conform to his preconception of what the original manuscript must have said, according his notion of Jesus as a Hindu-style avatar. (It should be noted that the section of the Swami's travelogue translated for Prophet's *The Lost Years of Jesus* relates that he *did* see the original from which Notovitch's book was transcribed. This particular section was, however, written in the third person, indicating that it had been added to the 1954 second edition by a later editor over a decade after Abhedananda's death.)

Being aware of the standards of Western scholarship, however, the Swami would have been reluctant to present his discovery in English to a Western audience. Knowing that there was no real text on the shelves of the Hemis Monastery library (or doubting that such a text existed), and knowing further that the monks themselves would deny the manuscript's existence, Abhedananda would have been aware that any claim of discovering the original Notovitch text would embroil him in the same controversies that greeted the initial publication of *The Unknown Life of Jesus Christ* in 1894. (The Swami was, as noted earlier, an acquaintance of the noted scholar Max Müller, who wrote an article (1894) condemning *The Life of Saint Issa* as a fraud.) The Swami therefore, with regret, decided to restrict the publication of his rewritten passages from *The Life of Saint Issa* to a Bengali book that would be unlikely to attract the attention of Western critics.

Had Abhedananda found a real text at Hemis containing the ideas expressed in his *In Kashmir and Tibet*, he would certainly have broadcast his findings to the widest possible audience, both scholarly and popular, for the reasons mentioned above. That he did not is strong evidence that the Swami never, in fact, laid eyes on such a manuscript. At the same time, Abhedananda's "re-forging" of *The Life of Saint Issa* falls into the category of a "true lie"—a falsified document expressing what the author felt were profound truths.

OTHER SOURCES

Nicholas Roerich, another man viewed as honorable, also entered into complicity with the Notovitch legend, but stopped short of claiming to have seen the original manuscript at Hemis Monastery. Instead, he, first, mentions the story of the earlier Russian traveler who transcribed the story of Jesus; second, recounts local legends about Issa's visit; third, implies that the monks know the details of Issa's Indian travels but keep them secret; and, fourth, provides quotations from other (unnamed) sources and documents that repeat—and often paraphrase—*The Life of Saint Issa*. This set of strategies allowed Roerich to confirm Notovitch's basic story while simultaneously avoiding the criticism that might have been evoked had he claimed to have actually seen texts on Jesus' Indian sojourn in the library at Hemis.

Like Abhedananda's Issa, Roerich's Issa is less antagonistic to Hindu and Buddhist religiosity than Notovitch's Issa. Specifically, although Roerich's Jesus attacks idolatry and the caste system, he does not condemn Jains, Hindus, or Buddhists as following "counterfeit" traditions. Unsurprisingly, the Jesus one encounters in Roerich's writings is closer to the theosophical view of Jesus (Roerich's own religious persuasion) than to either Notovitch's Deist or Abhedananda's Vedantist Jesus.

Interestingly, in the book *Altai-Himalaya* (1929), Roerich also paraphrases passages from *The Aquarian Gospel of Jesus Christ,* passages which, he claims, were taken from "Another source—historically less established—[that] speaks also about the life of Jesus in Tibet." This other source is never named, for obvious reasons. *The Aquarian Gospel* is a broad-ranging work, only a portion of which is devoted to Jesus' alleged studies in South Asia. The India and Tibet sections of *The Aquarian Gospel* are, however, directly inspired by *The Unknown Life of Jesus Christ,* although, as I have already noted, Levi Dowling was not guilty of actual plagiarism. Like Notovitch's Issa, Dowling's Jesus travels to eastern India, preaches against the caste system and idolatry, and then moves on to the Himalayas. To cite a few relevant passages from *The Aquarian Gospel*, "And Jesus was accepted as a pupil in the temple Jagannath; and here learned the Vedas and the Manic laws. The Brahmic masters wondered at the clear conceptions of the child, and often were amazed when he explained to them the meaning of the laws" (Dowling 1916, 21:19–20). Here one can see the direct influence of Notovitch's story, but not his wording. In only a very few short lines does one find Notovitch's language reflected in Dowling's text. Notovitch, for instance, has Jesus say, "Worship not the idols, for they hear you not" (5:26). Dowling is obviously working from this same passage when his Aquarian Jesus similarly asserts, "Tear down your idols; they can hear you not" (26:21).

Roerich's use of Dowling is less sophisticated than Dowling's use of Notovitch. For example, the Aquarian Jesus becomes interested in traveling to Buddhist Lhasa (an anachronism, as Buddhism did not become established in Tibet until the seventh century) where he meets the Chinese sage Ming-tse: "In Lassa of Tibet there was a master's temple, rich in manuscripts of ancient lore. The Indian sage had read these manuscripts, and he revealed to Jesus many of the secret lessons they contained; but Jesus wished to read them for himself. Now, Meng-ste, greatest sage of all the farther East, was in this temple of Tibet" (36:1–3). Roerich's clumsy paraphrase is lifted directly from *The Aquarian Gospel:* "Near Lhassa was a temple of teaching, with a wealth of manuscripts. Jesus wanted to acquaint himself with them. Ming-ste, a great sage of all the East, was in this temple" (1929a, 153). In addition to supplying his narrative with details taken from a source other than Notovitch, Roerich was likely attracted to Dowling's work because the Aquarian Jesus was far more compatible with his own theosophical beliefs. Reincarnation, for instance, is one of the core tenets of

Theosophy. For this reason, Roerich neglects to cite *The Life of Saint Issa* where Notovitch's Issa says, "Never would [God] so humiliate his child as to transmigrate his soul" (6:11). Instead, he is more attracted to Jesus' discourse on reincarnation in *The Aquarian Gospel of Jesus Christ*, where he comments on the source of singing talent:

> From whence this talent and this power? In one short life they could not gain such grace of voice, such knowledge of the laws of harmony and tone. Men call them prodigies. There are no prodigies. All things result from natural law. These people are not young. A thousand years would not suffice to give them such divine expressiveness, and such purity of voice and touch. Ten thousand years ago these people mastered harmony. In days of old they trod the busy thoroughfares of life, and caught the melody of birds, and played on harps of perfect form. And they have come again to learn still other lessons from the varied notes of manifests. (37:11–15)

Once again, Roerich simply paraphrases Dowling's passage, attributing it to the same unnamed source as the story of Jesus' trip to Tibet: "Said Jesus of skilled singers: 'Whence is their talent and their power? For in one short life they could not possibly accumulate a quality of voice and the knowledge of harmony and of tone. Are these miracles? No, because all things take place as a result of natural law. Many thousands of years ago these people already moulded their harmonies and their harmonies. And they come again to learn still more from varied manifestations'" (1929a, 156). While it is easy to see what Roerich did, it is less clear why he did it. Perhaps, to extend him the same benefit of the doubt we gave Abhedananda, Roerich traveled to South Asia sincerely expecting to find ancient manuscripts not only confirming Jesus' Indian sojourn, but also containing a record of Jesus' "real" teachings—teachings which would confirm Roerich's own theosophical views. Instead, all he encountered were a few legends scattered about here and there.

Disappointed in his quest, perhaps he became convinced that the documents he sought really existed, but that the Buddhist monks had misplaced them or were hiding them from outsiders. He suggests that he believes the latter when he describes how each "silent" lama at Leh "knows much" about the stories he "secretly and cautiously" guards (1929a, 120). He may also have convinced himself of the ultimate reality of the Hemis manuscript because of the prevalence of the legend among the ordinary people: "In what possible way could a recent forgery penetrate into the consciousness of the whole East?" (119). In any event, we can infer that Roerich eventually decided to work up a story about the Jesus whom he is certain must have visited India, and who must have taught esoteric truths.

Rather than rewrite the tale from scratch, however, Roerich made liberal use of *The Life of Saint Issa* and *The Aquarian Gospel of Jesus Christ*. Perhaps he felt that these two narratives were both somehow real, or at least based on real documents. After reading Roerich, one gets the impression that he believed Notovitch had actually seen a real manuscript, but inferred that his fellow Russian inserted his own prejudices into *The Life of Saint Issa*. Thus, like Swami Abhedananda, Roerich would have felt comfortable editing Notovitch's work so as to present only the passages free of Notovitch's "additions." Roerich also apparently believed that Dowling, another esotericist like himself, had really accessed the Akashic Records and had presented an accurate account of Jesus' life. He thus felt he could paraphrase details of Jesus' Indian travels from the *Aquarian Gospel* because he "knew" Dowling's narrative was true. Thus while Roerich's sense of honor prevented him from actually forging new documents from scratch, he gave in to the temptation to fudge the facts in order to spread the truth.

But why, we might ask at this point, was confirming Jesus' India trip so important that a man of Roerich's stature would fall victim to the "true lies" syndrome? In terms of our earlier discussion, it appears that Roerich was attracted to the possibility of legitimating his occult beliefs at the expense of traditional Christianity: "But who can fail to recognize that many of the so-called 'Apocrypha' are far more basically true than many official documents?" (1929a, 126). In this passage, it is not hard to realize that the "official documents" being referred to are Christian scriptures. Roerich, in other words, is asserting that the Jesus he found in India is the real Jesus and that the biblical account of Jesus' life and teachings is flawed. Although understated, the above statement captures the central premise of Roerich's entire edifice and provides the key to understanding his motive.

CONCLUDING REMARKS

As we have seen, the story of Jesus in India is rather like a psychologist's inkblot test, in that each successive promoter of the tale anticipated discovering his own religious beliefs reflected in Jesus' teachings. When he failed to do so, he either supplied the missing components or edited pre-existing texts to fit his preconception of what Jesus must have said and done. Each successive person who perpetuated the Issa tradition was attracted to the legend for the same reason—the Indian Jesus could be deployed to legitimate their own brand of spirituality as well as to undermine the legitimacy of the dominant Christian tradition.

This same attraction explains why so many Indian gurus, New Age teachers, and the like have adopted and propagated the legend, though sometimes they modify it further. In the final section of Elizabeth Clare Prophet's *The Lost Teachings of Jesus*, for instance, Prophet asserts that the "texts and legends" (e.g., Notovitch, Abhedananda, Roerich, and others) examined in her book indicate that Jesus "prayed, meditated, practiced yoga, studied and taught" (1984, 353). None of these texts, however, mention either meditation or yoga. Rather, it seems Prophet has simply inferred that Jesus *must* have practiced these spiritual techniques, based on her own preconception of what Jesus was like.

Through the case study of the legend of Jesus' journey to India, the present chapter analyzed the phenomenon of the fabrication of a pseudo-tradition as a legitimation strategy. The larger significance of this particular discussion for religious studies is that the history of religions contains innumerable examples of forged scriptures—including documents in the scriptural canons of major world religions like Christianity and Buddhism. This legitimation strategy is thus a concrete example of how the study of contemporary new religions potentially sheds light on our understanding of traditional religions, if only because such an approach compels us to view familiar phenomena against the backdrop of unfamiliar comparisons.

4

SCIENCE, TECHNOLOGY, AND THE SPACE BROTHERS

New Religious Movements . . . articulate themselves, often with a popular fluency, in the discourses of the natural sciences and seek to justify their beliefs by means of para- or pseudoscientific investigation or argument.
—Bryan Sentes and Susan Palmer, "Presumed Immanent"

In one of the opening chapters of Aldous Huxley's *Island,* Will Farnaby, the novel's protagonist, awakens to the voice of Mynah birds crying, "Attention! Here and now, boys!" Once fully awake, Will recalls the frightening experiences that accompanied his arrival on the island of Pala.

After miraculously making his way to shore in a sinking boat, he had scaled a sheer cliff along a tiny ravine. During what turned out to be a difficult climb in dark, stormy weather, he almost stepped on a snake. Then, in an effort to avoid the serpent, he lost his balance and fell a short distance, flailing wildly in the air before catching himself on a small tree. Scratched, bruised, and badly frightened, Will finally reached the top. Exhausted, he immediately fell asleep on the ground.

Shortly after awakening, he is discovered by two of Pala's young residents, Tom Krishna and Mary Sarojini MacPhail. Mary, who is about nine or ten, sends the younger Tom to bring some help for the injured stranger. Then, while waiting for others to arrive, Mary prompts Will to relate the story of his arrival. After recalling his nightmarish experience, the weakened Will breaks into a violent trembling.

> Mary Sarojini listened attentively and without comment. Then, as his voice faltered and finally broke, she stepped forward and, the bird still perched on her shoulder, kneeled down beside him. "Listen, Will," she said, laying a hand on his forehead, "We've got to get rid of this." Her voice was professional and calmly authoritative. (Huxley 1972, 11)

Mary then directs him to go back over the experience in detail, a directive Will initially refuses. Mary, however, insists until finally he complies.

> "I almost stepped on him," he whispered obediently. "And then I . . ." He couldn't say it. "Then I fell," he brought out at last, almost inaudibly. All the horror of it came back to him—the nausea of fear, the panic start that had made him lose his balance, and then worse fear and the ghastly certainly that it was the end.
> "Say it again."
> "I almost stepped on him, And then . . ."
> He heard himself whimpering.
> "That's right, Will. Cry—cry!" (12)

Mary compels the resistant Will to recount his frightening experience over and over again until, finally,

> The words came more easily and the memories they aroused were less painful.
> "I fell," he repeated for the hundredth time.
> "But you didn't fall very far," Mary Sarojini now said.
> "No, I didn't fall very far," he agreed.
> "So what's all the fuss about?" the child inquired.
> There was no malice or irony in her tone, not the slightest implication of blame. She was just asking a simple, straight-forward question that called for a simple, straightforward answer. Yes, what *was* all the fuss about? The snake hadn't bitten him; he hadn't broken his neck. And anyhow it had all happened yesterday. Today there were these butterflies, this bird that called one to attention, this strange child who talked to one like a Dutch uncle [and] looked like an angel out of some unfamiliar mythology. . . . Will Farnaby laughed aloud. The little girl clapped her hands and laughed too. (13)

Island is a utopian novel embodying Huxley's personal vision of paradise. An important component of this ideal society is the kind of informal therapy—one character refers to it as "psychological first aid"—described in the opening chapters. The thrust of this therapeutic technique is to remove the debilitating emotional charge associated with memories of traumatic experiences. It is a technique practiced by everyone on the island. Mary Sarojini MacPhail alludes to its omnipresence in Palanese society when she informs Farnaby that it is the "usual way" of dealing with such traumas. This psycho-technology did not, however, spring fully formed from the fertile imagination of Aldous Huxley. Rather, Huxley based his fictional account of Palanese therapy on the then-popular therapeutic movement known as Dianetics.

Dianetics was the brainchild of L. Ron Hubbard, writer and founder of the Church of Scientology. Before initiating the Dianetics movement, Hubbard had successfully pursued a number of unusual careers, from explorer to stunt pilot. By 1934, his major vocation was as a prolific and successful fiction writer. Within science fiction circles, he is remembered as one of the authors of the genre's golden age (the 1940s).

Dianetics, a system of mental health that grew out of Hubbard's personal experiences, reading, and experiments, can roughly be described as a synthesis of modern psychology and Oriental philosophy. Hubbard initially thought his new therapy would be enthusiastically embraced by the psychological-psychiatric mainstream. However, after being rebuffed by the psychotherapeutic establishment, he turned to the general public, where he found a ready audience.

Following a positive response to his ideas after they appeared in the *Explorer's Journal* (winter/spring 1950), he published *Dianetics: The Modern Science of Mental Health* (1950). The book quickly became

FIGURE 4.1. L. Ron Hubbard, founder of the Church of Scientology. Grateful acknowledgment is made to the L. Ron Hubbard Library.

FIGURE 4.2. Dianetics counseling, one of the core techniques of Scientology, uses an E-meter as part of the procedure of "auditing." Courtesy of the Church of Scientology International.

a national bestseller, and Dianetics became a movement. Groups were soon formed so that individuals could assist each other in the application of the techniques, called "auditing," described in *Dianetics*. Dianetics was especially popular within the film industry, at colleges, and within avant-garde intellectual circles.

Dianetics: The Modern Science of Mental Health describes techniques that, it is claimed, can be applied to the mind to rid the individual of dysfunctional emotions, irrational fears, and psychosomatic illnesses. The basic concept in Dianetics is that the mind has two distinct parts. Hubbard called the conscious part the "analytical mind." The second, termed the "reactive mind," comes into play when the individual is fully or partially unconscious. "Unconsciousness" could be caused by the shock of an accident, the anesthetic used for an operation, the pain of an injury, or the deliriums of illness.

According to Hubbard, the reactive mind stores particular types of mental image pictures he called "engrams." Engrams are a complete recording of every perception present in a moment of partial or full unconsciousness. This part of the mind can produce unevaluated and unwanted fears, emotions, pains, and psychosomatic illnesses. The goal of Dianetics therapy is a mental state in which the warping power of one's engrams has been decisively defeated. The analytical mind can then process information effectively and efficiently. Hubbard termed this state "clear," after the *clear* button on electronic calculators. By employing a discourse saturated with images of technological devices and analogies to phenomena studied by natural science, Hubbard was able to convey the sense that Dianetics was a truly scientific enterprise.

As the Dianetics movement expanded, Hubbard began to articulate a system of religious ideas—which included, for instance, the notion of reincarnation—that complemented the more practical focus of Dianetics therapy. (Hubbard felt he had discovered a scientific basis for reincarnation because some individuals undergoing auditing reported engrams from past lifetimes.) These ideas became the basis of Scientology as a religion. In 1954, a group of Dianetics and Scientology enthusiasts established the first church in Los Angeles, California.

One of the interesting aspects of the Church of Scientology is how certain elements of the popular culture of the 1950s were preserved within the church subculture. For instance, even female members typically refer to other adult women as "girls"—a linguistic convention the larger society has abandoned. Also, the majority of full-time church members smoke cigarettes, as did much of the majority of adults in the 1950s.

A more subtle, but far more significant mid-century theme preserved in the time capsule of the church's subculture is reflected in its name. Prior to the blossoming of cold war nuclear concerns and the emergence of the ecology movement's critique of runaway technology, the general populace accorded science and science's child, technology, a level of respect and prestige enjoyed by few other social institutions. Science was viewed quasi-religiously, as an objective arbiter of "Truth." Thus any religion that claimed its approach was in some way *scientific* drew on the prestige and perceived legitimacy of natural science. Religions such as Christian Science, Science of Mind, and, of course, Scientology claim just that.

There are, however, a number of differences between popular notions of science and science proper. Average citizens' views of science are significantly influenced by their experience of technology. Hence, in most people's minds, an important goal of science appears to be the solution of practical problems. This aspect of our cultural view of science shaped the various religious sects that incorporated "science" into their names. In sharp contrast to traditional religions which emphasize salvation in the afterlife, the emphasis in these religions is on the improvement of this life. Groups in the metaphysical (Christian Science–New Thought) tradition, for example, usually claim to have discovered spiritual laws which, if properly understood and applied, transform and improve the lives of ordinary individuals, much as technology has transformed society.

The notion of spiritual laws is taken directly from the laws of classical physics. The eighteenth- and nineteenth-century mind was enamored by Newton's formulation of the mathematical order in the natural world. A significant aspect of his system of physics was expressed in the laws of gravity. Following Newton's lead, later scientists similarly expressed their discoveries in terms of the same legislative metaphor—for example, the "law" of evolution.

One of the first and, at the time, most influential of the nineteenth-century new movements to adopt a rhetoric of establishing religion on a scientific basis was Spiritualism. Spiritualism was and is a religious movement emphasizing survival after death, a belief Spiritualists claim is based upon scientific proof through communication with the surviving personalities of deceased human beings by means of mediumship.

The belief in the possibility of communication with the spirit world has been held in most of the societies about which we have records. Spiritualism thus has many parallels and predecessors among traditional, tribal peoples, in the miracles of world religions, and in certain phenomena associated with shamanism and possession. In Christianity, these manifestations were not always associated with the spirits of deceased people, but, rather, were traditionally associated with angelic or diabolic possession, most frequently with the latter. By reinterpreting such phenomena as communications from the dead, one could view mediumship as an avenue for conducting empirical (in the broadest sense) research.

Like the later New Thought movement, Spiritualism also expressed its discoveries in the spiritual realm in terms of a series of laws. These have rarely been formulated systematically and tend to vary from writer to writer. Thus, for example, a relevant reading on the official web site of the National Spiritualist Association of Churches lists twenty laws, which are said to be "just a few" of the many universal laws. In addition to such familiar items as the law of gravity and the law of evolution, some of the less familiar laws listed are the laws of "harmony," "desire," "mind," "vibration," and so on (http://www.nsac.org).

This legislative rhetoric was carried over into metaphysical religions, particularly New Thought. Rather than presenting themselves as empirically investigating the spiritual realm via communications from the dead, groups in the metaphysical tradition view themselves as investigating the mind or spirit in a practical, experimental way. The self-perception of the early New Thought movement as "science" is expressed in lesson 1 of Ernest Holmes's 1926 classic, *Science of Mind,* in the following way:

> Science is knowledge of facts built around some proven principle. All that we know about any science is that certain things happen under certain conditions. Take electricity as an example; we know that there is such a thing as electricity; we have never seen it, but we know that it exists because we can use it; we know that it operates in a certain way and we have discovered the way it works. From this knowledge we go ahead and deduce certain facts about electricity; and, applying them to the general principle, we receive definite results. . . . The discovery of a law is generally made more or less by accident, or by some one who, after careful thought and observation, has come to the conclusion that such a principle must exist. As soon as a law is discovered experiments are made with it, certain facts are proved to be true, and in this way a science is gradually formulated; for any science consists of the number of known facts about any given principle. . . . This is true of the Science of Mind. No one has ever seen Mind or Spirit, but who could possibly doubt their existence? Nothing is more self-evident. (1944, 38)

The Church of Scientology is in this same lineage, though Scientology takes the further step of explicitly referring to their religio-therapeutic practices as religious *technology*—in Scientology language, the "tech." In much the same way as the 1950s viewed technology as ushering in a new, utopian world, Scientology sees their psycho-spiritual technology as supplying the missing ingredient in existing technologies—namely the therapeutic engineering of the human psyche.

UFO RELIGIONS

UFO religions represent in some ways continuity with, and in other ways a departure from, this line of development. Although UFO religions also appeal to science to legitimate themselves, their focus is not generally on developing a pragmatic science of the mind in the tradition of New Thought. In fact, the initial forms of religiosity to manifest in the UFO contactee movement represented little more than a recasting of pre-existing forms of occultism in technological guise.

Whereas metaphysical religions and UFO religions are both interested in drawing on the social legitimacy of science as the perceived arbiter of "truth," UFO religions also draw from the sacred overtones of science and technology as ultimate *power.* This latter appeal can be understood in terms of the phenomenology of religious consciousness. As analyzed in Rudolf Otto's classic *The Idea of the Holy* (1992), humanity's naked confrontation with the sacred (which he analytically separates from the other components of religion) can itself be analyzed into component parts. According to Otto, one encounters the sacred as a powerful, alien reality that does not belong to the world of ordinary human existence. This experience contains components of both fear and attraction: The sacred simultaneously repels and fascinates; it is "uncanny" and "awesome." The sacred is also mysterious—something we cannot grasp with our rational minds, yet which we endlessly attempt to understand.

The parallels between religious experiences and UFO experiences are straightforward enough. UFOs are uncanny and mysterious. Because of the tremendous technological power they represent, they also evoke fear. If the reader has seen Steven Spielberg's 1977 film *Close Encounters of the Third Kind,* she or he will recall the penultimate scene in which the mother ship appears: This enormous piece of alien machinery is experienced by the gathered officials and technicians as both beautiful and frightening—an incomprehensibly awesome power before which they feel like helpless children. This is very similar to the kind of encounter that Otto characterizes as religious.

That flying saucers and their inhabitants have come to be invested with religious meaning should not, therefore, come as a surprise. This religious meaning can be manifested overtly in such explicitly religious organizations as Heaven's Gate, the Raelian Movement, the Unarius Academy of Science, the Aetherius Society, and others. And it can manifest less obviously, in the form of themes of redemption and transformation that—when cloaked in the guise of flying machines—are not immediately recognized as religious, but which fulfill religious functions for members of our society. One often comes across films and literature that portray the "space brothers" (UFO pilots) as working to rescue humanity—either by preventing a nuclear Armageddon or by taking select members of the human race to another planet to preserve the species. The psychologist Carl Jung was referring to this portrayal of ufonauts (flying saucer pilots) as friendly, redemptive beings when he coined the expression "technological angels." The idea of positive, helpful extraterrestrials has been a common theme of much science fiction, from *Superman* (who, it will be remembered, was from another planet) to the "cute" alien of Spielberg's 1982 film *ET.*

Jung postulated a drive toward self-realization and self-integration, a drive that he referred to as the individuation process. The goal of this process was represented by the Self archetype, an archetype characterized by wholeness and completeness. One of the concrete symbols of this archetype can be a circle, and it was various forms of the circle that Jung called mandalas (from the meditation diagrams of Hinduism and Buddhism). According to Jung, mandala symbols emerge in dreams when the individual is seeking harmony and wholeness, which frequently occurs during periods of crisis and insecurity. Jung interpreted the phenomenon of flying saucers—which often appear in the form of circular disks—as mandala symbols, reflecting the human mind's desire for stability in a confused world. Whatever the influence of this psychological predisposition may be on our tendency to construe the space brothers as spiritual beings, it should also be noted that there was a tradition of viewing extraterrestrials as sources of spiritual wisdom prior to Kenneth Arnold's celebrated 1947 sighting (the event generally regarded as initiating the modern UFO era). This tradition is contained in certain lineages of occultism that claim contact with spiritual masters from other planets.

A useful example of this form of occultism is the "I AM" Activity. The "I AM" Religious Activity is a popularized form of

Theosophy, reformulated to appeal to a broader audience than earlier theosophical organizations. The founder of the movement, Guy Ballard, had long been interested in occultism and had studied theosophical teachings. One New Year's Eve, Ballard claimed he joined the famous occult master Saint Germaine at a gathering inside a cavern in Royal Teton Mountain. The individuals at this assembly were said to have hosted twelve Venusians who appeared in their midst in a blaze of light, not unlike a "Star Trek" beam-in. These Venusian "Lords of the Flame" played harp and violin music and showed the gathered terrestrials scenes of advanced technological achievements from their home world on a great mirror. The narrative of these events from the early 1930s was reported in Ballard's *Unveiled Mysteries* ([1935] 1982), which was published twelve years before Kenneth Arnold's celebrated encounter.

The first noteworthy prophet to emerge in the wake of the postwar flying saucer sightings was George Adamski. In the early 1940s he became intrigued with unidentified flying objects (UFOs) long before they were much discussed by the public. He even claimed to have seen a UFO for the first time on October 9, 1946, the year before Arnold's sightings. Adamski further reported that on November 20, 1952, he experienced telepathic contact with a human-like Venusian, and the following month he reported another contact in which a hieroglyphic message was given. These encounters were reported in *Flying Saucers Have Landed* (Adamski and Leslie 1953) one of the most popular flying saucer books ever written. Adamski gained a broad following and was a much sought-after lecturer.

As we can see from Ballard's report of the Royal Teton gathering, religious revelations from Venusians were nothing new. Adamski was thus not an innovator in this regard. Rather, Adamski's contribution was to connect the earlier notion of receiving information from extraterrestrials with the emergent interest in flying saucers. It is clear that Adamski believed that by giving them shiny new technological chariots, the masters of traditional occultism would be more appealing to the modern mind. Adamski stands at the font of a line of development that would expand into numerous "contactees," as they were referred to, claiming to receive occult wisdom from extraterrestrials. (For a fuller discussion of the transition from occult contactees to UFO contactees, refer to Melton 1995.)

One line of thought regarding religious interpretations of the UFO phenomenon is that the Western tradition's marked propensity to imagine God as somehow residing in the sky gives us a predisposition to view unusual *flying* objects as well as beings from outer space—the further reaches of the sky—in spiritual terms. It should also be noted that the God of the Bible is, in a certain sense, an extraterrestrial being. The West's religious tradition that contributes to the tendency to invest religious meaning in UFOs comes full circle when ufologists read a record of alien contact back into biblical stories and other ancient mythologies. This interpretive slant has been taken up by a number of UFO religions, such as the Raelian Movement. The following excerpt from Rael's first book, *The Book Which Tells the Truth* (1974) exemplifies this pattern:[1]

> *In the beginning, Elohim created the heaven and the earth*, Genesis 1:1.
>
> "Elohim," translated without justification in some Bibles by the word "God" means in Hebrew "those who came from the sky" and furthermore the word is a plural. It means that the scientists from our world searched for a planet that was suitable to carry out their projects. They "created," or in reality discovered the Earth, and realized it contained all the necessary elements for the creation of artificial life, even if its atmosphere was not quite the same as our own.
>
> *And the spirit of Elohim moved across the waters*, Genesis 1:2.
>
> This means the scientists made reconnaissance flights and what you might call artificial satellites were placed around the Earth to study its constitution and atmosphere. (Rael 1998, 20)

The Raelian Movement was founded in France in 1973 by Claude Vorilhon, better known as Rael. Like the classic UFO contactees of the 1950s and 1960s, Rael claimed to have encountered humanoid space aliens. These beings explained to Rael that the human race was created with sophisticated genetic engineering techniques by extraterrestrial scientists (the Elohim) in their laboratories.

Rael asserts that a cultural memory of these contacts has been preserved in certain myths and that many figures in traditional religious mythologies were actually space aliens. Satan, for example, was the head of a party of opinion on the home planet of the Elohim opposed to genetic experiments; that party believes that humanity poses a potential threat and should be destroyed.

FIGURE 4.3. Rael, founder of the Raelian Movement. Courtesy of the International Raelian Movement.

According to Rael, in *Let's Welcome Our Fathers from Space:* "Satan thought that one could not expect anything good from these scientifically-created creatures, and that out of man only evil could come. Satan was like the head of a political party on the planet of the Elohim, which was opposed to the creation of any type of be-ings in their image by other Elohim, who thought that they could create beings who would be positive and non-violent" (Rael 1986, 94–95). Certain biblical stories, such as the Flood, are explained in terms of the intervention of Satan's party: "The group who be-lieved that nothing but evil came out of man, presided over by one of the Elohim named Satan, finally triumphed, and the destruction of all life on Earth came about by the flood" (4). According to this narrative, Noah's Ark was actually a spaceship within which an-other party of Elohim preserved humanity.

Making a positive use of Satan's negative attitude toward hu-manity, Satan became responsible for testing the faithfulness of the prophets chosen to relay the message of the Elohim: "Once a per-son had been contracted by the Messengers of the Elohim, telling

FIGURE 4.4. Rael with scale model of the embassy for extraterrestrials. Courtesy of the International Raelian Movement.

him of his mission, Satan, or one of his men, would contact the prophet-to-be and by slander would destroy the Elohim in his mind (98). Rael interprets both the story of Job and the story of Satan tempting Jesus in the wilderness as examples of this role (98–102). Rael was also approached by Satan during a visit to the home world of the Elohim. In exchange for riches and an agreement to preach hatred rather than love, Satan promises to take Rael and his compatriots on board their spacecraft when planetary-wide conflict breaks out and, after everything is destroyed, bring

Rael back to rule the earth. Rael declines the offer, thereby passing the test that had been orchestrated by Yahweh, Rael's extraterrestrial father.

The Raelian Movement perceives itself as a scientific religion, founded to spread the truths revealed to Rael. One of the major goals of the movement is to build an extraterrestrial embassy in Israel in order to receive the Elohim when they land (some Raelian sources mention the year 2025, others 2035). Rael denies the existence of a "spiritual" realm, including the existence of the soul and of any immaterial god or devil. Members of the movement may, however, look forward to immortality in the form of cloning by alien scientists.

According to the Elohim, the world's religions were founded as a result of their direct communication with a series of human prophets for the purpose of implanting the idea of humanity's celestial origins and other notions in the human race. In this way, humanity would, in a later, scientific age (that is, the current age), be able to look back over traditional scriptures and perceive what had "really" happened. Rael, the "last of the forty prophets," is the bearer of this message.

The Raelian appeal to the authority of science is not, as noted earlier, part of an effort to legitimate a science of the mind. Unlike Christian Science, Scientology, and other groups that claim to model their approach after the *methods* of science, Rael's strategy is to base his "atheistic religion" in the secularist *worldview* derived from natural science. The appeal to this worldview legitimates Rael's critique of Christianity and other forms of supernatural spirituality. In other words, Rael claims that the Raelian Movement is a legitimate religion because—to refer to the terms of Weber's analysis—it is *rational* (meaning specifically, in this case, aligned with a secularist appropriation of science). As a corollary, traditional religion is *irrational* (again in the specific sense of unscientific) and therefore illegitimate. This particular strategy will be discussed at greater length in the next chapter.

5

ANTON LAVEY,
THE SATANIC BIBLE,
AND THE
SATANIST TRADITION

LaVey describes Satanism as a secular philosophy of rationalism and self-preservation (natural law, animal state), gift-wrapping these ideas in religious trappings to add to their appeal.

—Blanche Barton,
The Secret Life of a Satanist

The status of *The Satanic Bible* as an authoritative scripture—or, perhaps more accurately, as a kind of *quasi-scripture*—within the Satanic subculture was initially brought to my attention during my first face-to-face encounter with Satanists in the spring of 2000. Via the internet, I had found a small Satanist group in Portage, Wisconsin, which was about an hour south of where I resided at the time. This group, the Temple of Lylyth, distinguishes itself from Anton LaVey's brand of Satanism chiefly by its emphasis on the feminine nature of the dark power. I arranged to meet with them in Portage on a Friday evening.

Over the course of our conversation, the founder and then leader of the group mentioned that on Friday evenings he was usually downtown where a small group of fervent Christians regularly set up what might be called a "preaching station" to spread the Gospel. This young fellow (he was nineteen at the time) would confront them as a practicing Satanist. He always carried a copy of *The Satanic Bible* with him, not just so he could quote some of accusations LaVey leveled against Christianity, but also so he could correct anything these evangelists might say about Satanism by citing an authoritative source. I am sure this is something of a caricature, but I was left with the impression of dueling religion-ists, Christians hurling Bible verses at my informant as he matched them blow for blow with quotes from *The Satanic Bible*. This expe-rience led me to pay attention whenever other Satanists men-tioned *The Satanic Bible*.

The Temple of Lylyth is part of a loose, decentralized Satanic movement that coheres as a distinct religious community largely by virtue of adherence to certain themes in the thought of Anton LaVey, founder of modern Satanism, though few movement partic-ipants outside the Church of Satan would regard themselves as "or-thodox LaVeyans." Following the dissolution of the Church of Satan's grotto system in 1975 and before the explosion of the in-ternet in the mid-1990s, the Satanic movement was propagated al-most entirely by *The Satanic Bible*, which has continuously been in print as a widely available, mass-market paperback. Rather than a guide to Devil-worship, LaVey's work advocates a blend of Epicure-anism and Ayn Rand's philosophy, flavored with a pinch of ritual magic. Couched in iconoclastic rhetoric, *The Satanic Bible* has al-ways held particular appeal for rebellious adolescents. The title seems to have originally been chosen for its shock value rather than from any pretense to scriptural status.

The present chapter focuses on issues of the legitimation of au-thority within the Satanist movement and among Anton LaVey's

FIGURE 5.1. Anton LaVey, founder of Church of Satan, with pet. Courtesy of Zeena Schreck, Walter Gallo Archives.

successors in the Church of Satan. LaVey was a charismatic individual who appealed to the authority of reason and attacked the authority of tradition. However, the figure of LaVey and, particularly, *The Satanic Bible* almost immediately became sources of authority for a new Satanic "tradition" after LaVey's passing.

SATANIC LEGITIMACY

Satanists do not consciously regard *The Satanic Bible* in the same way traditional religionists regard their sacred texts. In fact, the title seems to have originally been chosen for its shock value rather than from any pretense to scriptural status. However, *The Satanic Bible* is treated as an authoritative document that effectively *functions* as scripture within the Satanic community. In particular, LaVey's work is quoted to legitimate specific positions as well as to delegitimate the positions of other Satanists. This legitimation strategy appears to have been unconsciously derived from the Judeo-Christian tradition, which locates the source of religious authority in a sacred text. In other words, being raised in a religious tradition that emphasizes the authority of scripture creates an attitude that can be unconsciously carried over to other, very different kinds of writings.

When LaVey founded the Church of Satan in 1966, he grounded Satanism's legitimacy on a view of human nature shaped by a secularist appropriation of modern science. Unlike Christian Science, Scientology, and other groups that claimed to model their approach to spirituality after the *methods* of science, LaVey's strategy—like that of the Raelian Movement—was to base Satanism's "anti-theology" in a secularist *worldview* derived from natural science. The appeal to a worldview based on "our scientific and technological advances" provided LaVey with an atheistic underpinning for his attacks on "obsolete" Christianity and other forms of supernatural spirituality (Barton 1990, 13). As noted in the preceding chapter, the Raelian Movement similarly appeals to the worldview of secular science for its legitimacy and, like Satanism, attacks other religions as unreasonable because of their lack of a scientific basis (Chryssides 1999, Sentes and Palmer 2000). At the same time, LaVey went beyond contemporary secularism by suggesting the reality of mysterious, "occult" forces—forces he claimed were not supernatural, but were, rather, natural forces that would eventually be discovered by science. In his notion of mysterious forces that could be manipulated by the will of the magician, LaVey was really not so far from the mentalistic technology of Christian Science, Scientology, and other religious bodies in the metaphysical tradition.

The human nature to which LaVey appealed was humanity's animal nature, viewed through the lens of Darwinism. The human being in this view is little more than an animal with no ultimate morality other than the law of the jungle and no purpose other than the survival of the fittest. In terms of Weber's schema, we would say that LaVey's appeal to human nature (meaning, for LaVey, the Darwinist vision of human nature) was a rational legitimation of authority. In other words, LaVey claimed that Satanism was a legitimate religion because it was rational (i.e., congruent with science). As a corollary, traditional religion was irrational (unscientific) and therefore illegitimate.

Beyond this explicit appeal to science, LaVey was a charismatic individual and this charisma was undoubtedly crucial for the successful birth of the Church of Satan. In addition to his personal magnetism, LaVey also consciously amplified his charismatic status by creating an impressive pseudo-biography in which he was able to convincingly portray himself as an extraordinary individual. However, LaVey's charismatic authority soon began to wane, particularly after he dismantled the Church of Satan (CoS) as a functioning church in 1975 (discussed below). This led to a number of interesting—though somewhat paradoxical—developments. In addition to numerous splinter groups, a decentralized, anarchistic movement emerged, shaped by the central themes in LaVey's thought, particularly as expressed in *The Satanic Bible*. This book became a doctrinal touchstone of the movement, though independent Satanists felt free to selectively appropriate ideas from *The Satanic Bible* and to mix them with ideas and practices drawn from other sources. LaVey's book became, in a sense, an actual scripture (or, perhaps more accurately, a kind of quasi-scripture), and sacred texts are a form of what Weber meant by traditional authority. However, many independent Satanists also adhered to LaVey's program of the authority of rationality, feeling free to criticize and even to reject aspects of the LaVeyan tradition. Thus the contemporary Satanic movement's legitimacy is based on a dual appeal to independent rational authority and to the authority of the LaVeyan tradition.

In contrast, the remnants of LaVey's church—which is still technically the largest Satanist group in terms of formal membership—quickly solidified into a doctrinally rigid organization focused on maintaining the purity of LaVeyan Satanism. This was partly in response to the challenge presented by non-CoS Satanists. In the ongoing argument over legitimacy, LaVey's successors have come to place excessive stress on their role as bearers of his legacy, even asserting that only CoS members are "real" Satanists and characterizing Satanists outside the fold as "pseudo" Satanists. In terms of Weber's analysis, one would say that CoS's legitimation strategy has narrowed to focus almost exclusively on CoS's claim to traditional authority.

ANTON LAVEY AND MODERN RELIGIOUS SATANISM

To comprehend religious Satanism, one must first understand that Satan has become an ambivalent symbol within the modern world. Part of the reason for the attractiveness of LaVeyan Satanism is its ability to hold together a number of diverse meanings found in this symbol. In the Western cultural tradition, the Devil represents much more than absolute evil. By default, the Prince of Darkness has come to embody some very attractive attributes. For example, because traditional Christianity has been so anti-sensual, Satan became associated with sex. The Christian tradition has also condemned pride, vengefulness, and avarice and, when allied with the status quo, has promoted conformity and obedience. The three former traits and the antithesis of the latter two traits thus became diabolical characteristics. LaVeyan Satanism celebrates such "vices" as virtues and identifies them as the core of what Satanism is really all about.

LaVey founded the Church of Satan in 1966, the first organized church in modern times devoted to Satan. As a consequence, Anton LaVey has sometimes been referred to as the "St. Paul of Satanism" (Wright 1993, 122). LaVey has two biographies, one historical and one legendary. This dichotomy has only become apparent in recent years. His real life was far more prosaic than the story he fabricated for the benefit of the media. LaVey effectively promoted his carefully crafted pseudo-biography through conversations with his disciples, media interviews, and two biographies, by associates, that he appears to have dictated—Burton Wolfe's *The Devil's Avenger* (1974) and Blanche Barton's *Secret Life of a Satanist* (1990). LaVey's fictional biography was clearly meant to legitimate his self-appointed role as the "Black Pope" by portraying him as an extraordinary individual.

According to the official Church of Satan biography, he was born Howard Anton Szandor LaVey in Chicago, Illinois. His parents, Joseph and Augusta LaVey, moved to San Francisco while LaVey was still an infant. He was introduced to the occult by his Transylvanian gypsy grandmother. As a teenager he pursued various avenues of occult studies, as well as hypnotism and music. He also played an oboe in the San Francisco Ballet Orchestra. He dropped out of high school at seventeen to join the Clyde Beatty Circus and worked as a calliope player and big cat trainer, later learning stage magic as well. While an organist in a burlesque theater, he had an affair with the young Marilyn Monroe shortly before she became famous.

He married in 1950 and about that time took a job as a police photographer, but in 1955 returned to organ playing. Until he formed the Church of Satan in 1966, he was the city of San Francisco's official organist. He divorced in 1960 in order to marry Diane Hegarty. He purchased his house—which eventually became the Church of Satan headquarters, later dubbed the "Black House"—after he found out it had been the former brothel of the madam Mammy Pleasant.

Drawing on his circus and occult backgrounds, he began to conduct "midnight magic seminars" at his house. This proved popular enough for him to found the Church of Satan in 1966. The basis for his rituals was Nazi rituals recorded on top-secret films he had seen as a teenager. LaVey's showmanship encouraged significant media coverage of such events as the first Satanic wedding and the first Satanic funeral, worship with a nude woman as the altar, and his cameo appearance as the Devil in the movie "Rosemary's Baby." LaVey made much of being a close friend of Sammy Davis Jr. and of having had an affair with Jayne Mansfield, two celebrity members of the Church of Satan. At its peak, he claimed that the church had hundreds of thousands of members. LaVey passed away in 1997.

LaVey's historical biography overlaps his legendary biography at several points. He was born in Chicago and his family did move to San Francisco. He did make his living as a musician and, of course, he actually did found the Church of Satan and died in 1997. He had several marriages. Almost everything else, however, seems to have been a fabrication.

LaVey's self-created legend was not seriously challenged until a 1991 interview in *Rolling Stone* magazine, entitled "Sympathy for the Devil." The author of that article, Lawrence Wright, did a little investigative footwork and discovered that LaVey was born Howard Stanton Levey to Gertrude and Mike Levey; there never was a "San Francisco Ballet Orchestra"; no one by the name Levey or LaVey worked as a musician or cat trainer for the Beatty Circus during the period he claimed to have been an employee; neither he nor Monroe ever worked for the Mayan "burlesque" theater; he never worked for the San Francisco Police Department; and there was no such thing as an official San Francisco city organist. These discoveries led Wright to remark toward the end of his article, "Later, as I began to take apart the literary creation he had made of his life, I would realize that "Anton LaVey" was itself his supreme creation, his ultimate satanic object, a sort of android composed of all the elements his mysterious creator had chosen from the universe of dark possibilities" (Wright 19921). Wright later expanded his expose of LaVey into a chapter for his *Saints and Sinners* (1993).

These findings were considerably amplified in "Anton LaVey: Legend and Reality," a nine-page "fact sheet" compiled two or three months after LaVey's passing by his estranged daughter, Zeena LaVey Schreck, and her husband, Nikolas Schreck (1998). In addition to repeating the points made by Wright, the fact sheet dismissed most of Anton LaVey's other claims, such as his claims to have had a Gypsy grandmother, seen films of secret German rituals, purchased the "Black House" (it was given to him by his parents, who had lived there, and had never been a brothel), appeared in "Rosemary's Baby," had affairs with Monroe and Mansfield, and so forth.

The current leadership of the Church of Satan has disputed some of these challenges to LaVey's official biography. Their strategy has been to vigorously dispute undocumented challenges while ignoring LaVey's documented fabrications. As one might anticipate, splinter groups from CoS as well as other independent Satanists have seized upon these revelations to challenge the church leadership's implicit claims to be the only authentic Satanist religious body.

Thinly disguised claims to exclusive legitimacy are peppered throughout CoS documents, such as in some of Blanche Barton's remarks in her "Sycophants Unite!" essay (composed prior to LaVey's death) posted on the CoS official web site: "We're lucky to have a leader like Anton LaVey. He has ensured that his philosophy will not die with him; it has been and will continue to be codified, expanded and applied in new areas *by his organization* [emphasis in original]." The scope and significance of this dispute is reflected in the *many* attacks on non-CoS Satanists found on the Church of Satan web site, particularly in the "Satanic Bunco Sheet," "Sycophants Unite!" "The Myth of the 'Satanic Community,'" "Pretenders to the Throne," and "Recognizing Pseudo-Satanists." Even a superficial perusal of these documents makes it clear that CoS is *obsessed* with shoring up its own legitimacy by attacking the heretics, especially those who criticize LaVey. For example, the unnamed author of the "Satanic Bunco Sheet" blasts non-CoS Satanists for "LaVey–baiting," and then goes on to assert that such pseudo-Satanists deal with LaVey and the Church of Satan by playing "the Christian game of handing out laurels with one hand while stabbing their progenitor in the back with the other. . . . [and] they must somehow convince you that the author of *The Satanic Bible* wasn't practicing pure Satanism [and] that his Church has gone awry in the hands of his successors."

The Church of Satan began generating splinter groups as early as 1973 when the Church of Satanic Brotherhood was formed by group leaders in Michigan, Ohio, and Florida. This church lasted only until 1974, when one of the founders announced his conversion to Christianity in a dramatic incident staged for the press in St. Petersburg. Other members of the Church of Satan in Kentucky and Indiana left to form the Ordo Templi Satanis, also short lived. As more schisms occurred, LaVey decided to disband the remaining grottos, the local units of the Church of Satan, which left the church as little more than a paper organization generating a meager income for LaVey through sales of memberships (one could, and still can, become an official member by paying a one-time $100 fee to the Church of Satan).

LaVey's disbanding of CoS as a functioning church in 1975 struck many observers—both then and now—as an impulsive, erratic act. It is, however, quite understandable from the perspective of the audience cult–client cult–cult movement distinction and the central role religious experience plays in the founding of a religion (themes discussed earlier in chapter 2). In terms of this analysis, LaVey made the mistake of founding the Church of Satan as a full-blown religion. His motivations were, however, commercial (the *profit* motive) rather than religious (the *prophet* motive); he not only lacked profound religious experiences, he completely rejected anything like a spiritual reality. Thus when he got to the hard part of running his religion—administering an expanding organization, dealing with schisms and so forth—he was not up to making the necessary personal sacrifices that being a founding prophet and leader required because his pecuniary and self-aggrandizing motives for forming CoS were so shallow. It was at this juncture that he collapsed the Church of Satan as a religion and turned it into an audience cult.

There are many presently existing groups that derive directly or indirectly from CoS, the most important of which is the Temple of Set. Unlike LaVey, the founder of the Temple of Set, Michael Aquino, initiated his organization in the wake of a religious experience. (Refer to Aquino's account of this experience in his history of the Church of Satan, 1999.)

The conflict (mostly on the internet) between the original Church of Satan and new Satanist groups accelerated after LaVey's death. In addition to attacking non-CoS Satanists as illegitimate, LaVey's organizational successors have also sought to legitimate their positions by appealing to the authority of LaVey and his writings. These kinds of appeals are rather ironic, given the Black Pope's rejection of traditional religious authority. As indicated earlier, LaVey himself did not attempt to legitimate his new religion with appeals to tradition or to the supernatural. Rather, his explicit strategy was to ground Satanism's legitimacy on a view of human nature shaped by a secularist appropriation of modern science.

GENESIS OF *THE SATANIC BIBLE*

The most significant single document for the Satanic tradition is *The Satanic Bible*. The idea for this volume came not from LaVey, but from an Avon Books editor named Peter Mayer. As a direct result of the success of the popular film "Rosemary's Baby" and the subsequent increase of popular interest in Satanism and the occult, Mayer decided that "the time was right for a 'Satanic bible,'" and he approached LaVey about authoring it (Aquino 1999, 52).

LaVey and his wife took the material they had on hand, wove it together, and expanded on these writings to form what became the core of *The Satanic Bible*. This pre-existing material consisted of the following:

A short, mimeographed paper that they had been distributing as an "introduction to Satanism."

The so-called "rainbow sheets," which were "an assortment of polemical essays" that the LaVeys had been mimeographing on colored paper (Aquino 1999, 52).

A handout describing and containing instructions for the conduct of ritual magic.

Articles previously published in the church periodical *The Cloven Hoof.*

The LaVeys then ran into a problem, which was that, even after expanding upon all of their available material, they were still *substantially* short of having a manuscript of sufficient length to satisfy their publisher. So, either because the deadline was coming up quickly or because LaVey just didn't want to write anything else at the time (Aquino describes their situation in terms of the former), LaVey tacked materials written by other authors onto the beginning and end of his manuscript.

Without acknowledging his sources, he took sections of "an obscure, turn-of-the-century political tract," *Might Is Right,* by New Zealander Arthur Desmond (writing under the pseudonym Ragnar Redbeard 1910), added in a few sentences of his own, and incorporated it as a prologue. He also added the Enochian Keys ("a series of Elizabethan magical incantations"), as they had been modified by Aleister Crowley, and "further altered them by replacing their Heavenly references with diabolical ones." Traditional occultists immediately recognized LaVey's source for the Enochian Keys, but it was not until 1987 that the source of LaVey's prologue was discovered (Aquino 1999, 65).

LaVey's second daughter, Zeena Schreck, described the genesis of *The Satanic Bible* in the following way:

> I'm pretty sure that ASL [Anton Szandor LaVey] intended to include the *Might Is Right* part from the beginning as he'd always liked it and wanted to use it somehow. From memory of what my mother told me years ago, the Enochian was added at the last minute when the deadline was breathing down their necks. Writing did not come easily to my progenitor, and he often suffered from extremely inhibiting writer's block, a side-effect of his chronic depression, which is another reason I believe he tended to "borrow" the writings of other authors so liberally. . . . My mother also synthesized material from many of the old CoS newsletters, *The Cloven Hoof* to round out *The Satanic Bible*. She did type the manuscript and even added some of her own writing and much editing of the manuscript. If one takes away what came out of the old newsletters, other plagiarized sources and the Enochian, as well as many blank "decorative" pages, and such filler as the list of Satanic names, there was very little original material written for it at all. . . . The title of the book itself, which I believe is far more responsible for its image of "authority" than its rather thin contents, was a last minute decision. (Schreck 2002)

It should also be mentioned that, in circles critical of CoS, one often comes across the accusation that LaVey's "Nine Satanic Statements," one of the church's central doctrinal statements, is an unacknowledged "paraphrase . . . of passages from Ayn Rand's *Atlas Shrugged*" (Schreck and Schreck 1998), specifically a paraphrase of the character John Galt's lengthy speech in the latter part of Rand's novel. However, when one actually examines these parallels (which are conveniently laid out in appendix 11 of Aquino's *The Church of Satan*), one finds that this is a caricature of LaVey's indebtedness to Rand. For example, the first Satanic statement is: "Satan represents indulgence, instead of abstinence!" (LaVey 1969, 25). The Rand passage presented as the source of this statement is: "A doctrine that gives you, as an ideal, the role of a sacrificial animal seeking slaughter on the altars of others, is giving you death as your standard. By the grace of reality and the nature of life, man— every man—is an end in himself. He exists for his own sake, and the achievement of his own happiness is his highest moral purpose" (1957, 940). This passage is rather lengthier than LaVey's supposed paraphrase. The second Satanic statement is as brief as the first statement: "Satan represents vital existence, instead of spiritual pipe dreams!" (LaVey 1969, 25). The Rand passage said to correspond with this statement, though shorter than the first, is similarly distant in style and content from LaVey: "My morality, the morality of reason, is contained in a single axiom: existence exists—and in a single choice: to live. The rest proceeds from these" (944). And there is a similar disparity in the other parallels between the Satanic statements and Rand. Thus, even if it were true that LaVey was looking at *Atlas Shrugged* when he composed the "Nine Satanic Statements," it would be more proper to say that he was *inspired* by Rand rather than to assert that he *paraphrased* her work.

I should finally note in this regard that the title of the appendix (which originally appeared as an article by George C. Smith in 1987) in which the LaVey–Rand connection is delineated, "The Hidden Source of the Satanic Philosophy," similarly implies that Rand's philosophy was the *un*acknowledged core of LaVey's thought (Aquino 1999). This is, however, incorrect; LaVey himself explicitly acknowledged that his religion was "just Ayn Rand's philosophy with ceremony and ritual added" (cited in Ellis 2000, 180). (Refer also to the "Satanism and Objectivism" essay on the Church of Satan web site, where this connection is examined at length.)

Despite the book's diverse source material and piecemeal assembly, it nevertheless coheres as a succinct—and, apparently, quite attractive—statement of Satanic thought and practice. As Aquino observes, "the *Satanic Bible* was somehow 'more than the sum of its parts.' Its argument was an argument of common sense, assembled in part from pre-existing concepts, but the excellence of the book lay in its integration of these into a code of life meaningful to the average individual—not just to occultists and/or academic-level philosophers" (1999, 52).

One measure of *The Satanic Bible*'s appeal is that it has continuously been in print since it first appeared in 1970 and has been translated into a number of other languages. I have been unable to obtain recent figures, but in his *In Pursuit of Satan*, Robert Hicks mentions a sales figure of 618,000 copies (1991, 351). There were also a number of illegal foreign-language editions. These include a

Spanish translation published in Mexico in the 1970s and a Russian translation in the late 1990s. Legal editions include Czech and Swedish translations in the mid 1990s and a 1999 German edition. The French translation has been completed but not yet printed. Also, the rights for a Greek translation were purchased, but the book does not seem to have appeared.[1]

THE ROLE OF *THE SATANIC BIBLE* IN MODERN SATANISM

Although religious Satanism is interesting, academics have almost entirely ignored it. (The relevant academic literature consists of a handful of articles—e.g., Alfred 1976; Harvey 1995—and passing mentions in studies of the ritual abuse scare.) The principal reason for the lack of attention appears to be that Satanism is perceived as a trivial phenomenon rather than as a serious religion. The tendency seems to be to regard Satanists as nothing more than immature adolescents who have adopted a diabolical veneer as a way of acting out their rebellion against parents and society. Does the phenomenon of adolescent rebellion, however, exhaust the significance of religious Satanism? Are most Satanists, in other words, just angry teenagers who adopt diabolical trappings to express their alienation, only to renounce the Prince of Darkness as soon as they mature into adults? Though many youthful Satanists undoubtedly fit this profile, through my fieldwork I came to feel that this was, at best, only a partial picture. Instead, I hypothesized that there must be a core of committed Satanists who—for whatever reasons they initially become involved—had come to appropriate Satanism as something more than adolescent rebellion.

In order to test this hypothesis—and also because so little had been written on religious Satanism—I collected some basic demographic data in connection with a larger study of contemporary Satanism. I constructed a simple questionnaire that could be answered in five or ten minutes and began sending out questionnaires in early August 2000. By the end of February 2001 I had received 140 responses, which I felt were adequate to use as the basis for constructing a preliminary profile.[2]

When I sought feedback on preliminary write-ups of my findings from informants, a few voiced objections to the central role I assigned LaVey and his best-known work, *The Satanic Bible*, in the formation of modern Satanic religion. I was, furthermore, encouraged to shift my emphasis to the work of earlier literary figures ultimately responsible for fashioning the positive image of the Devil that LaVey later adopted for his Church of Satan. My survey findings, however, consistently indicated the centrality of LaVey to modern Satanism. This finding was a surprise, as I had initially assumed that contemporary Satanism had moved well beyond LaVey. I was thus led to conclude that—despite his dependence on prior thinkers—LaVey was directly responsible for the genesis of Satanism as a serious religious (as opposed to a purely literary) movement. Furthermore, however one might criticize and depreciate it, *The Satanic Bible* is still the single most influential document shaping the contemporary Satanic movement. As one of my informants noted, "I do not think Satanists can get away from LaVey, although some seem to take a real issue with him or try to downplay his importance. He wrote the book that codified Satanism into a religion, and for that he should be considered the central figure of the religion."

I do not intend to review all of my survey findings here (they are the subject of Lewis 2001; a summary of this research can be found in appendix A), but I do want to note that I was surprised to find that the average respondent had been a Satanist for seven to eight years. I also found that over two-thirds of the sample had been involved in at least one other religion beyond the tradition in which they were raised—usually Neopaganism or some other magical group. Both of these statistics indicate a level of seriousness I had not anticipated.

Because most respondents became involved during their teens, I inferred that many had initially become Satanists as an expression of teenage rebelliousness. It was clear, however, that their involvement did not end after they left home. Rather, they went on to appropriate Satanism as a serious religious option. The fact that the great majority of Satanists have looked into other religions shows that this was not an unconsidered choice, undertaken solely as a reaction against established religions. Also, though a reaction against Christianity may well have been a factor for some, too many respondents indicated that their religious upbringing was superficial, nominal, or nonexistent for this factor to explain why most people become Satanists.

Before I began collecting questionnaire data, I had received the impression, from perusing the internet, that contemporary Satanism had developed in different directions from the specific formulation developed by Anton LaVey in the 1960s. In particular, at the time it appeared to me that many contemporary Satanists had moved to a position of regarding Satan as a conscious being and had legitimated their claims to authority on the basis of direct communications from dark forces. I was thus surprised to discover that LaVey's humanistic approach—which rejects the real existence of personal spiritual beings, diabolical or otherwise—was the dominant form of Satanism professed by respondents.

At least part of the reason for this state of affairs appears to be the pervasive influence of *The Satanic Bible*. A full 20 percent of respondents explicitly noted *The Satanic Bible* as the single most important factor attracting them to Satanism. For instance, in response to a questionnaire item asking how they became involved, a number of people simply wrote, "I read the *Satanic Bible*." It is also likely that this book played a major role in the "conversion" of other Satanists in my sample. One respondent elaborated by noting that she had been a Satanist in her "heart first, but [she] couldn't put a name to it; then [she] found *The Satanic Bible*."

Similar stories attributing their infernal "conversions" to *The Satanic Bible* can be found in other sources. The popular book *Lucifer Rising*, for instance, recounts the story of how Martin Lamers, founder of the CoS-affiliated Kerk van Satan (Holland), was initially inspired by his discovery of LaVey's volume (Baddeley 1999, 104). However, not everyone who is converted to Satanism via *The Satanic Bible* feels prompted to join the Church of Satan. *Lucifer Rising* also notes that "the Church of Satanic Liberation was established in January 1986 after its founder, Paul Douglas Valentine, was inspired by reading *The Satanic Bible*" (153). Other stories of conversions directly inspired by *The Satanic Bible* can be found in Michael Aquino's *The Church of Satan*—e.g., the conversion of Robert DeCecco, who would later become a master of the temple (69); and Lilith Sinclair, who would eventually become a priestess and Aquino's wife (82).

To return to the survey, LaVey's influential publication was also referred to a number of times in response to other questionnaire items. For example, one person noted, "Because I agree with and practice the majority of the beliefs set forth in *The Satanic Bible* and other works of Dr. LaVey, I VERY MUCH consider myself just as valid a Satanist as any 'official' priest." Another respondent wrote, "Satan is merely a word, a representative concept that encompasses all that the *Satanic Bible* teaches." And yet another individual stated, "To me, Satan is the personification of mankind's carnal nature. More information can be found in *The Satanic Bible* by Anton Szandor LaVey."

My strong impression was that *The Satanic Bible* was a doctrinal touchstone for most participants in this movement, despite the fact that the great majority of my sample were not formal members of Anton LaVey's Church of Satan. (One respondent, noting that he was not a member of any organization, wrote, "[It's] just me and my *Satanic Bible*.") And whatever LaVey had in mind when he entitled this publication, in certain ways *The Satanic Bible* has truly come to play the role of a "bible" for many members of this decentralized, anti-authoritarian subculture. (As indicated in Schreck's comments cited earlier, the title was "a last minute decision." She further noted in the same communication that "earlier titles proposed included such awkward possibilities as *The Bible of the Church of Satan, The Bible of Satanism* and so forth" [2002].)

In a follow-up questionnaire, respondents were explicitly asked how they regarded *The Satanic Bible* and to what extent their personal philosophies were congruent with the ideas expressed in its pages. Most stated that their view of the world aligned significantly with *The Satanic Bible*. One Satanist said *The Satanic Bible* was about the realities of human nature, so that there was "nothing [in *The Satanic Bible*] that I didn't already know or believe myself prior to reading it." Only one respondent completely rejected the LaVeyan tradition. Two respondents asserted that they regarded *The Satanic Bible* as just another "self-help book." Some respondents diminished (without disparaging) *The Satanic Bible* as an "introductory text" or "primer" of Satanism. Most hastened to add that they did not regard it as "dogma."

One can acquire a sense of how *The Satanic Bible* is regarded as a doctrinal touchstone by perusing the official web site of the Church of Satan (http://www.churchofsatan.com). For example, the "Satanism FAQ" section of the "Church of Satan Information Pack" states that "critically reading *The Satanic Bible* by Anton Szandor LaVey is tantamount to understanding at least the basics of Satanism." Similarly, the church's "Church of Satan Youth Communiqué" asserts that "LaVey wrote *The Satanic Bible* so that people could pick up a copy, read it, and know everything they need to know about Satanism and how to put it to work in their own lives."

In addition to these general assertions, one can find on the Church of Satan web site other essays in which authoritative tenets are cited from *The Satanic Bible,* as when the "Satanic Bunco Sheet" notes that "*The Satanic Bible* advises to 'question all things,'" or when, in an essay entitled "Satanism Needs an Enema!" an individual writing under the pseudonym Nemo introduces a series of citations from *The Satanic Bible* to support a point he is arguing with the words, "Other quotes from LaVey's own pen in *The Satanic Bible* reiterate this theme." The clear implication of this statement is that because these quotations come from "LaVey's own pen in *The Satanic Bible,*" they are authoritative; thus there can be no further discussion of the issue. Toward the end of the same essay, Nemo also asserts, "We have a bible. We have a *pro-human* dogma. We have a church. We have a tradition. We have ceremonies and rituals. We have a High Priestess." In other words, with respect to the theme being pursued in this book, Nemo is asserting that CoS has an authoritative scripture, dogma, and tradition that support his argument. And it is obvious that Nemo regards his appeal to CoS *tradition* as stronger than direct appeals to science or common sense, which were the touchstones of LaVey's philosophy.

It is also interesting that one of the accusations leveled against non-CoS Satanists in Nemo's "Recognizing Pseudo-Satanism" essay is that, in such groups, "The words of *The Satanic Bible* become twisted and distorted until they no longer have useful meaning!" Furthermore, in his "Satanism Needs an Enema!" essay, the same writer exclaims, "I am calling for a closing of the ranks and a throwing out of the heretics. I am asking for the Purge! I am asking for a *reverse* Inquisition." Both of these sets of passages—the first quoting *The Satanic Bible* to make a point and the second accusing heretical breakaways of warping *The Satanic Bible*'s meaning (even going so far as to call for an "Inquisition" against heretics within the ranks)—exemplify all-too-familiar patterns found in the theological conflicts of traditional religions.

Quoting *The Satanic Bible* to legitimate a point of argument is not, however, confined to representatives of the Church of Satan. The so-called "Xloptuny Curse" is an interesting example of how some of the "heretics" have turned the message of LaVey's writings to their own purposes. A short essay, "The Xloptuny Curse," written by Joe Necchi, was posted on the official web site of the First Church of Satan in the summer of 2000. (The First Church of Satan [FCoS] is a newer Satanist organization founded by a former member of CoS whose brand of Satanism is very close to *The Satanic Bible*.) The text discusses the circumstances of a seemingly effective suicide curse that was leveled by Lord Egan, founder/leader of the FCoS, against Xloptuny (John C. Davis), an internet pugilist and member of the CoS. Less than a year before Davis took a gun to his head, Egan had cursed Davis, specifying in a public, on-line communication that he would die by shooting himself. The passage to focus on for present purposes is where Necchi remarks,

> What is interesting, however, is the way in which some have predictably tried to rationalize Xloptuny's suicide as a Yukio Mishima–inspired act of heroism. Ironically, those trying so hard to canonize Mr. Davis thusly now have decided to conveniently ignore the book they are always waving about like a black flag at most other times: *The Satanic Bible*. In this sense, we see that many Satanists really behave exactly like Christians: they follow the precepts of their religion when it's easy to do so, when it suits them, but are quick to abandon them when it really counts.
>
> *The Satanic Bible* specifically states: "Self-sacrifice is not encouraged by the Satanic religion. Therefore, unless death comes as an indulgence because of extreme circumstances which make the termination of life a welcome relief from an unendurable earthly existence, suicide is frowned upon by the Satanic religion." There is little ambiguity in this passage. As there is no reason to believe that Xloptuny was in "extreme circumstances that make the termination of life a welcome relief"; he died as a traitor to the Church whose cause he so often trumpeted, the defense of which he used as a rationale for his often black and bilious attacks on his enemies. Apparently "the great Dr. Anton LaVey's" words meant little or nothing to John C. Davis when he arrived at the moment of truth. (quotes from LaVey 1969, 94)

Here again we see *The Satanic Bible* being quoted as an authoritative document in a manner similar to the way sacred texts are quoted in comparable conflicts within other religious traditions. In other words, "The Xloptuny Curse" is yet another example of how *The Satanic Bible* functions as quasi-scripture within the Satanic community.

Almost all Satanists would deny that *The Satanic Bible* is an inspired document in anything like the sense in which the Christian Bible is regarded as an inspired book. Interestingly, however, there are a few individuals—most notably Michael Aquino, a former CoS leader and founder of the Temple of Set—who *would* regard this book as inspired. For example, in the relevant chapter in his history of the Church of Satan, Aquino asserts,

> The *Satanic Bible* [clothes] itself in the supernatural authority of the Prince of Darkness and his demons. Less this element, the *Satanic Bible* would be merely a social tract by Anton LaVey—not High Priest of Satan, but just one more 1960s'-counterculture-cynic atop a soapbox.
>
> The substance of the *Satanic Bible* therefore turns upon Anton LaVey's sincerity in believing himself to be the vehicle through which the entity known as Satan explains the mysteries of mankind's existential predicament. To the extent that he did, the *Satanic Bible* deserves the dignity of its title. . . .
>
> Despite the haphazard nature of its assembly, . . . we may therefore consider the *Satanic Bible* in its totality not as argumentative, but as inspired writing. Thus it assumes an importance by its very *existence*, not just by its content. (1999, 53)

Although Aquino's position would be rejected by most other professing Satanists, something approaching this position seems to be unconsciously informing their attitude toward *The Satanic Bible*.

CONCLUSION

Anton LaVey's primary legitimation strategy was to appeal to the authority of science, specifically to the secularist worldview derived from natural science and to an animalistic image of the human being derived from the Darwinian theory of evolution. In light of his radically secularist legitimation strategy, it is ironic that his organizational successors have subsequently attempted to legitimate their positions by appealing to LaVey as if he had actually been some kind of "Black Pope" and to *The Satanic Bible* as if it was truly a diabolically revealed scripture. It appears that being raised in a religious tradition that locates the source of authority in religious figures and sacred texts creates an unconscious predisposition that can be carried over to other kinds of persons and books—even in the unlikely context of contemporary Satanism.

Outside the institutional bounds of the Church of Satan, modern Satanism has become a loose, decentralized movement that coheres as a distinct religious community largely by virtue of participants' adherence to certain themes in the published words of Anton LaVey, particularly in *The Satanic Bible*. Despite this volume's patchwork quality and haphazard genesis, it has come to play an authoritative, quasi-scriptural role within the larger Satanic movement. Unlike members of the Church of Satan, however, non-CoS Satanists feel free to criticize and even to reject aspects of the LaVeyan tradition by appealing to the authority of rationality—a criterion of legitimacy LaVey himself put forward as the very basis of Satanism.

6

HEAVEN'S GATE AND THE LEGITIMATION OF SUICIDE

On March 26, 1997, the bodies of thirty-nine men and women were found in a well-appointed mansion outside San Diego, victims of a mass suicide. Messages left by the group indicate that they believed they were stepping out of their "physical containers" in order to ascend to a UFO that was arriving in the wake of the Hale-Bopp comet. They also asserted that this comet, or parts of it, would subsequently crash into earth and cause widespread destruction.

Heaven's Gate—formerly known as Human Individual Metamorphosis (HIM)—originally made headlines in September 1975 when, following a public lecture in Waldport, Oregon, over thirty people vanished overnight. This disappearance became the occasion for a media feeding frenzy. For the next several months, reporters generated story after story about brainwashed cult groupies abandoning their everyday lives to follow the strange couple who alternately referred to themselves as "Bo and Peep," "the Two," "Do and Ti," and other bizarre names.

Bo (Marshall Herff Applewhite) and Peep (Bonnie Lu Nettles) met in 1972 and founded one of the most unusual flying saucer religions ever to emerge out of the occult–metaphysical–New Age subculture. Preaching an unusual synthesis of occult spirituality

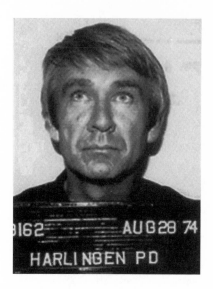

FIGURE 6.1. Mug shot of Marshall Applewhite, founder of Heaven's Gate, 1974.

and UFO soteriology, they began recruiting in New Age circles in the spring of 1975. Followers were required to abandon friends and family, detach themselves completely from human emotions as well as material possessions, and focus exclusively on perfecting themselves in preparation for a physical transition to the next kingdom (in the form of a flying saucer)—a metamorphosis that would be facilitated by ufonauts.

Bo and Peep were (perhaps surprisingly) effective at recruiting people to their unusual gospel, though their activities did not attract much attention until the Waldport, Oregon, meeting. Six weeks later, the group was infiltrated by University of Montana sociologist Robert Balch and a research assistant, David Taylor. Balch and Taylor presented themselves as interested seekers and became pseudo-followers in order to clandestinely conduct field research. As they would later report in subsequent papers, the great majority of the people who became involved with Bo and Peep were either marginal individuals living on the fringes of society or people who had been deeply involved with occult spirituality for some time before their affiliation with the Two (Balch 1995).

However, as useful as the "marginal seeker" characterization of the Two's recruits might be, our minds still recoil in incomprehension at the transparent absurdity of Bo and Peep's teachings—How could any sane human being buy into such silliness? And how could a "prophet" who looked like Mickey Mouse and sounded like Mr. Rogers lead a group of over three dozen people to their deaths? Mind control notions that portray "cultists" as suffering from damaged powers of reasoning are little more than expressions of social disapproval that substitute disparaging labels for real understanding. Perhaps we should consider the alternate hypothesis that, from the viewpoint of participants, the Two's teaching was actually quite plausible.

Applewhite and Nettles appealed to a wide variety of sources—particularly to a number of facets of New Age ideology, but also to certain aspects of the Christian tradition—to legitimate their authority and their unusual religious vision. This mix of sources is evident in their claim to be Jesus returned (Applewhite) and God the Father (Nettles), while simultaneously asserting that they were extraterrestrial "walk-ins" (a New Age notion). A number of observers have emphasized Heaven's Gate's Christian component, to the point of characterizing the Two's teaching as "space-age neo-Christian" (Hall 2000, 178). However, although the Christian component of their ideological synthesis should not be downplayed, it seems clear that the Christian elements were grafted onto a basically New Age matrix. The simple fact that Heaven's Gate attracted seekers from the New Age subculture rather than from the Christian subculture—that "New Agers" rather than Christians could entertain the Two's ideology as a viable, appealing teaching—underscores this point.

In the midst of a society in which the belief system propagated by the Two seems absurd, it is also appropriate to ask how they legitimated their unusual worldview to followers. And finally, after Nettles passed away from cancer, which elements of their belief system was Applewhite able to draw upon to legitimate a group suicide? In view of the dramatic end of Heaven's Gate, it might well repay our efforts if we examine the relevant aspects of the larger spiritual subculture within which such teachings might sound plausible rather than absurd. While not all aspects of Applewhite's theological synthesis were drawn from New Age thinking, most components of the group's overarching worldview were characteristically New Age, as shall be demonstrated.

ASCENDED MASTERS AND UFOS

Despite the existence of some formal organizations in the New Age movement, the core of this ambiguous subculture is constituted by a largely unaffiliated population of "seekers" who drift promiscuously from one spiritual group to another, never committing themselves to any single vision of truth. One result of the general weakness of doctrinally oriented organizations is that this subculture can be infiltrated by almost any interesting new idea not overtly antagonistic to the basic tenets of New Age ideology (Lewis 1992).

As an unusually fascinating form of rejected knowledge that mainstream scientists tend to classify as paranormal, UFOs have always attracted considerable interest within the occult–metaphysical–New Age subculture. Almost from the beginning, however, this subculture transformed flying saucers and their presumed extraterrestrial pilots into spiritual beings who had come to earth to help us along the path. To accomplish the transformation of ETs into wise, esoteric beings, "ufonauts" were assimilated into earlier models of spiritual sages, particularly the so-called ascended masters.

The concept of ascended masters or the Great White Brotherhood was codified within Theosophy by Helena Petrovna Blavatsky in the 1880s, and from there was passed on to the various religious groups that descend from the Theosophical Society. The ascended masters, in turn, were derived from the earlier notion of "secret chiefs" (Hutton 1999, 58), to whom a wide variety of different occult lodges—including the well-known Hermetic Order of the Golden Dawn—appealed as their primary "source of legitimation" (76). Many people in the New Age movement believe that the ascended masters guide the spiritual progress of humanity. The equation of ascended masters with ufonauts seems to have developed out of an earlier idea, which was that at least some of the masters were from other planets in our solar system, such as Venus. (This line of development was discussed in chapter 4.)

Even much secular thinking about UFOs embodies quasi-religious themes, such as the crypto-religious notion that the world is on the verge of destruction and that ufonauts are somehow going to rescue humanity. As mentioned in an earlier chapter, Carl Jung was referring to the latter portrayal of ufonauts when he called them "technological angels." Jung interpreted the phenomenon of flying saucers—which often appear in the form of circular disks—as Mandala symbols, reflecting the human mind's desire for stability in a confused world. From a depth psychological point of view, it is thus no coincidence that the chariots of the gods should manifest in the form of a circle, which is a symbol of wholeness (Jung 1956, 1978).

But if UFOs are the chariots of the gods, then why do the space brothers not just land and communicate their ideas to humanity in person? Basically the same question has sometimes been asked with respect to the Great White Brotherhood. One of the salient characteristics of the ascended masters was that they preferred to communicate their occult teachings through the medium of telepathic messages sent to select individuals. These chosen vessels then relayed the masters' messages to the larger public, either vocally in a form of mediumship later called "channeling" or in written form via automatic writing. Because the ascended masters were the primary model for the space brothers, it comes as no surprise that later-day UFO prophets should employ the same methods for communicating the wisdom of the ufonauts to the larger public.

George King, for example, the founder of the Aetherius Society, proposed that these masters were actually extraterrestrials who were members of a "space command" managing the affairs of the solar system (Saliba 2000). This concept has been built upon by other channelers and groups, such as Michael and Aurora El-Legion, who channel the "Ashtar Command." It was from this tradition that Applewhite and Nettles took the idea of spiritually advanced ufonauts. And it is easy to connect the Two directly to the theosophical tradition: before meeting Applewhite, Nettles had belonged to the Theosophical Society and had attended New Age channeling sessions at which extraterrestrial beings may have been channeled.

THE JOURNEY OF BO AND PEEP

In addition to teaching that ufonauts were spiritually advanced beings, Applewhite and Nettles also taught that aliens had come to pick up spiritually evolved human beings who would join the ranks of flying saucer crews. Only a select few members of humanity would be chosen to advance to this transhuman state; the rest would be left to wallow in the spiritually poisoned atmosphere of a corrupt world. Applewhite would later teach that after the elect had been picked up by the space brothers, the planet would be engulfed in cataclysmic destruction. When, in 1993, under the name of Total Overcomers Anonymous, the group ran an advertisement in *USA Today,* their portrayal of the post-rapture world was far more apocalyptic than Applewhite and Nettles had taught in the 1970s: "The Earth's present 'civilization' is about to be recycled—'spaded under.' Its inhabitants are refusing to evolve. The 'weeds' have taken over the garden and disturbed its usefulness beyond repair" (cited in Balch 1995, 163). For followers of the Two, the focus of day-to-day existence was to adhere to a disciplined regime referred to as the "overcoming process" or, simply, the process. The goal of this process was to overcome human weaknesses—a goal not dissimilar to the goal of certain spiritual practices followed by more mainstream monastic communities.

Experiences that seemed to disconfirm the Heaven's Gate worldview were addressed by attributing them to the machinations of evil aliens, who were referred to as "Luciferians" by the Two. For this aspect of their teaching, Applewhite and Nettles adopted a strategy deployed within certain conservative Christian sects, namely, to dismiss any challenges to their theology as motivated by demons. However, their vision of a world under assault by evil aliens who keep human beings bound to continuous reincarnations on the earth plane through delusion and through the distraction of physical pleasures is more clearly related to certain strands of traditional Gnosticism than to Christian demonology—though it should immediately be added that Bo and Peep's group does not otherwise exhibit enough relevant traits to be classified as Gnostic (Hall 2000, 177).

Details about how the group came to attach apocalyptic significance to the Hale-Bopp Comet are scanty. (Refer to discussion in Hall 2000, 171–172.) For whatever reason, someone outside the group had come to the conclusion that a giant UFO was coming to earth, "hidden" in the wake of Hale-Bopp. When Heaven's Gate heard this information, Applewhite took it as an indication that the long awaited pick-up of his group by aliens was finally about to take place. The decision that the time had come to make their final exit could not have been made more than a few weeks before the mass suicide. Applewhite had rethought his theology after his beloved partner died in 1985 because, in order to be reunited with Nettles, her spirit would have to acquire a new body aboard the spacecraft. The death of Nettles seems to have been the decisive influence leading him to later adopt the view that the group would ascend together spiritually rather than physically (Wessinger 2000, 237–239).

Applewhite may have chosen the option of a group suicide because there seemed to be no other viable solution to the problem of what followers would do after he passed away. This quandary relates Heaven's Gate to one of the more well known themes in Max Weber's analysis of religion, namely, that the death of the founder of a religion represents a crisis typically addressed via the routinization of the prophet's charisma—by which Weber meant the transmission and regularization of her or his charisma in the form of new institutions. Heaven's Gate, however, was never large enough to prompt the Two to consider setting up anything like an institution. And the teaching that the space brothers would pick them up within their lifetimes effectively prevented Applewhite from considering the option of appointing a successor (Wessinger 2000, 244). So in the end, getting older, and failing in health (Perkins and Jackson 1997, 81), Applewhite—having already decided some years before that they would make their exit via a group suicide—seems to have been predisposed to interpret any indication that the space brothers were coming as a sign it was time to leave. Hence, the rumor that a large UFO was approaching earth in the wake of Hale-Bopp—a rumor widely repeated among UFO buffs on the internet and discussed in such popular forums as the Art Bell radio show (Perkins and Jackson 1997, 76–79)—provided Applewhite with the sign he was waiting for to set in motion the final solution to his quandary.

GRADUATING TO THE NEXT LEVEL

The idea that the group might depart via suicide had emerged in Applewhite's thinking only within the last few years. The Two's earlier idea—an idea that had set Heaven's Gate apart from everyone else in the New Age–metaphysical subculture—was that a group of individuals selected to move to the next level would bodily ascend to the saucers in a kind of technological rapture (Hall 2000, 155). Applewhite and Nettles had originally taught that the goal of the process they were teaching their followers was to prepare them to be physically taken aboard the spacecraft where they would enter a cocoon-like state, eventually being reborn in a transformed physical body.

The notion of resurrection is central to chapter 11 of the Book of Revelation, the biblical passage that Applewhite and Nettles came to view as describing their particular ministry. This chapter recounts the story of two prophets who will be slain. Then, three and a half days later, they will be resurrected and taken up in a cloud: "At the end of the three days and a half the breath of life from God came into them; and they stood up on their feet to the terror of all who saw it. Then a loud voice was heard speaking to them from heaven, which said, "Come up here!" And they went up to heaven in a cloud, in full view of their enemies. At that same moment there was a violent earthquake" (Revelation 11:11–13). In the early phase of their movement, Applewhite and Nettles prophesied that they would soon be assassinated (Hall 2000, 153). Using the above passage as a script for future events, they further predicted that they would be resurrected three and a half days later and taken up into a flying saucer. The Two asserted that this event would prove the truth of their teachings. As for their followers, they taught that Heaven was the literal, physical heavens, and those few people chosen to depart with the Two would, after their physical transformation, become crew members aboard UFOs.

Although the basic teachings seem to have remained constant, the details of their ideology were flexible enough to undergo modification over time. For example, in the early days, Applewhite and Nettles taught their followers that they were extraterrestrial beings. However, after the notion of walk-ins became popular within the New Age subculture, the Two changed their ideas and began describing themselves as extraterrestrial walk-ins.

A "walk-in" is an entity who occupies a body that has been vacated by its original soul. An *extraterrestrial* walk-in is a walk-in who is supposedly from another planet. The walk-in situation is somewhat similar to possession, although in possession the original soul is merely overshadowed—rather than completely supplanted—by the possessing entity. The contemporary notion of walk-ins was popularized by Ruth Montgomery, who developed the walk-in notion in her 1979 book, *Strangers among Us*. According to Montgomery, walk-ins are usually highly evolved souls here to help humanity. In order to avoid the delay of incarnating as a baby, and thus having to spend two decades maturing to adulthood, they contact living people who, because of frustrating circumstances of life or for some other reason, no longer desire to remain in the body. The discarnate entity finds such people, persuades them to hand over their body, and then begins life as a walk-in.

The walk-in concept seems to be related to certain traditional South Asian tales about aging yoga masters taking over the bodies of young people who die prematurely. Another possible source for the contemporary walk-in notion is the well-known (in theosophical circles) teaching that Jesus and Christ were separate souls. According to this teaching, Jesus prepared his physical body to receive Christ and, at a certain point in his career, vacated his body and allowed Christ to take it over. An underlying notion here is that Christ was such a highly evolved soul that it would have been difficult if not impossible for him to have incarnated as a baby— and, even if he could have done so, it would have been a waste of precious time for such a highly developed soul to have to go through childhood.

Montgomery (1979), more than any other person, is responsible for popularizing the contemporary notion of walk-ins. In 1983 Montgomery published *Threshold to Tomorrow*, containing case histories of seventeen walk-ins. According to Montgomery, history is full of walk-ins, including such famous historical figures as Moses, Jesus, Muhammad, Christopher Columbus, Abraham Lincoln, Mary Baker Eddy, Gandhi, George Washington, Benjamin Franklin, Thomas Jefferson, Alexander Hamilton, and James Madison. In fact, it seems that Montgomery would identify almost everyone manifesting exceptional creativity and leadership as a walk-in.

In *Aliens among Us* (1985), Montgomery developed the notion of extraterrestrial walk-ins—the idea that souls from other planets have come to earth to take over the bodies of human beings. This notion dovetailed well with popular interest in UFOs, which had already been incorporated into New Age spirituality. Following Montgomery, the New Age movement came to view extraterrestrial walk-ins as part of the larger community of advanced souls that have come to earth to help humanity through a period of transition and crisis. It is easy to see how this basic notion fitted well into the Two's ideology, explaining away their human personal histories as the histories of the souls who formerly occupied the bodies of Applewhite and Nettles.

It should be noted that the walk-in idea—a notion implying a radical disjunction between soul and body—also provided Applewhite with an essential ideological component in his rethinking of the ascension scenario and ultimately legitimating their radical departure. In other words, after the death of Nettles, Applewhite had to come to grips with the fact that—under the physical ascension scenario that had been a cornerstone of their teachings for almost two decades—his spiritual partner would miss the chance to escape the planet with the rest of the group. This option was, however, unimaginable to Applewhite. Hence, by the time of the mass suicide, Applewhite had reconceptualized the ascension as an event in which Heaven's Gate members let go of their physical containers and ascended *spiritually* to the waiting saucers. Once on board, they would consciously "walk-into" a new physical body and join the crew of the next level spacecraft. This scenario is related in one of the group's internet statements: "Their final separation is the willful separation from their human body, when they have changed enough to identify as the spirit/mind/soul—ready to put on a biological body belonging to the Kingdom of Heaven. (This entering into their 'glorified' or heavenly body takes place aboard a Next Level spacecraft, above the Earth's surface.)" (Heaven's Gate 1996). Presumably, these new physical bodies would be supplied to Heaven's Gate members out of some sort of "cloning bank" kept aboard the spaceships.

ANCIENT ASTRONAUTS AND EARTH CHANGES

Another notion the Two picked up from the metaphysical subculture of their day was the ancient astronaut hypothesis. The expression "ancient astronauts" is used to refer to various forms of the concept that ufonauts visited our planet in the distant past. The basic idea that many, if not all, of the powerful sky gods of traditional religions were really extraterrestrial visitors intervening in human history had been around for many decades. However, it was not until the book *Chariots of the Gods?* authored by Erich von Däniken in 1969, that this notion was popularized. While later writers such as Zecharia Sitchin (1976, 1995) have developed this view with greater sophistication, none have been as influential as von Däniken.

This view, which seems to call into question the validity of religion, has been adopted by large segments of the New Age subculture in a way that is not seen as contradicting metaphysical spirituality. Instead, believers view the space brothers as working in cooperation with spiritual forces to stimulate the spiritual evolution of this planet. One aspect of the ancient astronaut hypothesis is the idea that the contemporary human race is the offspring of a union between aliens and native terrestrials. Some even believe that a distorted record of this event can be found in a few enigmatic verses in the book of Genesis about the sons of God copulating with the daughters of men. This union produced an intermediate species referred to in Genesis as the "Nephilim." In a different version of the same idea, ancient ufonauts stimulated the evolution of our ape-like forebears to produce present-day humanity. Our space "fathers" have subsequently been watching over us and will, according to some New Age notions, return to mingle with their distant offspring during the imminent New Age (Lewis and Oliver 1995).

Applewhite and Nettles taught a slightly modified version of the ancient astronaut hypothesis: aliens planted the seeds of current humanity millions of years ago and have come to reap the harvest of their work in the form of spiritually evolved individuals who will join the ranks of flying saucer crews. Only a select few members of humanity will be chosen to advance to this transhuman state. The rest will be left to wallow in the spiritually poisoned atmosphere of a corrupt world.

Applewhite would later teach that after the elect had been picked up by the space brothers, the planet would be engulfed in cataclysmic destruction. Though Applewhite's apocalyptic teachings might at first appear to be derived entirely from his biblical background, his decidedly "this-worldly" vision of our planet's end suggests that his ideology was decisively influenced by the New Age subculture and by the more recent discussion of colliding asteroids found in contemporary popular culture (Thomas 1997).

Particularly in the teachings of New Age channels, one often finds the theme of apocalyptic "earth changes" that are supposed to take place around the end of the millennium. This notion seems to have originally been introduced via the teachings of Edgar Cayce, as published by his son Hugh Lynn Cayce (1980). Furthermore, these upheavals in the earth's crust are often thought of as coming about as a direct result of a planetary "pole shift," a subsidiary notion that was popularized by Montgomery (1985). (Though in sharp contrast to Applewhite, New Age thinkers postulate that these dramatic earth changes will herald a terrestrial Golden Age.) The idea that global destruction would come about as the result of a wandering asteroid is a more recent notion that has been discussed in popular magazine articles and television specials only within the last dozen years or so.

Because these notions about walk-ins and earth changes would have been familiar to the seekers whom Bo and Peep attracted to Heaven's Gate, there would have been no need to explicitly legitimate or even to explain them to new recruits. As hard as it may be for most of us to grasp, such ideas were not only familiar, they were also plausible to many members of the New Age subculture. The same observation applies to most of the other key beliefs of the Two's ideological synthesis, such as the notion that the earth is a schoolroom for spiritual development.

OUR TERRESTRIAL CLASSROOM

Another major theme that Applewhite and Nettles absorbed from the metaphysical subculture was the view that the spiritual life is a graded series of learning experiences culminating—in the case of Heaven's Gate—in a "graduation" to the next evolutionary kingdom. Members of the group thought of themselves as "students," their fellows as "classmates," and Applewhite as their "tutor" (Heaven's Gate 1996). These educational metaphors would have been particularly comfortable and natural for a man who had been a popular university teacher during the first part of his adult life.

Like other religious and cultural systems, the worldview of the contemporary New Age movement is held together by a shared set of symbols and metaphors—shared images of life reflected in the discourse of participants as a set of commonly used terms. For example, due in part to a vision of metaphysical unity inherited from Theosophy and from Asian religious philosophy—but also due to this subculture's reaction against the perceived fragmentation and alienation of mainstream society—the New Age movement emphasizes the values of unity and relatedness. These values find expression in such common terms as "holistic," "oneness," "wholeness," and "community." This spiritual subculture also values growth and dynamism—an evaluation expressed in discourse about "evolution," "transformation," "process," and so forth.

The image of education is related to the growth metaphor (for example, one of our linguistic conventions is that education allows a person to "grow"). If we examine the metaphysical subculture through the lens of the education theme, we discover that, in contrast to many other religious movements, the dominant New Age "ceremonies" are workshops, lectures, and classes rather than worship ceremonies. Even large New Age gatherings such as the Whole Life Expo resemble academic conferences more than they resemble camp meetings (Lewis 1997).

It is also interesting to note the extent to which educational metaphors inform New Age thought. In terms of the way the Western metaphysical tradition has interpreted the ongoing process of reincarnation, spiritual growth and even life itself are learning experiences. To cite some of examples of this, Katar, a New Age medium, channels such messages as, "Here on Earth, you *are* your teacher, your books, your lessons and the classroom as well as the student" (Clark 1988, 7). This message is amplified by J. L. Simmons, a sociologist who, in his *The Emerging New Age,* describes life on the physical plane as the "Earth School" (1990, 91) and asserts that "we are here to learn . . . and will continue to return until we 'do the course' and 'graduate'" (73).

Similar images are reflected in the essay "The Role of the Esoteric in Planetary Culture," where David Spangler argues that spiritual wisdom is esoteric "only because so few people expend the time, the energy, the effort, the openness and the love to gain it, just as only a few are willing to invest what is required to become a nuclear physicist or a neurosurgeon" (Spangler 1977, 193–194). It would not be going too far to assert that, in the New Age vision of things, the image of the whole of human life—particularly when that life is directed toward spiritual goals—can be summed up as a learning experience:

> Each of us has an Inner Teacher, a part of ourselves which knows exactly what we need to learn, and constantly creates the opportunity for us to learn just that. We have the choice either to cooperate with this part of ourselves or to ignore it. If we decide to cooperate, we can see lessons constantly in front of us; every challenge is a chance to grow and develop. If, on the other hand, we try to ignore this Inner Teacher, we can find ourselves hitting the same problem again and again, because we are not perceiving and responding to the lesson we have created for ourselves. [It] is, however, the daily awareness of and cooperation with spirit [that] pulls humanity upwards on the evolutionary spiral, and the constant invocation and evocation of spirit enables a rapid unfolding of human potential. When the Inner Teacher and the evolutionary force of the Universe are able to work together with our full cooperation, wonders unfold. (Findhorn Foundation 1986–1987)

In these passages, we see not only the decisive role of the educational metaphor, but also how this metaphor has itself been reshaped by the New Age movement's emphasis on holism and growth. In other words, the kind of education this subculture values is the education of "the whole person," sometimes termed "holistic education," and this form of education is an expression of the "evolutionary force of the Universe" (a parallel to what, in more traditional language, might be called the redemptive activity of the Holy Spirit). Thus, despite the marked tendency to deploy images drawn from the sphere of formal education—a tendency that has created a realm of discourse saturated with metaphors of "classrooms," "graduations," and the like—the metaphysical subculture's sense of the educational process has tended to be more informal (more or less equivalent to learning in the general sense) as well as more continuous—a process from which there may be periodic graduations, but from which there is never a *final* graduation after which the learning process ceases. Even for Heaven's Gate members, graduation from the earth plane represented entering a new sphere of never-ending personal evolution—The Evolutionary Level Above Human.

Though some aspects of this view of the spiritual life as a

learning experience are based on tradition (e.g., the Pythagorean "school"), the widespread appeal of this image of spirituality is the result of the manner in which modern society's emphasis on education informs our consciousness. The various social, economic, and historical forces that have led to the increased stress on education in the contemporary world are too complex to develop here. Obvious factors are such things as the increasing complexity of technology and of the socioeconomic system. Less obvious factors are such considerations as the need to delay the entry of new workers into the economy. But whatever the forces at work in the larger society, by the time the baby boom generation began attending college in the 1960s, formal educational institutions had come to assume their present role as major socializing forces in Western societies. Being a college graduate and achieving higher, particularly professional, degrees became associated with increased prestige and the potential for increased levels of income. In other words, to a greater extent than previously, education and educational accomplishments had become symbols of wealth and status.

Because the generation from which the majority of participants in the alternative spiritual subculture have been recruited is the baby boom generation, the majority of participants in that subculture have been socialized to place a high value on education. Baby boomers, however, also tend to have been participants in the counterculture of the 1960s, which means that they come from a generation that was highly critical of traditional, formal education.

While some members of that generation revolted against the educational establishment by denying the value of education altogether, other college students of the time reacted against what they saw as an irrelevant education by setting up alternative educational structures such as the so-called "free schools." These educational enterprises, which could offer students nothing in terms of degrees or certifications, were viable, at least for a time, because they offered courses on subjects people found intrinsically interesting—including such metaphysical topics as yoga, meditation, and so forth. The free school movement, in combination with the adult education programs that emerged in the 1970s, provided the paradigms for independent, metaphysical educational programs that would eventually emerge.

As is evident from even the most casual perusal of the group's writings, Heaven's Gate was dominated by the educational imagery found in the contemporaneous New Age subculture. As has already been noted, Applewhite viewed himself as a teacher, his followers were students, their spiritual process was likened to an educational process (in their "metamorphic classroom"), and their goal was referred to as a graduation. In the group's writings published on the internet, they discussed how their "Teachers" on the next level had an "extremely detailed lesson plan" designed for their personal growth. Then, toward the end, they received signals that their "classroom time was over" and that they were ready to graduate to the next level (Jwnody 1996).

Thus, with the exceptions of, first, suicide being the means by which the transition to the next evolutionary sphere is to take place and, second, the next sphere being a literal, physical realm (a spacecraft), the basic concepts informing Heaven's Gate's thought world would be recognizable to any serious metaphysical seeker. However, even the notion of a physical spaceship being a quasi-heavenly realm is already implicit in the marked tendency of the New Age movement to portray ufonauts as spiritual beings—a tendency discussed in earlier sections. Furthermore, the widely accepted walk-in notion provides a readily understandable mechanism by which such a transition could be accomplished.

DEATH IN THE NEW AGE

This leaves only suicide as the one anomalous component of Applewhite's synthesis. We should note, however, that there are many phases of the New Age movement that portray death—if not suicide—in a positive light. For example, the basic metaphysical–New Age afterlife notion is reincarnation, although this process is regarded somewhat differently by the New Age than by the Asian religions from which the notion is derived. Whereas in a tradition like Buddhism reincarnation is viewed negatively, as a process that brings one back into the world to suffer, in the metaphysical subculture reincarnation is viewed as part of an extended education program stretched across many lifetimes, and is thus part of a positive process. In the same vein, the interest many participants in occult-metaphysical spirituality have displayed in learning about their past lifetimes in the hope of discovering that they were some famous or otherwise exalted personality would be anathema to a traditional Buddhist.

The New Age movement is also home to advocates of conscious dying. The expression "conscious dying" refers to an approach to dying in which death is regarded as a means of liberation of one's own consciousness—in other words, as a means of achieving enlightenment. This approach, ultimately inspired by Tibetan Buddhism, was popularized in the New Age subculture through the work of Baba Ram Das and Stephen Levine. In line with the New Age emphasis on spiritual-unfoldment-as-education, dying thus acquires a positive valence as part of the larger learning process (Bednarowski 1989).

Finally, it is within the metaphysical subculture that one finds the most interest in the near death experience. The expression "near death experience" (NDE), sometimes also called the "pseudo-death" experience, refers to the seemingly supernatural experiences often undergone by individuals who have suffered apparent death, and have been restored to life. (Some examples of NDEs were discussed in chapters 1 and 2.) The near death experience has attracted extensive public interest because of its seeming support for the notion of life after death.

The main impetus for modern studies on NDEs was the publication in 1975 of the book *Life after Life,* by psychiatrist Raymond Moody (1976), which followed earlier researches on this topic by other physicians such as Elizabeth Kubler-Ross and Russell Noyes. Moody's work describes the results of more than eleven years of inquiry into near death experiences and is based on a sample of about 150 cases. He lists nine NDE characteristics that make the dying process appear quite positive, even attractive. It should also be noted that Moody's fifth trait—rising rapidly into the heavens— sounds like it could have been (though I actually doubt that it was) the immediate source of Applewhite's idea that his group could die and ascend to a waiting spacecraft: "[N]ot all NDEers have a tunnel experience. Some report a "floating experience," in which they rise rapidly into the heavens, and seeing the universe from a perspective reserved for satellites and astronauts" (Moody 1989, 15). In this regard, in another one of his books (1989), Moody mentions an ecstatic vision Carl Jung experienced during an apparent NDE. Following a heart attack, Jung found himself a thousand miles

above the surface of the earth, on the threshold of entering a floating temple in a giant rock, where he would finally discover the answers to all of his questions. In this vision, Jung vividly describes
the terrestrial globe, his sense of letting go of everything associated
with earthly life, and his sense of anticipation of the glories await-
ing him upon his entrance into the temple:

> It seemed to me that I was high up in space. Far below I saw the
> globe of the earth, bathed in a gloriously blue light. I saw the
> deep blue sea and the continents. . . . A short distance away I
> saw in space a tremendous dark block of stone, like a meteorite.
> . . . As I approached the steps leading up to the entrance into the
> rock, a strange thing happened: I had the feeling that everything
> was being sloughed away; everything I aimed at or wished for or
> thought, the whole phantasmagoria of earthly existence, fell
> away. . . . I had the certainty that I was about to enter an illumi-
> nated room and would meet there all those people to whom I be-
> long in reality. . . . There I would at last understand . . . what
> historical nexus I or my life fitted into. (Jung 1965, 289–291)

Finally, Jung notes his profound disappointment when his doctor
brings him back to his body before he has a chance to cross the
threshold.

Again, with only a little interpretation (for example, the floating rock as the spacecraft), the whole experience could be taken as
almost a blueprint for what Heaven's Gate members believed
would happen after their deaths. This is not, of course, to assert
that either NDE research or the writings of Carl Jung encourage
people to take their own lives. It is, however, clear that, if taken seriously, reports of near death experiences paint a positive enough
portrait of dying to take the sting out of death. Thus, far from being crazy or irrational, even the final dramatic exit of Heaven's
Gate becomes understandable in terms of the thought world of the
metaphysical subculture from which Applewhite drew his theological synthesis.

CONCLUSION

As noted at the end of chapter 2, the personal charisma of the
founder is not the glue that holds together alternate views of reality. No matter how charismatic the prophet, his or her message

must somehow address the concerns of potential followers in a satisfactory manner if he or she is to convince more than a handful of close associates. In other words, to repeat an earlier point, a new vision has to have more going for it than merely the personality of the revealer.

Although the prophet's charisma may be necessary for giving life to the vision during the nascent stages of the new movement, the actual adoption of an emergent religion by a group of followers recruits the forces of social consensus to the side of the new revelation—forces that tend to maintain the alternate vision of reality independently of the charisma of the founder. To think of this in terms of the micro-sociology of knowledge (Berger and Luckmann 1966), the plausibility of a particular worldview and its accompanying lifestyle is maintained by the ongoing "conversation" that takes place among the members of a particular community. Thus as long as a new religion continues satisfactorily to address the concerns of followers, even things like a failed prophecy or a leader's blatant hypocrisy will not induce a crisis of faith.

Prophets themselves do not rely upon their personal charisma as their sole source of legitimation. Instead, they plant their new visions on the familiar foundations of pre-existing religious ideas, allowing their new teachings to appear plausible to potential recruits; in spite of what critics sometimes allege, founders of new religious movements do not invent their religious systems ex nihilo. With respect to Heaven's Gate—and although it may seem counterintuitive to anyone not familiar with the many exotic ideas floating around in the New Age subculture—the Two's message was really not all that weird to the people who became their followers. Similarly, the notions that death is a potentially positive experience and that one can exit one's body to consciously reemerge in another realm are simply not odd or irrational within a religious community, New Age or otherwise. It was thus a relatively small step for Applewhite to legitimate a group suicide. In other words, the group's dramatic exit was a completely plausible scenario undertaken willingly—not the exceptional act of a mesmeric cult leader pushing his blind sheep over the edge of an abyss.

7

THE AUTHORITY OF
THE LONG AGO AND
THE FAR AWAY

It is impossible for me to describe the happiness I feel at the idea that so great a body of free, enlightened, and powerful people, like your country-men, have engaged in purifying the religion of Christ from those absurd, idolatrous doctrines and practices, with which the Greek, Roman, and Bar-barian converts to Christianity have mingled it from time to time.
                    —Letter of Rammohan Roy to Henry Ware, February 2, 1824

I know not any more about your Hindu convert [Roy] than I have seen in the *Christian Register*, and am truly rejoiced that the Unitarians have one tro-phy to build upon the plain where the zealous Trinitarians have builded thousands.
                    —Letter of Ralph Waldo Emerson to his aunt, June 10, 1822

The great bulk of the scholarship on "revitalization movements" has been confined to religions originating in oppressed or relatively de-prived communities (for example, Wallace 1956). Only rarely have elite religious movements—meaning movements that attract indi-viduals who are economically and socially advantaged—been viewed from this perspective. There are, of course, distinct differ-ences between popular and elite movements. For example, elite movements have access to a broader range of material, institu-tional, and intellectual resources than do popular movements. The analysis that will be undertaken in the present chapter will argue that the intensity of the relationship between Eastern and Western Unitarians can best be understood in terms of the *ideological resource* that they were able to provide for each other—legitimation. Over the course of this analysis, we will also discuss how these move-ments invoked the authority of tradition to legitimate innovation.

Although these two movements were responding to different

configurations of influences, they were both nourished in the new intellectual atmosphere fostered by the Enlightenment, and this common climate of ideas was responsible for the bulk of their theological similarities. These shared characteristics were the foundation for the kind of mutual admiration expressed in the above citations. Ram Mohan Roy, the father of Hindu modernism as well as the principal founder of the Calcutta Unitarian Committee, held a fascination for British and New England Unitarians far out of proportion to the influence he was able to exercise on his own country people during his lifetime. This was because Roy's existence in a remote corner of the world seemed to legitimate Unitarian claims for the universal reasonableness of their position. Roy in turn depended, particularly in his debates with Trinitarian missionaries, on the moral and intellectual support of Anglo-American Unitarians.

While charismatic authority is a key category for understanding the legitimating process that occurs in the formative period of phenomena like cargo cults, it is less illuminating when applied to such elite religious movements as Unitarianism and the Brahmo Samaj. Elite movements depend, of course, on the charisma of their leaders to some extent, but the role of personal charisma tends to be less crucial in the case of movements generated out of religious modernism than in popular movements.

In both kinds of movements one often finds appeals to tradition, although these appeals are, as indicated in prior chapters, different from what Weber had in mind by the traditional legitimation of authority. Nascent movements often attempt to justify a new idea or a new social order by attributing to it the authority of tradition, but it is usually only through a radical reinterpretation of the past that they are able to portray themselves as the true embodiment of "tradition." One of the reasons why this particular legitimation strategy should have so much attraction is tied up with the prestige given to origins in almost all societies (as discussed in, for example, Eliade 1972). Consequently, the reinterpreted past appealed to by revitalization movements is presented as the "original" tradition—a tradition their contemporaries have allegedly lost or corrupted. This process is especially clear in certain phenomena in Western history, such as the Renaissance appeal to the authority of the Ancients and the Reformation appeal to the New Testament

FIGURE 7.1. Ram Mohan Roy (1774–1833). Painting by Atul Bose.

church. In a more subdued and diffused form, the same basic strategy was utilized by the Enlightenment.

THE ENLIGHTENMENT AS A NEW RELIGIOUS MOVEMENT

The Enlightenment was, from a certain point of view, itself an elite revitalization movement representing European culture's initial response to the scientific revolution. Science by itself cannot "create a world view" in the sense that people "do not live, suffer, exult and die by defining themselves in terms of a strictly scientific account of reality" (Mazzeo 1978, 135). Only an interpretation of the scientific enterprise that transforms science into a secular analogue of religion can provide human beings with an existentially satisfying view of the world, and this is precisely what the Enlightenment was. Instead of being the "story to end all stories" (Wiggins 1975, 3), it represented the recasting of the scientific revolution in terms of a mythic narrative. Part of this transformation of historical events into mythology was accomplished unintentionally, via the irreducible narrative quality of historical explanation. In other words, the mode of interpretation of historical explanation is inevitably "explanation by emplotment" (Ricoeur 1981, 290), and, with the right plots, it was thus only a short step for these narratives to take on the status of "myths" for the new "faith" in science. Many of the new narratives were variations on the Christian Fall-Redemption story.

For example, the Enlightenment developed its own origin myths. In some versions, we read about the early scientists and their primordial battles to bring the modern world out of the dark chaos of the Middle Ages. In other versions, the ancient Mediterranean civilizations were Edens that fell into ignorance and superstition at about the same time Constantine declared Christianity the official religion of the empire. Although the hagiographies of the great scientists gave them the status of culture heroes, the redeemer in all stories was ultimately Progress, which worked invisibly, like God's Providence, to bring about the redemption of the earth. And finally, the "judge" of this new faith was either history in the form of posterity, as in the phrase "posterity will judge" (Becker 1932, 142–144), or history itself in semi-reified form, as in the phrase "history will judge" (Ellul 1975, 98).

Enlightenment thinkers also utilized the West's historical past, particularly the Greek and Roman periods (but also, in its Deist phase, the moral teachings of Jesus), as a background to legitimate the criticisms they leveled against their own society. In their hands, the classical period became both a highly idealized reflection of their own aspirations and the opposite of everything they criticized in eighteenth-century Europe. This idealization was easy to accomplish because their principal sources of knowledge about classical civilization were the great works of literature and philosophy bequeathed to them by the ancients.

By the time of the Enlightenment the West had also become intensely aware of the non-Western world, and these other cultures were incorporated into the critique of eighteenth-century Europe. The Enlightenment thinkers believed, "That far the greater part of mankind, during far the greater period of recorded history, had lived (except, indeed, when oppressed and corrupted by Christian powers) more happily and humanely, under laws and customs more free and equitable, more in accord with natural religion and morality, than the peoples of Europe had done during the centuries of ecclesiastical ascendancy" (Becker 1932, 107–108). Examples of this iconoclastic use of other cultures are especially easy to find in Voltaire's writings: "[T]he Christian people have never observed their religion, and the ancient Indian castes always practiced theirs. . . . [I]n a word, the ancient religion of India, and that of literary men in China, are the only ones, wherein men have not been barbarous" (Voltaire 1965, 76). In this passage we see a clear example of how other civilizations were employed to legitimate their criticisms of contemporary Europe.

It should further be noted that many of the ideas of the Chinese, Greeks, and Indians bore, in the eyes of the Enlightenment, a remarkable resemblance to their own ideas. Lord Teignmouth (Sir William Jones's biographer), for instance, discovered that the Hinduism revealed in the Sanskrit classics was "pure Deism" (cited in Fields 1981, 42). The picture of ancient civilizations, Western as well as non-Western, which emerged in the eighteenth century, was thus shaped by two different sets of comparison-contrasts: First, it was the inverse image of everything that people like Voltaire criticized in their contemporaries, and, second, it reflected the Enlightenment's own ideas. These two comparisons, in turn, are most meaningfully understood as being derived from a more primary comparison—the contrast Enlightenment thinkers perceived between themselves and their unenlightened contemporaries.

The legitimating strategy being deployed here is, as was stated above, an extension and elaboration of the older "appeal to tradition" strategy. One might usefully conceive of it as adding a "spatial" dimension to what was primarily a "temporal" argument. However, the idealized India of the enlightened thinkers was also located in a past period of classical greatness. Enlightenment-inspired Orientalist scholars, such as Sir William Jones, who "discovered" India's golden age often ignored the living Hindu peoples and practices that surrounded them except to express the same kind of disdain for them that they expressed toward their European contemporaries. This split attitude engendered two Indias, an admirable India located in a "classical period somewhere in long-gone India" and a degenerate India that "lingered in present-day Asia" (Said 1979, 99).

RAM MOHAN ROY AND THE ANGLO-AMERICAN UNITARIANS

The larger part of the discussion up to this point has been given over to an analysis of the Enlightenment because of its exemplification of certain legitimation strategies as well as because of its decisive impact on Eastern and Western Unitarianism. Although New England Unitarianism was in many ways the end product of developments internal to Puritanism (Wright 1955), it is difficult to miss the continuities between Unitarianism and some of the characteristic themes of Deism. For instance, the New England innovators appealed to the authority of both reason and Jesus' moral teaching—legitimation tactics they shared with the Deists. Also like the Enlightenment thinkers, the Unitarians legitimated their innovations by portraying them as a recovery of tradition and implicitly or explicitly criticized other forms of Christianity as less faithful to "pure primitive Christianity" (Williams 1967, 71).

Rammohan Roy's reforming efforts adopted a similar pattern. His image of an "authentic Hindu tradition or golden age which he sharply set off against a dark age of popularized religion and social abuses" (Kopf 1979, 11) was directly inherited from the British Orientalist scholars. Furthermore, Roy's dependence on this

Enlightenment-informed scholarship for his "ideological recon-
struction" of Hinduism guaranteed that his religious vision would
be strongly colored by Deism. (The Orientalist scholar H. H. Wilson, for instance, thought that Roy considered Hinduism to have
originally been "pure Deism" [Crawford 1987, 111], although this
is an exaggeration of Roy's position).

Rammohan Roy's spiritual interests were, however, not confined to a reformation of Hinduism. He was first and foremost a
religious rationalist who adhered to a conception of "natural religion" resembling Herbert of Cherbury's position (Das 1974, 85). It
is within this more universalist framework that one should understand his advocacy of Hindu reform as well as his promotion of
Unitarian Christianity.

Roy was originally attracted to Christianity because of what he
regarded as its superior ethical teachings, and this interest led him
to associate with the Baptist missionaries at Serampore. After a period of study during which he is said to have learned to read the
Old and New Testaments in their original languages, Rammohan
Roy compiled a collection of the moral sayings of Jesus. Though
Roy had probably not intended to insult his Baptist friends, the
publication of this small volume was the first step in a conflict that
eventually pushed him into the Unitarian fold. The Serampore
missionaries objected, among other things, to the exclusion of miracle stories—an exclusion that seemed to diminish Jesus to the
stature of a mere human being. Roy did not, as a matter of fact, believe in the divinity of Jesus; and, within a year of the publication
of his compilation, he was able to evoke the same conviction in
one of the Baptists, William Adam. Within another year (in 1823),
Roy, Adam, and Dwarkanath Tagore established the Calcutta Unitarian Committee. This remarkable series of events took place
without any direct influence from either American or British Unitarians. At most, Roy had probably done some reading in Unitarian
writings (Kopf 1979, 7).

Roy's and Adam's activities naturally evoked harsh reactions
from the missionaries. One missionary writer, for example, encouraged a vigorous response to the new movement so that Trinitarian
Christianity would not be "driven from this land of heathen darkness, by the joint forces of the Hindoo Unitarians, and Free-Think-
ing Christians" (cited in Majumdar 1983, 80). The actual situation,

however, was that the Bengal Unitarians were relatively few in number and weak in influence. Roy's reform efforts had made him the enemy of Orthodox Brahmins, and his and Adam's other activities had provoked the enmity of many Englishmen. The hostility was great enough that Roy felt he had to employ a bodyguard, and at least one Trinitarian writer threatened to bring blasphemy charges against him (a legally punishable offense). Also, Adam's former colleagues attempted to persuade the Bengal government to deport him. This difficult situation was further exacerbated by Roy's far-from-irenic temperament. After his break with the Serampore Baptists, for example, he regularly challenged the missionaries to written debates. Roy also began undiplomatically to compare Trinitarianism with Hindu polytheism (Parekh 1927, 64).

On the positive side, however, these polemics were responsible for attracting the attention, and eventually the support, of Anglo-American Unitarians (Lavan 1977, 4). As early as June 1822, for example, the *Christian Register* gave an account of Roy and his conflict with the Trinitarians. In February 1823, it recounted the conversion of Adam and the formation of the Calcutta Unitarian Committee. After this, the *Register* as well as other Unitarian periodicals carried frequent reports of the movement. As a result of this attention, Anglo-American Unitarians began giving Roy and Adam strong moral (and some financial) support (Lavan 1977, 56–57).

Considering the tenuous position of Bengal Unitarianism, they were more than happy to establish links with the English and American movements. The importance of this relationship for the Calcutta movement is evident in a retrospective statement made some years later, on the occasion of the formation of the Calcutta Unitarian Mission, that "the first endeavour of the Committee after its institution was to secure foreign co-operation" (cited in Majumdar 1983, 77). Even before the formation of Indian Unitarianism, Roy had sought the support of English Christians for his efforts to reform Hinduism (Lavan 1977, 37), so this pattern of strengthening his position through outside support was already familiar to him. However, considering the relatively modest financial support that the Bengal Unitarians received from the Anglo-American movement, one might well wonder what Roy and Adam perceived as being so valuable about their links with the British and the Americans.

At least part of the answer to this seems to be the legitimation that these links offered. If, for example, the threat to invoke penal statutes against blasphemy (Singh 1983, 247–248) had actually been carried out, Roy would have been able to defend his writings on Jesus as embodying the teachings of a recognized English denomination. More important, however, was the less tangible *moral support* that British and American Unitarians offered. In other words, the knowledge that there were people in different parts of the world who held the same beliefs (which had apparently been reached independently of one another's influence) would tend to reinforce one's convictions about the veracity of these beliefs. This would particularly be the case for a movement influenced by the Deist notion of "natural religion"—the idea that human beings everywhere, in their natural state, should be able to arrive at the propositions of rational religion independently of supernatural revelation. The self-legitimating utilization of distant co-religionists comes through in such expressive actions as the inclusion of "excerpts of letters of support from Unitarians in Boston and London" (Lavan 1977, 69) in the minutes of a reorganization meeting of the Calcutta Unitarians. While actions like these probably did little to legitimate the movement in the eyes of critics (though it most likely discomfited them), we can surmise that it would have increased the participants' sense of their own legitimacy.

The *drive* for this kind of self-legitimation is particularly evident in the responses of Anglo-American Unitarians to the discovery of the Bengal movement. The extensive coverage of Rammohan Roy's activities in Unitarian periodicals has already been mentioned. In the United States, Roy's publications were "eagerly reprinted" (Majumdar 1975, 104), and libraries such as Harvard acquired extensive collections of Roy's writings (109). It would not be an exaggeration to say that Rammohan was "idolized" by many of his non-Indian admirers (Kopf 1970, 26). For instance, when he visited England, the speaker at a Unitarian welcome meeting said that he was "as glad to meet and welcome Ram Mohan Roy as he would have been if a Plato or a Socrates had come from the dead" (Parekh 1927, 147–148). The lively interest that Anglo-American Unitarians took in Roy is difficult to explain in any way other than in terms of the encouragement they found in what appeared to be a spontaneous breaking forth of the light in a distant land. Enlightened thinkers seized upon the writings and activities of a "stranger in a far off land not only as furnishing intellectual verification and justification of their own ideas, but as happy augury of the universal triumph of a rational religious outlook" (Singh 1983, 269). This "verification and justification," which has been termed *legitimation* throughout the present analysis, probably had little impact outside of enlightened circles. Hence the support that Rammohan Roy was able to provide to American and English Unitarians was almost entirely in the area of self-legitimation.

CONCLUDING REMARKS

The present chapter examined two legitimation strategies utilized by the Enlightenment, early Western Unitarianism, and early Eastern Unitarianism. First, the invocation of the authority of tradition, a tradition reinterpreted so as to legitimate innovation; and, second, the invocation of the image of distant societies or movements, the existence of which appear to reinforce the claims of one's own movement. A characteristic of both of these modes of legitimation was that they were (as far as we can infer) generally ineffective outside of each movement's own membership and its supporters. Instead, it appears that their principal function was to legitimate each respective movement in the minds of its own participants.

PART II

LEGITIMATING REPRESSION

8

ATROCITY TALES AS A DELEGITIMATION STRATEGY

The preceding chapters have discussed a variety of ways in which new religions seek legitimacy by drawing on the authority of charisma, tradition, and rationality. The balance of the study will examine the complementary notion of delegitimation. Conflicts over the legitimacy or illegitimacy of religious groups can be understood as an argument over *classification*. In the context of such controversies, the authority of governmental agencies and courts, authority that potentially threatens new religions, is taken for granted. What is at issue, therefore, is not whether the government has the authority legitimately to intervene in the affairs of a given religious group, but, rather, whether the group in question should be classified as a legitimate religion and left alone or classified as a harmful pseudo-religion and repressed.

The present chapter discusses anti-cult atrocity tales from two distinct perspectives: On the one hand, the common themes that current apostate narratives share with nineteenth-century anti-Catholic and anti-Mormon apostate narratives will be analyzed in terms of a deep structure that is derived from the projections of the dominant society. On the other hand, using the results of a survey of former members of controversial religious groups, the sharp contrast between the post-involvement attitudes of deprogrammed ex-members and voluntary apostates will be examined.

ATROCITY TALES PAST AND PRESENT

A phenomenon that can often be observed in the wake of a dynamic social movement is the emergence of a countermovement that comes into being for the sole purpose of opposing the original movement. Of particular interest for students of the contemporary cult controversy who would like to set this phenomenon in historical perspective are the anti-Catholic and anti-Mormon movements that emerged in the United States during the nineteenth century. Both of these movements produced extensive bodies of literature that show distinct parallels with anti-cult literature, particularly if one focuses on the genre of apostate stories.

Contemporary themes of the "psychological kidnapping" and exploitation of young people by sinister cults are paralleled in anti-Catholic literature by the themes of the "captivity" (Slotkin 1973, 444) and abuse of young females in nunneries. This Protestant fantasy led to the production of numerous apostate tales authored by "escaped" nuns. These women were sometimes genuine ex-nuns who presented highly embellished accounts of their experiences (for example, Reed 1835) or fake ex-nuns who fabricated their stories from whole cloth (for example, Monk 1997).

For nuns to escape, however, they first had to be in a state of bondage, and this state required a certain amount of explanation because Catholics did not bodily carry off their "prisoners." The initial "capture" was explained in terms of flattery and in terms of devious indoctrination designed to influence impressionable young ladies to take the veil. Once inside the convent, the means of retaining captives varied from one author to another. In cruder narratives, inmates were physically imprisoned in the institution and controlled by threat of corporal punishment, and especially reluctant nuns were locked up in subterranean dungeons. In more nuanced accounts inmates were controlled by subtler, psychological means, such as fear of hell and the belief that any doubts were inspired by Satan: "[The bishop] said the Devil would assail me, as he did Saint Teresa, and make me think I ought to go back to the world; and make me offers of worldly pleasures, and promise me happiness. In order to prevent this, I must watch and pray all the time, and banish entirely worldly thoughts from my mind" (Reed 1835, 89).

These tales typically consisted of the recounting of one atrocity after another, held together by a thin strand of narrative. In the more extreme stories, these atrocities ranged from sexual abuse to murder. Maria Monk, for example, claimed that infants born to nuns (a supposedly frequent event because of regular sexual intercourse with priests) were murdered. Monk recounted observing two infants who, after being baptized, "were then taken, one after another, by one of the old nuns, in the presence of us all. She pressed her hand upon the mouth and nose of the first so tight that it could not breathe, and in a few minutes, when the hand was removed, it was dead. She then took the other and treated it in the same way. No sound was heard, and both children were corpses. The greatest indifference was shown by all present during this operation; for all, as I well knew, were long accustomed to such scenes" (Monk 1997, 155–156). Apostate tales were designed to evoke and to legitimate public reaction, and they often succeeded in this purpose. For example, very soon after ex-nun Rebecca Reed began to tell her story, a Protestant mob burned her former convent to the ground. These narratives usually also contained calls for governmental action. At the conclusion of one ex-nun's story, for example, she pleaded that "the Legislature [should] enact laws for the inspection of Convents. . . . Let the prison doors of monasteries and Convents be thrown open to their deluded inmates" (O'Gorman [1881], 131).

In anti-Mormon literature, polygamous wives played essentially the same role that nuns played in anti-Catholic literature, and apostate (and pseudo-apostate) Mormon females composed similar captivity narratives. However, a conceptual problem emerged in Mormon apostate stories: How could one make the case for a state of bondage in a situation where the alleged captive was apparently free to walk out at any time? Nunneries could be portrayed as prisons, but Mormon women were obviously not so confined. Thus, in addition to the deluded follower theme used to characterize Catholic bondage, one finds the first theory of "hypnotic mind control" in anti-Mormon literature. For example, in the totally fabricated apostate tale *Female Life among the Mormons,*

Maria Ward described her entrapment in terms of mesmerism (the original term for hypnosis):

> At the time I was wholly unacquainted with the doctrine of magnetic influence; but I soon became aware of some unaccountable power exercised over me by my fellow traveler. His presence seemed an irresistible fascination. His glittering eyes were fixed on mine; his breath fanned my cheek; I felt bewildered and intoxicated, and partially lost the sense of consciousness, and the power of motion...I became immediately sensible of some unaccountable influence drawing my sympathies toward him. In vain I struggled to break the spell. I was like a fluttering bird before the gaze of a serpent-charmer. (Ward 1855, 12)

Via such pseudo-scientific notions—precursors to more recent theories of cult "mind control"—the captivity motif could be extended to situations where it would normally have been inappropriate except as a metaphor.

The Mormon apostate tales, like the Catholic apostate stories, were loosely connected accounts of one sensationalistic atrocity after another, containing many crudely crafted descriptions of violence and the same kinds of sexual allusions found in convent tales. The violence in anti-Mormon tales was often quite vivid. For example, in the totally fictional apostate tale *Boadicea; The Mormon Wife*, Alfreda Eva Bell describes the following cold-hearted murder: "'Will you go with me?' asked he. 'No,' answered the dying woman. 'Then you are done for,' said Yale; and deliberately, before my very eyes, in spite of my wild screams for his mercy, he fired at her and scattered her brains over the floor" (Bell 1855, 55). Lurid descriptions of violence against women can also be used to suggest sexual assault. In Ward's account, for instance, a female who dared raise her voice in dissent against the Mormon hierarchy was "gagged, carried a mile into the woods, stripped nude, tied to a tree, and scourged till the blood ran from her wounds to the ground" (Ward 1855, 429).

As already noted with respect to Catholic captivities, this kind of sensationalism was mixed with propagandistic themes calling for the repression of Mormonism. Even in some of the fictional tales, this theme was overtly set forth, as, for instance, toward the end of Bell's story: "I prayed that I might be permitted to reach the States, and, by my pen, put forth the horrors I had witnessed, in order to swell the outcry for the speedy destruction of such a hell of vice as the Mormon colony, and do my "little all" towards arresting further horrors" (Bell 1855, 69). The portrayal of mesmeric captures was supplemented by the accusation that Mormons bodily carried off Gentile women to fill their "harems," and this particular accusation was one of the more scandalous themes in anti-Mormon propaganda. The kidnapping accusation seemed, to the minds of some of the authors of anti-Mormon tales, to legitimate the physical extermination of all Mormons. For example, one of the heroes of *The Prophets,* after rescuing his wife from the clutches of Joseph Smith, vows to kill every Mormon in Nauvoo, Illinois: "I swear by the heaven above me, I will shoulder my rifle, and never lay it down until Nauvoo is razed to the ground. It makes me feel like a demon to think they should dare raise their polluted thoughts to my wife; but they shall rue the deed, for devastation shall follow them until there shall not be one left in a week's travel from Nauvoo" (Belisle 1855, 312). Like sensationalistic anti-Catholic stories, anti-Mormon tales were capable of evoking violent, vigilante-style activity—as is evident in such events as the murder of Joseph Smith—and governmental intervention—as witnessed by such actions as the 1857 invasion of Utah by federal troops.

Contemporary anti-cult literature replicates this same structure, but here the metaphor of captivity is even more strained: Nuns were behind walls and Mormons were at least geographically isolated, but the stereotypical cult member is out on the streets every day hustling strangers and is thereby fully immersed in the non-cult world. Contemporary anti-cult proponents are thus forced to rely upon pseudo-scientific theories of brainwashing and cult mind control—notions of mental enslavement that we saw in embryo in anti-Catholic and anti-Mormon literature. The link with notions from earlier eras is quite evident, especially in more popular tales. For example, compare the following passage from Christopher Edwards's *Crazy for God* with the description of Mormon mesmerism cited earlier: "She took my hand and looked me straight in the eyes. As her wide eyes gazed into mine, I felt myself rapidly losing control, being drawn to her by a strange and frightening force. I had never felt such mysterious power radiate from a human being before . . . touching something within me that undermined thought itself" (1979, 60). Although the stage settings are different, the plot has not changed. Former "cult" members recount the same stories of deception and exploitation, which in turn evoke vigilante-style violence in the form of kidnappings of current members of controversial religions (Patrick and Dulack 1977) and, in some instances, attacks upon cult facilities (Terry and Manegold 1984). Success in stimulating governmental intervention eluded the anti-cult movement during the height of the cult scare, with the exception of a few isolated incidents such as the Branch Davidian fiasco.

BRAINWASHING AS AN IDEOLOGICAL WEAPON

Despite the clear parallels between current anti-cultism and the passions of earlier conflicts, the negative stereotype of cults is so widely accepted that most nonspecialists would disagree with the characterization of cult mind control as pseudo-scientific. It is thus important to note that almost all mainstream academic researchers reject the popular stereotype of new religions deceptively recruiting and brainwashing their members, and that almost all of the studies supporting the notion of cultic mind control are so obviously biased that mainstream social scientific journals routinely do not publish them.

Since the mid-1970s, mainstream scholars—particularly sociologists—have been steadily churning out studies directly relevant to this controversy. At this point in time, a collection of the books devoted to this controversy plus books on new religions containing at least one full chapter directly relevant to the controversy—and I mean a collection of mainstream scholarly works, not popular accounts—would fill a standard library bookcase. This does not include the significant number of relevant articles published in academic journals. For a long time, the anti-cult movement chose to ignore this significant body of scholarly literature because it refuted the negative stereotypes they relied upon to justify their continued existence. In more recent years, anti-cultists have deployed the delegitimation strategy of dismissing any study that debunks the cult stereotype as being the product of "cult apologists," as if the many mainstream researchers who have weighed in on this subject were all on the payroll of powerful cults.

The operative question that social scientists have asked about mind control is, How does one distinguish cultic brainwashing from other forms of social influence—forms of social influence like advertising, military training, or even the normal socialization routines of public schools? Some anti-cultists have theorized that cult members are trapped in a kind of quasi-hypnotic trance, while others assert that the ability of cult members to process certain kinds of information has "snapped" (Conway and Siegelman 1979).

The problem with these and similar theories is that if cultic influences actually overrode the brain's ability to logically process information, then individuals suffering from cultic influences should perform poorly on IQ tests or, at the very least, should manifest pathological symptoms when they take standardized tests of mental health—and, when tested, they do not. In point of fact, such empirical studies indicate that members of new religious movements are actually smarter and healthier than the average member of mainstream society (for example, Sowards, Walser, and Hoyle 1994).

Other kinds of studies also fail to support the view that new religions rely upon non-ordinary forms of social influence to gain and retain members. For example, if new religions possessed powerful mind-control techniques that effectively overrode a potential convert's free will, then everyone—or at least a large percentage of attendees—at recruiting seminars should be unable to avoid conversion. However, in her important study *The Making of a Moonie* (1984), Eileen Barker found that less than 10 percent of the people who visited centers run by the Unification Church—an organization many people regard as the evil cult par excellence—eventually attended recruitment seminars. Of those who attended such seminars, less than 10 percent ended up joining the church (a net recruitment rate of under 1 percent). Furthermore, of those who joined, more than half dropped out within the first year of their membership. In another important study, published as *Radical Departures: Desperate Detours to Growing Up* (1984), Canadian psychiatrist Saul Levine found that, out of a sample of over eight hundred people who had joined controversial religious groups, more than 90 percent dropped out within two years of membership—not the kind of statistics one would anticipate from groups wielding powerful techniques of mind control.

In the face of these and other empirical studies, social scientists have asked further questions: Given the lack of empirical support, where does the brainwashing notion come from? And what is the real conflict that the cult stereotype obfuscates? The general conclusion of sociologists (as analyzed, for example, in David Bromley and Anson Shupe's *Strange Gods: The Great American Cult Scare* [1981]) is that the principal source of the controversy is a parent-child conflict in which parents fail to understand the religious choices of their adult children and attempt to reassert parental control by marshaling the forces of public opinion against the religious bodies to which their offspring have converted.

This core conflict is then exacerbated by an irresponsible mass media less interested in truth than in printing exciting stories about weird cults that trap their members and keep them in psychological bondage with exotic techniques of mind control. Also, once an industry is established that generates enormous profits by "rescuing" entrapped cult members (I am here referring to deprogramming—the kidnapping of members for the purpose of inducing apostasy), special interest groups are created that have a vested interest in promoting the most negative stereotypes of alternative religions. These special interest groups add further fuel to the parent-child conflict by scaring parents with lurid stories of what will happen to their adult child if they fail to have her or him deprogrammed. In this manner, many otherwise reasonable and well-meaning parents are recruited into the controversy.

This, essentially, is the picture of the cult controversy that social scientists have pieced together over the last three decades. Because of its vested interest in maintaining the conflict, the anti-cult movement has been unresponsive to objective scholarly studies and has proceeded with business as usual, as if these studies were nonexistent. Rather than responding directly to mainstream social science, a handful of anti-cultists with academic credentials have instead conducted research in their own terms and have created alternative periodicals that feature pseudo-scientific studies supporting the cult stereotype.

For example, the *Cultic Studies Journal,* published by the American Family Foundation, creates the impression that it is a mainstream scholarly journal. One will, however, rarely find it on the shelves of university libraries. The *Cultic Studies Journal* fails to pass muster as a legitimate academic periodical because, among other things, the few empirical studies published by *Cultic Studies Journal* utilize unacceptably biased samples, namely, samples of deprogrammees and other former cult members who have been intensively indoctrinated in anti-cult ideology.

This sampling bias is usually justified by such assertions as, to cite from a representative article published in the *Cultic Studies Journal*, "It is *unlikely* [my emphasis] that cults will permit objective, scientific studies in the near future" (Dubrow-Eichel, Dubrow-Eichel, and Eisenberg 1984). What, however, do the authors mean by "unlikely?" When one reads between the lines, it is clear that what they really mean to say is that they refused to admit any evidence that might possibly contradict their presuppositions, so they did not bother to ask members of representative new religious movements. By way of contrast, more neutral researchers have found that alternative religions are almost always open to being studied. Psychiatrist Saul Levine, for example, studied dozens of controversial groups and found: "In spite of the fact that almost every group deeply suspects the motives of therapists in general . . . no leader has ever turned down my request [to be permitted to study members], nor has there ever been a lack of volunteers willing to cooperate with me" (1984). In response to the experience of Levine and other mainstream researchers who have found the same openness among controversial religions, anti-cultists have replied that, even if cults appear to be open to empirical studies, researchers must focus on former members because current members convey false information as part of their deceptive agenda. However, even within the population of ex-members, anti-cultists have confined their studies to former members of new religions who have been intensively indoctrinated in anti-cult ideology, namely, deprogrammed former members. The unacceptably prejudiced nature of this subpopulation was demonstrated in an important study by social psychologist Trudy Solomon (1981).

Solomon found that the negative attitude of ex-Moonies toward the Unification Church was a direct function of "method of exit and degree of contact with the anti-cult movement" (1981, 281). In other words, as one might anticipate, former Moonies who were forcibly deprogrammed and who continued to associate with the anti-cult movement were far more negative toward the church—and were far more likely to repeat anti-cult rhetoric about mind control and the like—than were ex-Moonies who left voluntarily and had little or no contact with anti-cult groups. In my replication of Solomon's research (Lewis 1986, 1990), I found essentially the same pattern among 154 former members of a half dozen different controversial religious movements.

Solomon divided her sample into eight subgroups across which post-involvement attitudes would vary (1981, 281). For a number of reasons (explained in Lewis 1986), I utilized a much simpler typology:

1. No Exit Counseling (NEC): Voluntary defection and no counseling connected with the anti-cult movement (N = 89).
2. Voluntary Exit Counseling (VEC): Some form of voluntary counseling at the hands of the anti-cult movement, e.g., exit counseling, reentry counseling, etc. (N = 29).
3. Involuntary Exit Counseling (IEC): Coercive deprogramming with or without other forms of treatment following their deprogramming (N = 36).

While there are, of course, other factors involved in anti-cult socialization, the intensity of the counseling process appeared to be the primary operant factor.

Four questionnaire items measured respondents' attitudes toward their former movements. These items asked respondents to evaluate the extent to which they felt that (1) they have been recruited deceptively, (2) they have been "brainwashed," (3) their leader was insincere, and (4) the group's beliefs were spurious. The fourth item, for example, was:

Evaluate the doctrine/ideas/world view of your former group:
1. Completely true
2. More true than false
3. More false than true
4. Completely false

The responses to each of these measures were treated as interval data for the purpose of analysis. All four attitude measures were found to be highly correlated with the degree of one's exposure to anti-cult counseling, which was also treated as a variable by assigning values to each of the treatment groups (NEC = 1, VEC = 2, and IEC = 3). The correlation coefficient (r) for deceptive recruitment was .392, for brainwashing .587, for leadership insincerity .407, and for spurious world view .551—all significant at the .001 level.

Three other variables that might possibly have been factors in shaping attitudes were computed as controls: (1) length of membership, (2) age at recruitment, and (3) time between exit and the point at which they completed the questionnaire. None of these calculations yielded significant correlations.

The four forced-choice items were replicated elsewhere in the survey instrument by open-ended questions that requested essentially the same information. For example, the open-ended question corresponding to the multiple-choice item cited above was: "How would you describe and/or evaluate the doctrine/ideas/world view of your former group?" Consistent with the quantitative data, qualitative expressions of post-involvement attitudes were found to vary according to the extent of one's anti-cult socialization: Ex-members who had experienced coercive deprogramming tended to express negative, stereotyped attitudes; voluntary defectors who had no links with anti-cultists tended to feel ambivalent or positive about their former movements; and the attitudes of respondents who were not kidnapped but who had experienced some form of voluntary counseling at the hands of anti-cultists tended to lie somewhere in between.

What follows is a qualitative analysis of some exemplary sample responses, which have been selected according to treatment group and according to the four cult-stereotypical attitudes for which I collected quantitative data. The pattern of responses to each of the four attitudes will be discussed in turn.

1. Recruitment

IEC: At the time of recruitment there were unethical techniques of coercion being utilized against me.

VEC: I was not lied to. However, I didn't really know what I was getting into.

NEC: The people were very sincere.

These three responses reflect the overall pattern of post-involvement attitudes with respect to the three categories of ex-member. Voluntary apostates tended to discount the idea of deceptive recruitment unless they had joined the Unification Church via the Oakland Family's well-known (but now defunct) recruiting operation. Many deprogrammees tended to draw on mind control type explanations to explain their recruitment, but others made use of less exotic notions of deception, such as, "I was lied to."

2. Brainwashing

IEC: I was hypnotized, also performed self-hypnosis to block out my old self, any doubts.

VEC: I was exposed to only one doctrine, and not encouraged to question or doubt.

NEC: Someone who says "I was brainwashed" has little self-esteem and/or sense of who they are.

As predicted, the IEC group supported the brainwashing notion, the NEC group rejected it, and the opinion of the VEC group fell somewhere in between. Individuals in the intermediate VEC group who said they had been brainwashed tended to describe brainwashing more in terms of indoctrination into a rigid, narrow belief system than as some type of hypnosis.

3. Leader

IEC: He has psychologically "raped" or taken advantage of thousands of people. I would like to see him dead.

VEC: I think he's sincere, but his sincerity gives him an excuse to use people and manipulate them because he believes in himself.

NEC: A spiritual teacher of considerable merit and great sincerity, somewhat limited by his own culture, and especially by many of his close disciples.

This item elicited a more complex range of responses than the recruitment and brainwashing questions. A number of individuals, for example, evaluated their former leader as "sincere but deluded." Also, the evaluation of the leadership by voluntary defectors tended to be far more ambivalent than their evaluation of mind control claims because difficulties or disenchantment with leaders often contributed to apostates' decisions to leave their movements. Voluntary defectors often made such remarks as, "I think he started out sincere, but became corrupted."

4. Worldview

IEC: The doctrine states that the world is a miserable prison and people are simply pigs, dogs, camels, asses in human form. They must be converted or killed.

VEC: There is much truth in the philosophy which I still believe in. There is also much I don't believe in.

NEC: Pure, just not represented in a perfectly pure way.

Deprogrammees described their former group's ideology as being fanatical, twisted, fabricated by the founder, and the like. Individuals in the VEC group, although they sometimes resorted to the same kind of stereotyped, anti-cult evaluations, often perceived that at least some portion of their former belief system overlapped their present belief-system, and thus tended to be less harsh in their criticisms. Voluntary defectors tended to express positive or ambivalent attitudes toward their former group's belief system. Like their attitude toward the movement's leadership, voluntary defectors' evaluation of the ideology tended to be critical at certain points. More often than not, voluntary defectors retained large portions of their former beliefs.

5. Anti-cult Movement

The questionnaire also contained forced-choice and open-ended items which solicited ex-members' evaluations of the anti-cult movement. To an open-ended question about the anti-cult movement, I received the following kinds of responses:

IEC: It warns people of the dynamics of cults and how they use unethical tactics.

VEC: The educational part is good. I think the deprogramming part has gotten out of hand.

NEC: Ignorant, closed-minded people who are unable to accept any ideas except their own.

The pattern was, as one could have predicted, an inverted mirror image of ex-member's attitudes toward their former movements, in that respondents at either end of the spectrum tended to express strong negative or positive evaluations, whereas subjects in the intermediate group tended to have mixed opinions ($r = .499$). There were also in each treatment group a number of people (though proportionately more in the NEC group) who described the anti-cult movement as an "anti-cult cult"; to cite an example: "The anti-cult movement appears to me to be a group of self-righteous do-gooders who have their own cult going on. They appear to have just as much, if not more so, of a 'savior complex' as Moon,

Wierwille, or any other charismatic religious leader." As reflected in this particular response, ex-members sometimes held negative attitudes toward both the anti-cult movement and their former religious groups.

In terms of the influential line of thought initiated by one of the founders of sociology, Emile Durkheim (1960), the labeling and persecution of minorities is usually more of a response to doubts and anxieties about norms and values within the dominant culture than a response to tangible threats from minority groups. In other words, in a society confronted with unsettling tensions such as arise in the wake of rapid social change (particularly in a society without pressing external threats), a subcommunity will be found that can be perceived as the larger community's "criminal opposite" and then persecuted "as a means of ritually reaffirming the group's problematical values and collective purposes" (Bergesen 1984, vii). The deviant group is thus forced to play a self-clarifying role for the dominant society by serving as a screen onto which the dominant society projects an inverted image of itself.

Because the image of the minority group is more of a projected "otherness" than an empirical otherness, one would expect to find a marked tendency on the part of "projectors" to blur the distinctions between various groups of "projectees." In other words, the empirical diversity should be obscured beneath a unitary projection (Gilman 1985, 21). This tendency is not difficult to document. One nineteenth-century figure asserted, for example, that "Brigham Young 'out-popes the Roman' and described the Mormon hierarchy as being similar to the Catholic" (Davis 1960, 207). Even racial otherness seemed to blend rather easily with religious otherness in the minds of certain mainstream citizens, as is clear in the statement of one anti-Mormon who asserted, "The Lord intends that WHITE FOLKS, and not Mormons shall possess that goodly land [Utah]" (cited in Bunker and Bitton 1983, 86). And, to shift forward into the contemporary period for one more example, in the heyday of deprogramming, archdeprogrammer Ted Patrick asserted, regarding the diversity among the movements he attacked, "You name 'em. Hare Krishna. The Divine Light Mission. Guru Maharaj Ji. Brother Julius. Love Israel. The Children of God. Not a brown penny's worth of difference between any one of 'em" (Patrick and Dulack 1977, 11).

One of the results of this tendency to blur distinctions is that common sets of accusations are leveled against various groups which are empirically quite different. The four accusations, leveled against contemporary religious movements, that were reflected in the attitudes of deprogrammed ex-members—deceptive recruitment, brainwashing, insincere leadership, and bogus belief system—are examples of such common themes. If we turn back in time, it is not difficult to find parallel themes in anti-Catholicism and anti-Mormonism: Joseph Smith was often accused of fabricating the Mormon religion for the purpose of personal gain (for example, Belisle 1855); the Catholic confessional was frequently described as a mind control device (for example, Monk [1836] 1977); both Mormons and Catholics were accused of deceptively recruiting or kidnapping young Gentile-Protestant women; and so forth. Such themes seem to constitute part of a common "deep structure" through which the dominant social group perceives all forms of religious otherness (Cox 1978). Why, one might ask, should the same themes resurface time and again?

When a minority group forced to play the role of deviant is a religious movement, one of the first points of contrast with the dominant society is in the area of competing belief systems. Non-mainstream beliefs are "obviously" untrue to individuals securely enmeshed in the perspective of the dominant culture. But this obvious spuriousness presents certain problems, such as, Where did such weird ideas come from in the first place? The easiest solution to this quandary is to accuse the cult leader of having cynically concocted a false belief system. This approach also enables one to explain the genesis of the movement: The entire thing was dreamed up by the leader for the purpose of gaining wealth and power. The other two accusations arise naturally out of this picture: Why would anyone ever become part of such a nutty movement? It must be because they were recruited deceptively. And why, once they were actually inside the group and could see what it really was, did they not leave immediately? It must be because they were brainwashed. These four themes thus fit together into a neat package that delegitimates alternative religious movements and saves us from having to take them seriously. These themes also serve to legitimate the persecution of such groups.

The apostate fits into this structure as the chief source of evidence for its truth. In other words, the testimony of ex-members who have actually been there, and who have supposedly witnessed all of the horrors about which outsiders can only fantasize, provides the stereotype with its most important source of empirical evidence. What the above data indicates, however, is that the apostates who are paraded before the public by the anti-cult movement have been carefully selected. Though few if any apostates are ever completely objective about their former religion, ex-members who have been intensively "counseled"—especially those who were kidnapped—should be especially suspect as being less than neutral witnesses.

By relying upon this subset of ex-members, the anti-cult movement involves itself in a hermeneutic circle: Instead of forming generalizations based on a broad range of data, the anti-cult movement generates its own data by imposing an a priori ideology on a select number of individual cases (deprogrammees) and then "discovers" evidence for its ideology in the testimony of these same individuals. Anti-cultists depend upon this subset of former members for the ultimate proof of their accusations.

Without the legitimating umbrella of brainwashing ideology, deprogramming—the practice of kidnapping members of nontraditional religions and destroying their religious faith—cannot be justified, either legally or morally. Though advocates claim that deprogramming does nothing more than reawaken cult members' capacity for rational thought, any actual examination of the process reveals that deprogramming is little more than a heavy-handed assault upon a person's belief system. The vast majority of deprogrammers have little or no background in psychological counseling. They are, rather, "hired gun" vigilantes whose only qualifications, more often than not, are that they are physically large or that they are themselves deprogrammed ex-cult members.

To understand how deprogramming actually works, Stuart Wright's study of voluntary defectors—originally his dissertation (1983), later published in book form under the title *Leaving Cults: The Dynamics of Defection*—is a useful point of reference. Making use of the notion of socialization, Wright described defection as a process of "desocialization" and found that the first step in the deconversion process was a disruption of one's sense of the group's plausibility, which could be brought about by one of four situations:

1. A breakdown in members' insulation from the outside world.
2. The development within the group of romantic relationships that were expressly forbidden by the group.
3. Perceived lack of success in achieving the group's goals, particularly the goal of transforming the outer world.
4. Inconsistencies between the actions of the leadership and the ideals and values they claimed to represent.

Wright also found that, once the plausibility of the group had been disrupted in the follower's mind, certain secondary factors could come into play that would further increase the likelihood of apostasy. The secondary "defection factors" indicated by Wright were as follows:

5. The pull of family ties.
6. Conventional careers.
7. Alternative religious belief systems.

This general framework can be adapted for the purpose of understanding what happens during deprogramming.

At least four of Wright's defection factors are clearly present in deprogramming:

1. A breakdown in insulation from the outside world (accomplished by physically removing the member from her or his group).
2. A highlighting of the inconsistencies between group ideals and the actions of leaders.
3. The pull of family ties. (Deprogrammings are almost invariably paid for by other family members who then participate in the sessions.)
4. The presentation of an alternative belief system. (Though Wright's analysis of voluntary defection discussed this as the *discovery* of alternate *religious* belief systems, in deprogramming, the alternate belief system usually presented is some highly secular system of beliefs and values.)

In addition to these four factors, deprogramming seeks to shatter one's faith by the following:

5. Pointing out internal inconsistencies *within* the group's belief system (as differentiated from inconsistencies between ideals and practices).
6. By offering an alternative explanation for the individual's recruitment and membership—the familiar deception and/or mind control ideology.

These six factors effectively disrupt the plausibility of the deprogrammee's religious beliefs. Success is not, however, necessarily guaranteed, as the high failure rate of deprogramming—between a third to a half return to their respective movements—demonstrates.

The additional two factors explain certain systematic differences that exist between the attitudes of deprogrammees and the attitudes of voluntary defectors: Voluntary defectors tend to retain more aspects of the worldview and the ideals of their former movement than do deprogrammees. Also, as has already been demonstrated, voluntary defectors rarely rely upon notions of mind control to interpret their former group or their membership in that group.

These two special tactics of deprogramming are not difficult to document. One of the respondents to my survey, for example, said that his deprogrammers demonstrated to him that "the *Divine Principle* [a Unification Church scripture] was flawed, had contradictions and thus could not be absolute truth."

Indoctrination in brainwashing ideology is an essential component of deprogramming. Another deprogrammed respondent related, for instance, "After three days of dialogue I had a basic understanding of thought reform and how it had been applied to me." The attractiveness of this ideology was reflected in yet another deprogrammee's response: "It still makes me cringe to think of the 'witnessing' I did to co-workers during free times. But my deprogrammer made sure I knew it wasn't my fault." This last statement clearly indicates how anti-cult ideology's provision for a face-saving "absolution from blame" makes it attractive to ex-members.

Deprogramming is much more effective at destroying beliefs than at providing deprogrammees with new systems of meaning. Among questionnaire respondents, the deprogrammees who did not become crusading anti-cultists after their faith was broken reported experiencing a very bleak psychological landscape during the time period immediately following their exit; for example: "I felt as if my whole world had caved in." "I didn't know who I was, where I was going, why I should try. I just wanted to crawl into a dark corner and be put out of my misery." "I was kidnapped and deprogrammed, so my whole world was suddenly ripped out from under me. . . . [B]efore, every single action had cosmic importance, but, afterwards, I felt small and unimportant. Life had no meaning." Not unsurprisingly, deprogrammees frequently reported experiencing suicidal tendencies after their exits, and at least one of my deprogrammed contacts killed herself before the questionnaire reached her.

The one other characteristic of deprogramming that sets it apart from voluntary defection is its comparative rapidity. Voluntary apostates characteristically take a long time to reach a decision to leave, and, after leaving, they continue to reflect on their membership period in what Stuart Wright describes as a "sifting process in which favorable events or experiences are separated out from what is later perceived as wrong, immoral or theologically adrift" (Wright 1984, 180). As a result of this lengthy process of deliberation, their attitude toward their former movement is usually complex and ambivalent. Deprogrammees, on the other hand, frequently experience a sudden shift of perspective that resembles a classic conversion experience in its rapidity, totality, and one-sidedness. The motivation for making this sudden shift in perspective can be explained as a reaction to the intensity of the assault carried out by deprogrammers. If the attacks on their faith have a real impact on kidnapped cult members, they can resolve the conflict they feel by completely adopting the point of view of the deprogrammer.

Without claiming to be exhaustive, this description provides an outline of how deprogramming "works." In addition to avoiding pseudo-scientific notions of brainwashing, this account is able to explain why deprogrammees' understanding of their cult experience is so different from voluntary defectors.

Beyond shaping public opinion by recounting stereotyped atrocity tales, deprogrammees feed into the cult controversy in a number of other ways: At the level of basic research, these former members are interviewed in pseudo-scientific surveys designed to substantiate such claims as: that cultic brainwashing techniques induce mental illness in their members (for example, Conway and Siegelman 1982) and that child abuse is widespread in alternative religious groups (for example, Gaines et al. 1984). In a variety of different court battles, ex-members recruited by anti-cultists provide negative testimony against their former movements, such as in child custody cases where one of the parents is a cult member (for example, Driscoll 1983) and in cases where governmental agencies need evidence for cult violations of various governmental regulations (for example, *Cult Observer* 1986). The testimony of a deprogrammed Branch Davidian was, for example, part of the evidence used to obtain a search warrant before the assault on the Davidian community (Lewis 1994b).

Although few people would assert that there is nothing to be criticized in new religious movements, a careful consideration of the history of religious conflict should cause us to hesitate before accepting the more extreme accusations proffered by anti-cultists. The response that the present cult controversy is categorically different from earlier religious controversies is difficult to support, especially when one examines the continuities from one era to another in overall patterns of conflict. As demonstrated in the present chapter, the specific set of accusations leveled against religious groups in the past as well as in the present serves both to dismiss their claims to be legitimate religions and to legitimate their repression.

9

RELIGIOUS INSANITY

Unfortunately, in considering the effects of religion, it has been too common for authors to impugn opinions, merely because they differed from their own: consequences, therefore, have been ascribed, resting entirely upon gratuitous evidence. This is absolute intolerance, not induction; and when arguments assume this turn, controversy, not conviction, follows.

—George Man Burrows, *Commentaries on the Causes, Forms, Symptoms, and Treatment, Moral and Medical, of Insanity*

As noted in the preceding chapter, conflicts over the legitimacy or illegitimacy of religious groups can be understood as arguments over *classification.* In the context of such controversies, the issue is whether a given religion is legitimate and should be protected, or a harmful religion (often portrayed as a pseudo-religion) that should be repressed. Chapter 8 took a dual-pronged approach by examining the common themes between current apostate narratives and nineteenth-century anti-Catholic and anti-Mormon apostate narratives, and by contrasting the post-involvement attitudes of deprogrammed ex-members with voluntary apostates in terms of these shared themes.

The present chapter takes a roughly comparable approach to the pseudo-disorder of "information disease," a supposedly unique psychological disorder caused by prolonged exposure to cultic brainwashing. The first part of the chapter sets the stage for the discussion of this "cult disease" by examining the nineteenth-century attribution of "religious insanity" to converts of sectarian religion. In the second half of the chapter, using other findings from the survey referred to in chapter 8, the contrasting reports of cult disease symptoms between deprogrammed ex-members and voluntary apostates is examined.

RELIGIOUS INSANITY PAST

Although madness has long been attributed to certain forms of religious expression, it was only in the latter half of the eighteenth century that "religious enthusiasm" or "religious insanity" began to be generally accepted as a diagnostic category for a disorder treatable by medical means. It was in a professional atmosphere favoring such views that William Perfect, an English doctor who specialized in mental illness, published a compilation of his more "curious and interesting" cases, including four anecdotal accounts of religious enthusiasm. (The full title of Perfect's book was *Annals of Insanity, Comprising a Selection of Curious and Interesting Cases in the Different Species of Lunacy, Melancholy, or Madness, with the Modes of Practice in the Medical and Moral Treatment, as Adopted in the Cure of Each*—not unusually long for the eighteenth century!) Included in this compilation was the case of "Mrs. EH," who "had for some time been made a proselyte to a prevailing system of religion, that like an epidemic disease had long spread its baneful influence through many ranks of people, to the excitement of the most daring outrages, and the wildest extravagancies" (Perfect 1798, 87). While Perfect's disease rhetoric effectively conveys his distaste for revivalist religion, it is less clear how Mrs. EH's "enthusiasm" had been able to induce a state of madness. In this regard, he asserted,

> So humiliating a degradation of our reasoning faculties owes much of its accession to the absurd and ill-founded prejudices of that epidemic enthusiasm, which naturally excites the attention of weak minds to the discussion of religious points, which they too eagerly contemplate, without the power of clear comprehension, to the entire subversion of their intellectual discernment. Amongst this description was the unfortunate subject of this case; religious studies having so far gained the ascendancy over her reason, as to impel her to words and actions of a maniacal tendency. In this dangerous state of fanaticism she was committed to my care. (89–90)

From the scanty evidence available to us from his description of the case, it is difficult to determine with certainty whether Mrs. EH was genuinely unbalanced. Perfect superficially described a few of the unhealthy beliefs and behaviors that she had "contracted," but there is nothing in his description that would strike the modern reader as pathological. One is thus inclined to assume that she was committed to the good doctor's care because her family disapproved of her new faith.

Mrs. EH was subjected to a physiological course of treatment that included a new diet, regular bleedings, and laxatives. This treatment program may strike the reader as naive and even as amusing, but a perusal of the medical literature of earlier centuries turns up many instances where religious ravings were attributed to physiological problems; for example, the following from an 1869 article by Joseph Workman: "His bowels were obstinately constipated. Purgatives had a calming effect, but still his religious delusions persisted" (1869). Dr. Perfect noted, however, that the abatement of his patient's symptoms was "in great measure to be attributed to her sanctified sectaries not having it in their power to procure access to her person as usual" (1798, 92). (In other words, Perfect had her locked up.) It was this isolation from her coreligionists, in combination with the heavily disapproving atmosphere of her treatment environment, which eventually brought about a "cure": "No one being permitted to pay the least attention to her enthusiastic ecstasies and raptures, they began gradually to lose their influence on her mind; and in about eight months appeared to be nearly forgotten. Her reason thus completely restored, she returned home to her family, who carefully guarded against a future relapse by a firm and steady resolution to prohibit the visits of those zealous devotees, through whose principles she derived the first impression of her terrible affliction" (92).

When interpreting descriptions of religious insanity, we must be careful to distinguish between cases where a medical diagnosis was being used to legitimate the "treatment" of relatives who had converted to sectarian religion and cases of genuine disturbance. Perfect's compilation is a useful text in this regard because his unconcealed prejudices allow us to perceive that most of the instances of religious enthusiasm he cited belong to the former. For example, in the case of "Mrs. SJ," for whom his advice was consulted via the mail, his correspondent noted that the patient "converses rationally, but reluctantly, on any other subject [that is, any subject other than religion]" (239). The apparent rationality of victims of religious insanity on other topics, a tendency that was noted in a number of nineteenth-century studies, tends to corroborate the impression that many of these individuals were not actually imbalanced.

Perfect's anthology is also useful because of his etiology (the study of the cause of disease), an etiology which overtly contains a marked disapproval of sectarian belief in its native conceptualization of the connection between false belief and disease. For example, although a certain "Mr. GL" had a natural "disposition to melancholy," this predisposition did not become pathological until he became "acquainted with a gloomy fanatic teacher of the Methodist order." After imbibing the "poisonous tenets of his doctrine, he soon became enthusiastically mad" (295–296).

Such a naive etiology implies a similarly naive course of treatment, namely that one should attempt to dislodge diseased beliefs. Perfect soon discovered, however, that religious enthusiasts were unusually resistant to therapy. When responding to his correspondent in the case of Mrs. SJ, for instance, Perfect observed, "If she could be conversed with on any regular basis, her mistaken notions of religion might probably be corrected; but in religious melancholy I have repeatedly found that argument has but little weight, for it seems to be the nature of the disorder to involve the mind in the most miserable and inextricable mysteries. The patients thus influenced resist or evade every argument which the most sensible person can adduce from the most rational ground, to undeceive their blinded judgment and deluded mind" (240). Hence, rather than recommending a direct assault on Mrs. SJ's deluded beliefs, Perfect prescribed a course of physiological treatments combined with advice on how to distract her from thoughts and conversation on religion: "Perhaps she is not altogether inclined to company, although she may be to business or amusement. The mind, if possible, should be diverted, and kept in a calm unruffled state; and all conversation on her favorite topic be carefully avoided" (241). In yet another case, Perfect prescribed "a change of residence, prohibiting all intercourse with her *religious* friend" (365) as a way of weakening his patient's pernicious belief system. In this particular instance, a mainstream minister was called in to conduct what we in the present century might refer to as a "deprogramming" session: "At this crisis a truly pious divine of her acquaintance had free access to her, and succeeded in endeavoring to enlighten the dark gloom that had involved her mind, and brought it back to a clear sense of religious duties; and after the patient had continued completely rational for six weeks, . . . she became in every respect as well as at the period before her illness" (366).

Whatever one might think about Dr. Perfect's opinions, we can be grateful for his admirable candidness, which allows us to reconstruct a very different state of affairs underneath his medical discourse. In most if not all of the instances cited above, a medical model was being used to delegitimate deviations from accepted religious norms where a heresy model would have been utilized less than a hundred years earlier. Instead of being burnt at the stake, these "deviants" were sent to hospitals to be cured of their heretical notions. Despite the various physiological treatments to which the patients were subjected, it was obvious even to Perfect that separation from fellow believers was the key element in his program of therapy.

In terms of socialization theory, the plausibility of any given symbolic universe is maintained by the ongoing process of conversation with co-inhabitants of a particular belief system (as discussed in Berger and Luckmann 1966, 157ff). When our conversation partners change, and especially when we are entirely cut off from former associates, there is a natural (though not inevitable) tendency for our beliefs to undergo a process of modification in the direction of the beliefs of our new friends. This process is particularly effective when, as in this case, the desired change is in the direction of *re*socialization into the norms of mainstream society (Berger and Luckmann 1966, 114). Something of this sort almost certainly took place in the cases recounted by Perfect.

Despite the fascinating nature of the notion of religious insanity, few studies have done more than scratch the surface of this topic (for example, Bainbridge 1984). Because of the poverty of relevant studies, it will be useful to briefly lay out the religious insanity theory that one finds in the medical literature of the late eighteenth and nineteenth centuries. Although the conception of mental illness gradually changed over the course of the nineteenth century, the generally accepted theory was firmly physiological: "Insanity is a disease of the physical organism, principally of the brain and nervous system, though disease of the physical organism may be *brought on* by a thousand 'causes,' whether of the kind we logically distinguish as 'efficient' causes, or 'occasional' causes, and these too *both* moral and physical" ("Religious Insanity" 1876, 126–127). In the early part of the nineteenth century, one finds the notion that insanity is correlated with lesions in the brain (Rothman 1971, 110), whereas later in the century the tendency is more to see mental (as well as many physical) illnesses as resulting from a deficiency of "nerve force" (Haller and Haller 1977). Nonetheless, the etiology of insanity was remarkably constant: Though acknowledging certain predisposing factors such as heredity, the actual initiating cause was portrayed as some kind of shock to the system—either physical, as in the case of a blow to the head, or through what nineteenth-century alienists (the older term for psychiatrists) referred to as "moral" causes—bereavement, loss of employment, and so on. Within this schema, religious enthusiasm was viewed as a moral factor which, when taken to extremes, could result in physiological damage; in the words of Amariah Brigham, one early nineteenth-century theorist of religious insanity. "All long continued or violent excitement of the mind is dangerous, because it is likely to injure the brain and nervous system. Religious excitement, therefore, like all mental excitement, by affecting the brain, may cause insanity or other diseases" (Brigham 1835, 284–285).

Revivals were the paradigmatic context in which this "violent excitement of the mind" was experienced. For instance, William Sweetser, another nineteenth-century psychiatrist, observes, "At the field-meetings that are annually held among us I have been witness to the most frightful nervous affections, as convulsions, epilepsy, hysteria, distressing spasms, violent contortions of the body, not only in females in whom, from their more sensitive and sympathetic temperament, such affections are most readily excited, but also in the more hardy and robust of our own sex. Even spectators, such as attend for the purpose of amusement or merriment, will oftentimes be overtaken by the same nervous disorders" (1850, 196). Many alienists, however, continued to echo William Perfect's opinion that pernicious doctrines in and of themselves could induce insanity.

Such a vague and imprecise etiology was, however, only superficially physiological. With no way of measuring depleted nerve force, and no pre-mortem way of discovering brain lesions, the de facto criterion for determining mental illness was verbal and behavioral expression. The obvious problem with such a criterion was that any unusual expression of belief or behavior that "appeared to exceed the common deviations of human belief and conduct" (Arnold 1806, 219) could be labeled crazy and legitimate the incarceration of a nonconforming individual. This actually seems to have been the case with the majority of religious enthusiasts committed to asylums; the "high reported cure rate for religious insanity" as contrasted with other forms of insanity indicates that incarceration was probably being "used by families to punish deviant members" and bring them back into line with accepted norms (Bainbridge 1984, 235). This is not to say that either families or physicians cynically deployed medical labels that they knew were spurious, but rather that a medical explanation was seized upon because it "made sense"—it seemed to substantiate popular prejudice as well as to legitimate a vigorous response.

This kind of "medicalization of deviance" perspective (Conrad and Schneider 1980) seems especially likely when we consider some of the more unusual causes of insanity mentioned in the psychiatric literature of the nineteenth century: masturbation, spermatorrhea ("involuntary seminal discharges"), intemperance, hashish intoxication (Dewey 1899, 233), novel reading, "effeminate education" (McIntoch 1866, 522), tobacco use, onset of puberty, and dealing in lottery tickets (Earle 1848, 195–199). Even more to the point are the psychiatric disorders "discovered" among slaves by Samuel A. Cartwright, a southern physician: Drapetomania, the mental illness "that induces the negro to run away from service" (Cartwright, 1851, 707), and "Dysestheia Ethiopis, or hebetude of mind and obtuse sensibility of body—a disease peculiar to negroes—called by overseers, 'rascality'" (709). The recommended therapy for the latter disease was "to have the patient well washed with warm water and soap; then, to anoint it all over with oil, and to slap the oil in with a broad leather strap; then to put the patient to some hard kind of work" (712). Needless to say, the same course of treatment, minus water, soap, and oil, had been applied by overseers long before Dr. Cartwright's *remarkable* investigations.

There had been enough speculation about religious insanity by the beginning of the second quarter of the nineteenth century that another English physician, George Man Burrows, could devote considerable space to discussion of the subject in his 1828 study,

Commentaries on the Causes, Forms, Symptoms, and Treatment, Moral and Medical, of Insanity. The second chapter of this work, "Religion in Reference to Insanity," is one of the best treatments of its kind, and thus provides a useful point of reference for gaining a better sense of the intricacies of the theory of religious insanity. Burrows begins by noting that it is the excessive emotion associated with religion that is the chief causal factor: "As there is no single passion, when excited to excess, that may not induce mental derangement, so we may readily believe that religion, which influences the internal man more than the passions collectively, may be the cause of insanity" (25). Burrows immediately notes, however, that causality may be falsely attributed to religion merely because the lunatic raves about religious matters. He further points out that the whole subject has been brought into a state of confusion because of the tendency of physicians to attribute pathological consequences to religious systems with which they disagreed.

Early in the chapter, Burrows makes an important disclaimer that one finds in almost every extended treatment of religious insanity: "It is not, however, from the agency of the Christian faith, in its pure and intelligible form, but from the perversion of it, that many become victims of insanity" (26). This appears to be an innocent enough statement in itself, but the mere admission that there can be perverted versions of the Christian faith indicates that he has his own axes to grind.

Toward the end of the chapter, after he has gone over a number of case studies, Burrows observes that "misused" religion may be only the initiating cause in people who are otherwise predisposed to derangement: "Each of them certainly possessed a constitutional temperament highly susceptible of excitement, and consequently favourable to derangement. Religion, therefore, in these instances, can be considered as the agent only; and, as may be the case with any other agent, the effect was consequent on the misuse, and not on the fair and proper application of it" (54). Burrows observes that most theories impute causal efficacy to one of three factors: "Firstly, to the mysticism of the tenets inculcated; secondly, to the intenseness with which abstract theology has been studied or followed; and thirdly, from religion being over-ardently impressed on minds too tender or uninformed to comprehend it" (38). His own opinion, however, is that it is the transitional state from one religious system to another that is the efficient cause: "I do not recollect an instance of insanity implying a religious source in any person steadfast in his ancient opinions. Wherever it was suspected to emanate from such a cause, it was clearly to be traced to circumstances which had diverted the lunatic from the authority of primary principles, to the adoption of new tenets, which he had not comprehended, and therefore had misapplied. The Maniacal action appeared always to originate during the conflict in deciding between opposite doctrines; and the exacerbation arrived before conviction was determined" (39).

From this statement and most of the other passages cited above, it can be seen that Burrows is more careful than many of his contemporaries. He is, however, not immune from the prejudices of his age. For example, he attributes the higher percentage of women infected with religious excitement to the natural weakness of the female sex—a very common observation in the literature on the subject. To his credit, however, and in marked contrast to many other writers on this topic, Burrows *also* notes certain differences between the socialization and occupations of males and females as explanatory factors: "Many causes combine to make women more prone to such impressions. Physically, man is more robust, and has less sensibility, or irritability, than women; morally, his education is more solid, and his pursuits more active and definite. The education of females is generally showy, rather than substantial; and as they naturally possess more ardent and susceptible minds, want of active occupation becomes a most dangerous enemy to them" (55). This passage may not strike the reader as exceptionally enlightened, but contrast it with such statements as this: "History, as well as the experience of physicians of the present day, teaches us that in certain highly emotional women, that religious sentiment and venereal desires are convertible passions. Religious sexual delusions are common occurrences and even certain diseases, such as epilepsy and hysteria, predispose to abnormal fervour" ("Brinton" 1876).

Burrows is, however, less cautious when expressing his opinions about certain specific religions. Despite his assertion that "in these enlightened times, it is to be hoped" that just "because a deranged person is a Papist, or a Protestant of the established church, or a sectarian, or even a Pagan" it should not be imputed that he or she is consequently more prone to insanity (1828, 32), Burrows's own bias comes forward in the context of some of his case studies. For example, his dislike of Catholicism is ill-disguised in the following: "Upon going out, she witnessed, for the first time, the ceremonies of the Romish church with which she appeared much struck. From that moment she lost all her zeal for the Protestant faith; and nothing would satisfy her but that she would be a catholic. She was brought home. No care, however, removed this conceit; and she still continued so wild and unmanageable, that she was sent to a lunatic asylum" (51).

Nonetheless, it should be noted that the depreciating tone of his remarks contrast favorably with those of his contemporaries. One of the reasons Burrows was selected for detailed examination was because his analysis was relatively cautious and reflective. He was, however, only slightly less guilty of medicalizing religious groups he disliked. I have tended to speak kindly of Dr. Burrows because of his comparative moderation; few of his contemporaries exercised Burrows's restraint. (For contrasting examples, refer to Arnold 1806; MacCormac 1864; Sweetser 1850.) Finally, we might note among nineteenth-century psychiatrists a general lack of restraint that is evident in the wide variety of groups that were at one time or another accused of inducing mental derangement: Mormons, Methodists, Catholics, Anabaptists, Quakers, Spiritualists, Presbyterians, Millerites, and Christian Scientists.

RELIGIOUS INSANITY PRESENT

From the standpoint of the early twenty-first century, it is easy to be amused by the perceptions and theories of our predecessors. Our amusement should be tempered, however, by the realization that the notion of religious insanity was devised and promulgated by some of the more thoughtful and liberal minds of the age. Much like Perfect and Burrows, we are not immune to the propensity to label ideas with which we disagree or behaviors of which we disapprove as sick or crazy. This seems to be particularly true of the attitude of certain members of the mental health profession toward cults. When, for example, one prominent anti-cult psychiatrist can seriously assert that the question motivating his work is, "What kind of nutty people get into these crazy groups?" (cited in

Bromley and Richardson 1983, 5) and commit patients he has never examined to medical institutions on the basis of their membership in alternative religions, we should suspect that contemporary cult disease is a close relative of nineteenth-century religious insanity.

Because members of controversial religious groups fall within the normal parameters of objective tests of intelligence and social adjustment, attempts to demonstrate the baneful effects of cultic brainwashing "scientifically" have tended to focus on the psychological problems former members encounter after leaving their religion. This post-involvement syndrome, sometimes referred to as "information disease" (a term coined by Flo Conway and Jim Siegelman in their popular book *Snapping* [1979]), is supposedly a *unique* mental illness, allegedly caused by prolonged exposure to mind control techniques. The information disease notion occupies a central position in the scientific attack on nontraditional religions—a position comparable to the role played by apostate tales in more popular attacks (examined in the preceding chapter).

Both the popular and the scientific attacks on alternative religious groups are attempts to psychologize—to *medicalize*—a controversy that, on deeper examination, is clearly a controversy over ideology and lifestyle. Opponents of religious innovation have been so successful in their tactic of medicalizing the controversy that their viewpoint finds expression, and therefore legitimation, in the *Diagnostic and Statistical Manual of Mental Disorders* (the standard diagnostic reference for psychological disturbances, henceforth abbreviated *DSM*). For example, under the category "Atypical Dissociative Disorder"—a disorder which the manual characterizes as a "residual category" for dissociative responses that do not fit other, more specific, categories—we find that prospective candidates include "persons who have been subjected to periods of prolonged and intense coercive persuasion (brainwashing, thought reform, and indoctrination while the captive of terrorists or cultists)" (*DSM* 1980, 260). In addition to the totally unsupported assertion that alternative religions utilize "coercive persuasion," this statement also places cultists on equal standing with terrorists. Or, again, under the category "Paranoid Personality Disorder"—a disorder which the manual confesses "rarely comes to clinical attention"—we find the authors *speculating*, "It seems likely that individuals with this disorder are overrepresented among leaders of mystical or esoteric religions" (308). (Controversial leaders of new religious movements are often accused of being psychopaths; for example, for a recent book-length argument along these lines, refer to Stevens and Price 2000.) Like the nineteenth-century diagnostic category of religious insanity, such nonempirical speculation shows more about the biases of certain psychologists than about the personality of religious leaders.

This shifting of ground from ideological to medical is a not uncommon tactic employed by members of a dominant social group against minorities. As a general phenomenon, it has regularly been studied by social scientists under the rubric of the "medicalization of deviance" (Conrad and Schneider 1980). The use of psychological-medical labels to legitimate repression is, in other words, not unique to the contemporary cult controversy. For example, one of the methods by which the former Soviet Union dealt with dissidents was to commit them to mental asylums through the use of such exotic diagnoses as "manic reformism" and "paranoia with counter-revolutionary delusions" (35). The earlier discussion of drapetomania—the mental illness that made slaves so deranged that they wanted to "run away from service"—is another vivid example of the medicalization of a social conflict.

Most mainstream scholars who have studied the cult controversy have come to similar conclusions about the mind control and brainwashing accusations leveled against contemporary new religions. In other words, in the context of this controversy, it is clear that parents become concerned about their offspring because they adopt eccentric lifestyles and beliefs, rather than because they exhibit genuinely pathological behavior. These parents are literally unable to understand their adult children's rejection of secular career goals and conventional family life, and as a consequence readily adopt the medical model represented by brainwashing ideology (Melton and Moore 1982, 40–41). That the real issue is "heresy" from the values and lifestyle of mainstream society, rather than mental illness, is clear in descriptions of deprogramming. Although kidnappers like Ted Patrick assert that the essence of this practice is "simply to get the individual thinking again" (quoted in Conway and Siegelman 1979, 65), any actual examination of what happens during deprogramming reveals that the goal of the proce-

dure is to force the individual to abandon his or her religious beliefs, and a person is considered "cured" when he or she agrees to
give up allegiance to his or her religious group (Anthony, Robbins,
and McCarthy 1980; Kim 1979; Bromley and Shupe 1981).

Thus the role of our secular society in transforming a disagreement over lifestyles and beliefs into a psychological issue is two-
fold: On the one hand, parents of individuals who have joined
new religious movements are often so secularized themselves that
they are unable to comprehend intense religious commitment as
anything other than crazy. On the other hand, attacks on religious
innovation must be cloaked in secular garb because accusations of
heresy are powerless to legitimate the mobilization of a secular culture's repressive agencies. A major difficulty with psychologizing
the inquisition against alternative religions, however, is that the recruitment and indoctrination techniques of nontraditional religions are not demonstrably more deceptive or manipulative than
such socially approved activities as advertising (Cox 1983, 51) or
military recruitment and training (Bromley and Shupe 1981, 81,
107). Also, if members of new religions had truly undergone radical personality changes, if their minds had snapped, and if they
were actually victims of ongoing trances (all fairly standard accusations), then such pathological mental states should show up as
some kind of irregularity when standardized psychological tests are
administered. However, as both defenders and critics of alternative
religions will agree, members of such groups fall within the range
defined as healthy on objective tests.

Anti-cultists have thus been compelled to focus their attention
on the "syndrome" that former members experience following removal from their religious community. This syndrome is described
in various ways, depending on the source, and usually includes
such symptoms as poor attention span, "floating" in and out of altered states, amnesia, hallucinations, suicidal tendencies, guilt,
fear, violent outbursts, and lack of a sense of directedness. Anti-cult
researchers assert or imply that this psychological disorder is
specifically the result of exotic mind control techniques, parading
under the guise of religious practices—praying, meditating, and
Bible reading—to which cult members have been subjected. Concentration on the post-involvement period characterizes the
empirical work of such anti-cultists as Flo Conway and Jim Siegel-

man (1982) , Margaret Singer (1979), and John Clark (Clark et al. 1981).

Of these studies, the one that conveys the most substantial appearance to casual readers is Conway and Siegelman's survey of four hundred ex-members of controversial religions, a survey that was reported in a 1982 article entitled "Information Disease: Have Cults Created a New Mental Illness?" Conway and Siegelman presented data on seven symptoms—floating/altered states, nightmares, amnesia, hallucinations/delusions, "inability to break mental rhythms of chanting," violent outbursts, and suicidal or self-destructive tendencies—for which respondents reported long-term mental and emotional effects. More particularly, Conway and Siegelman claimed, "The psychological trauma cults inflict upon their members is directly related to the amount of time spent in indoctrination and mind control rituals" (1982).

Although one could critique many aspects of this study, the decisive weakness of the information disease notion—and it should be noted that Singer and Clark do not use the *term* "information disease," although the same basic *notion* of a "cult withdrawal syndrome" is implicit in their work—is that this supposedly new and unique syndrome is actually nothing more exotic than a traumatic stress response.

There are a number of syndromes with which information disease can be compared. Sociologist Brock Kilbourne, for example, has pointed out that a wide variety of psychological disturbances— from bereavement to the mourning symptoms which follow divorce—parallel the symptomatology of the post-cult involvement syndrome (1983, 35–36). Although any of these disorders could be used to point out the parallels between information disease and responses to traumatic stress, it is easiest to make a case for the connection between the cult withdrawal syndrome and what the *Diagnostic and Statistical Manual of Mental Disorders* calls the "Post-Traumatic Stress Disorder." The *DSM* describes the cause of the post-traumatic stress disorder (PTSD) as any "psychologically traumatic event that is generally outside the range of usual human experience," such as assault, military combat, natural disaster, or an accident (1980, 236). The trauma of deprogramming, particularly a deprogramming of the classic "snatch" type (Patrick and Dulack 1977), clearly fits the category of a stressful event outside the range of normal human experience. And, because two-thirds to three-fourths of the samples used by anti-cult researchers were deprogrammed (71 percent in Conway and Siegelman's 1982 "Information Disease" study and 75 percent in Singer's 1979 "Coming out of the Cults" study), it is reasonable to hypothesize that the difficulties which these individuals experienced would be partially—if not entirely—a response to traumatic stress.

Most of the overlap between the cult withdrawal syndrome and the post-traumatic stress disorder is quite straightforward: Simply compare the symptomatology of the PTSD—nightmares, guilt, memory impairment, difficulty concentrating, phobic response, explosive outbursts, suicidal tendencies, and so on—with the symptomatology (mentioned earlier) reported in anti-cult studies of ex-members. In addition to these obvious parallels, some of the more bizarre symptoms of the post-involvement syndrome, such as hallucinations and the tendency to slip into dissociated states, express another essential component of PTSD symptomatology.

The *DSM* describes this other symptom as "recurrent and intrusive recollections," and as the "sudden acting or feeling as if the traumatic event were reoccurring," which in some instances is experienced as "dissociative-like states, lasting from a few minutes to several hours or even days" (238). This intrusive recalling of the traumatic event—which can be experienced either as waking flashbacks or as unpleasant dreams—is the more central symptom of the post-traumatic stress disorder. This symptom is probably also related to the experience of "floating" described by former cult members.

The problem with the term "floating," however, is that it is a "technical" term coined by deprogrammers to refer to ex-members' alternation between the values and belief system of their former group and the values and beliefs of mainstream society. Thus when an individual drifts back into the perspective of her or his former faith, it appears to parents and deprogrammers that she or he has lost touch with the real world. Because a person who has gone through deprogramming has been indoctrinated to interpret her or his experience in terms of this perspective, it may be that former members of nontraditional religions who report experiencing this symptom are actually thinking about their alternation back and forth between their religious group's perspective and the perspective of mainstream culture, rather than any sort of actual trance or altered state of consciousness.

Similarly, the symptom described by Conway and Siegelman as the "inability to break mental rhythms of chanting" might also be an expression of what the *DSM* describes as "recurrent and intrusive recollections." Here once again, however, we have to reckon with the factor of indoctrination at the hands of deprogrammers, relatives, and other people in the anti-cult movement. As is commonly known in anti-cult circles, individuals being tormented by deprogrammers frequently respond to heavy-handed interrogation by breaking off the dialogue and attempting to enter a contemplative, prayerful, or meditative state. If these individuals' deprogrammings are later successful, they will subsequently reinterpret such strategies as part of their indoctrinated mental state (i.e., they were "unable" to prevent themselves from "trancing out"). Hence, with this symptom, it is likely that many of the individuals reporting an "inability to stop mental rhythms of chanting" are responding out of the interpretive framework of their counter-indoctrination.

Finally, the other characteristics of the post-involvement syndrome reported by anti-cult researchers—indecisiveness, a sense of meaninglessness, blurred mental acuity, and so forth—are symptomatic of a major depressive disorder, which the *Diagnostic and Statistical Manual of Mental Disorders* notes regularly accompanies the post-traumatic stress disorder (237). This analysis demonstrates that information disease symptoms are either exact parallels to the post-traumatic stress disorder or, where the parallel is weak, can be explained in terms of the influence of anti-cult indoctrination. We are thus fully justified in hypothesizing that information disease is the direct result of the traumatic transition out of a nontraditional religion rather than the result of anything experienced while in such a group.

If this line of reasoning is correct, it suggests that there should be a high correlation between the post-involvement syndrome and the experience of deprogramming. Though not all traumatic exits occur under the circumstances of forcible abduction and intensive counter-indoctrination, it seems reasonable to assume that the majority of exit traumas would be experienced by deprogrammed ex-members. In my research on former members of controversial religious groups, I indeed found this to be the case.

This survey, which was reported in a set of papers published in the 1980s (Lewis 1986; Lewis and Bromley 1987) and partially discussed in the preceding chapter, contained a section that asked subjects to compare their pre-involvement period (before joining their religious group) with their post-involvement period in terms of the various symptoms described in anti-cult literature. Using for the sake of simplicity only the seven symptoms for which Conway and Siegelman presented quantified data in their "Information Disease" article, and dividing the sample into the three treatment groups described in the preceding chapter, a distribution of information disease can be charted out, which, as anticipated, clearly links the post-involvement syndrome with deprogramming-exit counseling (see table 9.1). With the exception of the voluntary counseling category (which will be discussed momentarily), the resulting table requires little commentary. Though not all experiences of exit counseling need be excessively traumatic, and while defections not accompanied by deprogramming can be traumatic enough to produce certain symptoms of the stress response, the data clearly indicates a *high* correlation between the experience of deprogramming-exit counseling and the induction of information disease. Conway and Siegelman's claim of a correlation between information disease and time spent in such brainwashing activities as prayer and meditation failed to be verified.

Table 9.1.   Relationship between Mode of Exit and Incidence of Information Disease Symptoms (Percentage of Respondents Reporting Symptom)

SYMPTOM	NO COUNSELING	VOLUNTARY COUNSELING	INVOLUNTARY COUNSELING	CORRELATION COEFFICIENT*
Floating	11	41	61	.414
Nightmares	11	41	47	.358
Amnesia	8	41	58	.482
Hallucinations	4	24	36	.337
Chanting	3	55	56	.530
Violence	9	31	42	.301
Suicidal	9	34	41	.270

*All correlations significant at the .001 level.

The most unusual statistic in the table is the pattern of the symptom that Conway and Siegelman referred to as the "inability to break mental rhythms of chanting." It is possible that the steep rise from the non-counseled category to the voluntarily counseled category might be an indication of just how much this symptom is dependent on anti-cult indoctrination. On the other hand, the pattern could very well result from the manner in which this survey item was worded (which was quite different from the others). Most likely this skewed pattern is the result of both of these factors. Whatever the proper explanation, the chanting data does not call into question the more general correlation noted between deprogramming and information disease.

There is, however, a certain (and perhaps unavoidable) ambiguity in this study's conclusions. Other studies of post-involvement attitudes have found a high correlation between contact with the anti-cult movement and the tendency of ex-members to describe their cult experiences in a negative, stereotyped manner. This tendency makes it difficult to determine the extent to which these findings were the result of exit traumas and the extent to which deprogrammed ex-members—who clearly felt marked anger toward their former religions—simply wanted researchers to feel that they had been damaged by their membership.

Thus it might be possible to argue that negative indoctrination at the hands of anti-cultists accounts almost entirely for the post-involvement syndrome. However, though such indoctrination undoubtedly accounts for a portion of the syndrome, it is difficult to imagine that the experience of being snatched off the street and held against one's will until after one's religious beliefs were destroyed would *not* induce traumatic stress. Also, the many parallels observed between information disease and the post-traumatic stress disorder are too striking to be easily passed over. To resolve this ambiguity by changing tact and approaching the issue from a new angle, we can take the further step of examining evidence from a very different group of people—*un*successfully deprogrammed members of controversial religious movements.

In connection with my survey of *ex*-members, I interviewed or received questionnaires from twenty-four *current* members of non-traditional religions who had experienced deprogramming without abandoning their religion (most either escaped or faked apostasy and returned to their church). Respondents were asked to describe their post-deprogramming mental-emotional state, and especially to recount any experiences of vivid dreams or waking flashbacks connected with their deprogramming. The vivid reliving of the traumatic event is, as mentioned earlier, the defining symptom of the post-traumatic stress disorder. (The PTSD is the same syndrome former Vietnam veterans often experience.) Thus the marked presence of this symptom among *un*successfully deprogrammed individuals would support the view that the symptoms reported by deprogrammed ex-members were genuine responses to the trauma of being kidnapped and psychologically assaulted.

As anticipated, the most intense symptoms were reported by individuals who had experienced violent, snatch-type deprogrammings. Thus one respondent who had been "roped, taped, gagged, and handcuffed before being thrown in the deprogrammer's car at the start of the deprogramming" reported that for a long time afterwards the sound of a car door slamming was enough to cause him to relive the fear associated with his kidnapping. The most commonly reported pattern was a connection between what might be called "aggressive communication" and the tendency to recall the verbal harassment of the deprogramming. In such patterns, the triggering stimulus would often be loudly voiced anger. For example, one Hare Krishna devotee recounted, "If I hear someone yelling at me or if I hear someone yelling at someone else, I completely revert right back to the deprogramming. I can practically even see [name of one of her deprogrammers]. All I see is ill motivation and someone wanting to do harm to me." Many other such patterns are idiosyncratic to each individual's specific experiences. Thus, for example, one person who had tripped and fallen on a sidewalk as she was escaping later experienced a short but intense flashback when she tripped while jogging. Other deprogramming victims reported "van phobia" if they had been kidnapped in vans, and attacks of anxiety around people who resemble their deprogrammers.

The duration of symptom recurrence varied according to the brutality and duration of the deprogramming and according to the intangibles of each kidnapping victim's personality. At the time this research was being carried out, many of the respondents continued to suffer from their experiences. For instance, one individual reported, six years later, "[I still suffer from anxiety] if I'm a passenger in a car and suddenly I don't recognize where I am or I'm not sure where I'm being taken."

Closely related to such waking flashbacks are vivid dreams in which the trauma is relived. Most respondents reported experiencing nightmares following their deprogramming. Sometimes these dreams were fairly realistic, such as dreaming one is running away from pursuers (a frequently reported nightmare) or such as the person who dreamed: "I was kidnapped from my bed at night and dragged back to the hotel room for more mental torture. I would wake up seeing [name of her deprogrammer]'s face." More often, however, nightmares expressed the traumatic experience in exaggerated ways. For example, one person dreamed that his father threatened him with the statement, "This time, if you try to escape, we'll kill you." Another person dreamed that her parents "locked [her] in a box." Not infrequently this tendency of the dream state to embellish the deprogramming trauma resulted in surrealistic nightmares. One of the people in this category was a Hare Krishna devotee who went through a particularly brutal deprogramming at the hands of Ted Patrick. This individual described some of her dreams: "I've had dreams of people torturing me with fire and yelling at me, physically hurting me, trying to kill me . . . horror movie kind of things, really gross things, like people being murdered—other people in the background screaming—I'm being tortured, I'm being murdered, like a concentration camp. That's what it feels like. Being locked in and I can't get out. And I'm dying, and then I wake up because I start shaking." This person was still experiencing these kinds of nightmares ten years after her deprogramming. As with flashbacks, there is considerable variability in the length of time that such dreams recur following deprogramming.

These accounts and *many* others that could be cited are eloquent testimonies to deprogramming's capacity to induce trauma, and they clearly refute other interpretations of the stress symptoms reported by deprogramming victims. In light of these findings, the notion of a unique mental illness induced by cultic brainwashing evaporates. However, although the idea of cult disease can be dismissed, there remain a few unresolved ambiguities with respect to the question of the cause of the traumatic stress response.

These ambiguities are raised with respect to the category of *voluntary* defectors who experience traumatic stress symptoms after their exit. Where does this subsample fit into the explanatory schema outlined thus far? Deprogramming is obviously not the causal factor, but does the source of distress lie in the circumstances surrounding the exit or in cult life itself? With a little reflection, it is not difficult to imagine circumstances under which even voluntary exits could be extremely stressful. Psychiatrist Saul Levine, whose *Radical Departures* was referred to in the preceding chapter, observes, "The more intolerant the group has been to its departing member, the greater the difficulty in readjusting to life in the outside world and the more likely that professional help will be needed" (1984, 150). Levine also indicates that certain voluntary defections can induce a traumatic stress reaction. However, even under these circumstances—where interaction with the religious group is clearly responsible for the ex-member's distress—it is still clear that the cause of this distress is the trauma of a stressful *exit.*

It might be well to note that when conducting this research the possibility of finding the opposite state of affairs—that is, that a traumatic experience in an intensive religious group could induce defection—was not excluded. However, over the course of research on former members of controversial religions, very few examples were found of an extremely distressing experience that was not directly tied to the decision to leave or to deprogramming. The point being made here might become a little clearer if we look at a few concrete examples of individuals who linked up with the anti-cult movement only after they left their religious group.

At least four respondents in the survey combined their exit with a marital separation (that is, their spouse remained in the organization). Furthermore, three of them had become involved in litigation to gain custody of their children, and every one of these three individuals sought contact with anti-cult groups. (If, as will be discussed further in the next chapter, ex-members can get the "cultist" label to stick to their ex-spouse, they markedly increase their chances of obtaining custody of the kids.) Two of these three also underwent anti-cult counseling—counseling that would only have reinforced the negative attitude these ex-members held toward their former religious community. The distress this set of people experienced was clearly tied to traumatic events surrounding their exit. In other words, they decided to leave and their decision initiated a stressful series of experiences. It is the subcategory of individuals such as these who constitute the genuine exceptions to the assertion that it is deprogramming that causes the stress response, but they are *not* exceptions to the assertion that it is the trauma of defection (rather than the mind warping effects of brainwashing techniques) that is responsible for inducing the stress response.

Before bringing this chapter to a close, it would be useful to glance at one final example from this particular group of individuals (that is, people who experienced anti-cult counseling only after leaving). The example we will examine is the case of a former member of the Hare Krishna Movement who was forced to return home by the authorities (she was a minor during her term of membership). In addition to once again demonstrating the point that it is the circumstances surrounding the exit—rather than the group itself—that are responsible for inducing the stress response, this particular case is useful for illustrating the following:

1. How the anti-cult movement influences ex-members to reinterpret their cult experience,
2. How anti-cultists ignore certain obvious factors in their analysis of the cause of the post-involvement syndrome, and
3. How anti-cultists use the post-involvement syndrome in court cases intended to cripple nontraditional religions.

Over the course of a prolonged struggle with her parents, this individual—who we will call Linda Smith (not her real name)—was subjected to various forms of harassment and mistreatment in an effort to break her will and force her to conform to parental expectations. For example, at different points in time her father destroyed Linda's altar and other devotional items (while she was still living at home), slapped her across the face and jammed a hose of running water down her mouth to prevent her from chanting, threatened her with shock treatment, confined her to a juvenile hall, and chained her to a toilet for two weeks to prevent her from running away (she ran away twice, apparently for good reasons). On top of this, Linda's father died of a heart attack within a year of her final return, and she was made to feel that her rebellious behavior was the cause of her father's death.

As one might anticipate, Ms. Smith suffered a traumatic stress reaction. Interestingly enough, however, after undergoing counter-indoctrination at the hands of certain anti-cult counselors, Linda, in consort with her mother, brought suit against the Hare Krishna Movement and was eventually awarded almost $10 million in damages for psychological problems that she claimed were caused by her Krishna involvement (this judgment was later overturned). The plaintiff's expert witness—a prominent anti-cult psychologist whose mind control theories were subsequently rejected by the American Psychological Association—presented a diagnosis of Ms. Smith's difficulties. This diagnosis included, among other disorders, the post-traumatic stress disorder. The psychologist flatly asserted that Linda's mental problems were a *direct result* of the time she spent in the Hare Krishna Movement. The rather extreme actions of Mr. and Mrs. Smith were ignored as possible contributory factors.

To conclude with a brief summary of the discussion presented in the latter half of this chapter, attacks on nontraditional religions have been legitimated by the accusation that cult membership is psychologically damaging. To support this accusation, anti-cultists have been compelled to focus on the post-involvement syndrome (information disease) in their efforts to document the presence and harmful effects of cultic mind control. This syndrome was chosen because *every other standard procedure for detecting mental illness failed to discover psychopathology among members of nontraditional religions*. After a discussion of the issues involved, the analysis proceeded to demonstrate—through a comparison of symptoms and an analysis of data drawn from a survey of ex-members—that information disease was *not* a unique mental illness, but was instead almost always a traumatic response to deprogramming.

10

THE CULT STEREOTYPE
AS AN IDEOLOGICAL
RESOURCE

Some of the specifics of how the notion of delegitimation has been applied to the cult controversy were analyzed in chapters 8 and 9. The contribution of this discussion to the notion of legitimacy is the simple observation that conflicts over the legitimacy or illegitimacy of religious groups can be understood as an argument over *classification*. The authority of the governmental agencies that could be invoked against alternative religions is not at issue. Rather, opponents of religious innovation assert that new religious movements—almost always referred to as cults—are not "real" religions. Instead, cults are exploitative criminal organizations parading as pseudo-religions and should be repressed. As a consequence of the sharp contrast critics have drawn between cults and genuine religions, the term "cult" has come to *mean* a harmful pseudo-religion run by a self-seeking charlatan. The present chapter examines some concrete conflicts involving efforts to delegitimate a specific religious group by attempting to have it *reclassified* as a cult.

In prior studies of the cult controversy, sociologically informed observers have tended to focus on the efforts of the anticult movement to gain widespread social acceptance for its peculiar perspective on nontraditional religious groups. Because the consensus among mainstream new religions scholars is that the most dramatic claims made by anti-cultists against minority religions are inaccurate (e.g., Barker 1984; Bromley and Richardson 1983; Bromley and Shupe 1981; Melton and Moore 1982), analysts have focused on uncovering the deeper interests lying behind rhetoric about brainwashing, cultic manipulation, and the like. These discussions of the anti-cult movement and of the cult stereotype propagated by anti-cultists have drawn on theorizing about social movements—theorizing that has tended to focus on the macro dynamics of such movements. This tendency to emphasize what takes place at the broader levels of society has been prompted by, among other factors, a reaction among social scientists against earlier micro theorizing that gave excessive attention to explaining why individuals become involved in social movements.

One of the issues that gets missed by focusing excessively on either the individual participant or on the broader social dynamics is understanding how particular minority religions are drawn into the "cult wars," as well as how anti-cult ideology is used in specific conflicts involving individuals and groups who, for the most part, have no interest in the wider anti-cult crusade. To understand social dynamics at this level, which lies somewhere between the macro level of the larger anti-cult movement and the micro level of individual involvement, some adaptation of earlier theorizing is called for. The present discussion will undertake to examine some of the specific conflicts through which a particular minority religion—the Church of the Movement of Spiritual Inner Awareness (MSIA), which was also used as a case study in chapter 1—has been drawn into the cult controversy. After presenting a brief overview of the anti-cult movement, it will be argued that, for most of the people involved in conflicts with MSIA, the cult stereotype is an ideological resource, useful for legitimating support for their side of the struggle, but representing no deep involvement in the anti-cult cause.

The anti-cult movement itself exercises relatively little real direct power. Where it is most influential is in helping to construct and reinforce negative stereotypes about nontraditional religions in the mass media.[1] However, the popularity of the cult stereotype indicates that there is a pre-existing disposition to accept such stereotypes in American society. By attending to certain themes in anti-cult discourse, it should be possible to uncover some of the factors behind the receptivity of contemporary society to negative, stereotyped images of minority religions. Relevant social-psychological research also indicates that, once a stereotype has been accepted, it structures our perceptions so that we tend to notice information that conforms to our image of the stereotyped group and to neglect or forget other kinds of information. What this means for any given confrontation is that, as soon as the label "cult" has been successfully applied (that is, accepted as appropriate by outsiders not directly involved in the conflict), the information that the mass media gather is selectively appropriated so that almost every item of data conforms to the stereotype about cults, thus effectively marshaling moral support for the person or group locked in conflict with a minority religion.

THE ANTI-CULT MOVEMENT

In the early 1970s, opposition to religious innovation was centered around deprogrammers—individuals who forcibly abducted members of nontraditional religions, locked them up in motel rooms, and assaulted their beliefs until they gave up their religious faith (Kelley 1977; Shupe and Bromley 1980). Despite claims that deprogramming is a therapeutic intervention that breaks through cult members' "hypnotic trance" and forces them to think again (for example, Hassan 1988; Langone 1993; Ross and Langone 1988), it is clear that deprogrammers are little more than vigilantes acting at the behest of parents upset by the religious choices of their adult children (Bromley and Richardson 1983; Bromley and Shupe 1981). This negative evaluation of deprogramming is reinforced by the observation that, as a group, deprogrammers are largely uneducated individuals with little or no training in counseling.

Deprogramming, controlled entirely by independent entrepreneurs, could never have developed into a viable profession without the simultaneous development of secular "cult watchdog groups."[2] These organizations, despite vigorous public denials to the contrary, regularly referred concerned parents to deprogrammers. The evidence for this connection is overwhelming. For example, at the national gatherings of the Cult Awareness Network (CAN; formerly the Citizens Freedom Foundation, or CFF), one could always find a host of deprogrammers actively marketing their services to concerned parents in attendance. Deprogrammers, in turn, allegedly kicked back a certain percentage of their take to CAN. John Myles Sweeney, former national director of CAN/CFF, described this arrangement: "Because of the large amount of money they make due to referrals received from CFF members, deprogrammers usually kick back money to the CFF member who gave the referral. . . . The kick backs would either be in cash or would be hidden in the form of a tax-deductible 'donation' to the CFF" (Sweeney 1992, 1). One of the results of the financial alliance between anti-cult groups and deprogrammers was that anti-cult groups acquired a vested interest in promoting the worst possible stereotypes of nontraditional religions. In other words, if one was profiting from referring worried parents to deprogrammers, it made no sense to inform parents that the religion their child had joined was comparatively benign. Instead, the tendency was to paint such religions in the exaggerated colors of fear and fanaticism, creating the anxiety that, unless their child was "rescued" immediately, he or she could end up as a lobotomized robot, suffering from permanent emotional and psychological damage.

Similarly, it made little sense to propagate a balanced view of alternative religions to the press. If one profited from the fear surrounding such groups, then it was natural to take every opportunity to repeat frightening rumors. It was, in fact, the two-decade-long interaction between the anti-cult movement and the media that has been responsible for the widespread view that all cults are dangerous organizations—this despite the fact that comparatively few such groups constitute a genuine threat, either to themselves or to society.

However, with the exception of periodic attention from the mass media, the anti-cult movement (at least in North America) was and is relatively powerless. Even the influence that anti-cult spokespersons had in shaping public perceptions of cults was not based upon the intrinsic merit of their interpretations. Rather, anti-cultism feed upon—and in turn feed—a public *predisposition* to perceive nontraditional religions in a negative light. We might best understand this predisposition in terms of the social psychology of stereotyping.

SOCIAL FUNCTIONS OF THE CULT STEREOTYPE

What is a stereotype? Stereotypes are generalizations about other groups of people, but they are a peculiar type of generalization. "Stereotypes are used to ascribe incorrectly certain characteristics to whole groups of people and then explain or excuse social problems in light of these characteristics" (Rothenberg 1988, 253). Stereotypes are also usually held rigidly, in that we tend to ignore or to dismiss evidence that flies in the face of our generalization. Such rigidity indicates that our stereotype "may be relatively fundamental to our conceptual scheme, it may protect our self-esteem, it may help bring about some desirable situation, or it may shield us from facing [some] unpleasant fact" (Andre 1988, 257). Thus the stereotype of certain races as "lazy" for example, would simultaneously boost the self-esteem of society's dominant racial group as well as blind one to the inequalities of existing social arrangements. It is relatively easy to perceive that most generalizations about cults are little more than negative stereotypes, but what are the social forces that make such stereotypes about nontraditional religions peculiarly attractive to contemporary society?

Unless there are groups that are consciously anti-social or criminal, like the Mafia or like gangs, the deviations from the norm that a community chooses to perceive as threatening are somewhat arbitrary. The people that our culture have traditionally construed as "deviants" have been racial (for example, Blacks), ethnic (for example, Jews), and sexual (for example, homosexuals) minorities. In recent years, however, it has become socially unacceptable to persecute these traditional groups, at least in the overt manner in which they have been attacked in the past. This leaves few groups of any significant size to persecute. One of the few minorities that liberals have been slow to defend are nontraditional religions. This is due to a number of different factors, including the resistance of traditionally conservative religions to liberal change. The failure of normally open-minded people to protect religious pluralism has allowed contemporary witch hunters to declare open season on cults.

Groups of people experienced as threatening frequently become screens onto which a society projects its anxieties. If, for example, a culture is troubled by sexual issues (as is often the case), then its enemies are perceived as perverse, sexually deviant, and so on. Racial minorities, who have often been viewed as "loose" and sexually aggressive, have suffered from this projection (e.g., refer to Gilman 1985). This was also a dominant theme in nineteenth century anti-Catholic and anti-Mormon literature (Lewis 1990; Miller 1983). Contemporary "cults," of course, suffer from the same projection.

In his classical formulation of the notion of psychological projection, Freud (1938), who was especially concerned with sex and violence, viewed projection as a defense mechanism against unacceptable inner urges. Thus in a society with strict sexual mores, an individual constantly keeping a lid on his or her desires might perceive rather ordinary dancing, let us say, as sexually suggestive. Becoming enraged at such "loose" behavior, he or she might then attempt to lead a movement to have all of the dance halls in town closed down. It should be clear that this hypothetical individual's *inner* struggle is being projected outward to provide a script for an *outer* struggle (i.e., internally one is repressing one's desires while symbolically battling the same desires in the outer world). The same process is at work in the collective mind of society, perceiving marginal groups as sexually deviant. For instance, the stereotype of the sexually abusive cult leader, routinely forcing devotees to satisfy his or her sexual whims, perfectly captures the fantasy of many members of our society who desire to sexually control any person they wish.

The same kind of process occurs with respect to repressed aggressive urges. We live in a society with strict sanctions against overt violence; simultaneously, violence is glorified in the entertainment media. This sets up a cultural contradiction that is projected onto enemies and deviant groups, with the result that minorities are often perceived as violent and belligerent. This accusation is also regularly projected onto nontraditional religions. In particular, the violent actions of a tiny handful of members of alternative religions is mistakenly taken to indicate a widespread tendency among all such groups.

We can generalize beyond Freudian psychology's emphasis on sex and aggression to see that many other cultural anxieties/cultural contradictions are projected onto minority groups. For instance, our society gives us contradictory messages about the relative importance of wealth and material success. On the one hand, we are taught that economic pursuits should be secondary to higher moral, social, and spiritual concerns. On the other hand, we receive many messages from the surrounding society that the single-minded pursuit of wealth is the be-all and end-all of life. This inherent contradiction is typically ignored or overlooked with regard to mainstream religions where gross economic inequities exist within the same community or where religious elites enjoy favored status and privilege. Instead of being faced directly, this self-contradiction is examined only after it has been projected onto alternative religions, where it constitutes the basis of the stereotype of the money-hungry cult leader who demands that her or his followers lead lives of poverty while the leader wallows in riches.

One of the more important cultural contradictions projected onto alternative religions is reflected in the brainwashing–mind control notion that is the core accusation leveled against such groups. Discourse that glorifies American society usually does so in terms of a rhetoric of liberty and freedom. However, while holding liberty as an ideal, we experience a social environment that is often quite restrictive. Most citizens work as employees in highly disciplined jobs where the only real freedom is the freedom to quit. Also, we are daily bombarded by advertising designed to influence our decisions and even to create new needs. Our frustration with these forms of influence and control is easily displaced and projected onto the separated societies of alternative religions, where the seemingly (but often not actually) restricted flow of information offers a distorted reflection of the situation we experience as members of the dominant society.

The components of the cult stereotype that have been enumerated above, and others that could be mentioned, explain certain themes in anti-cult discourse, as well as why this stereotype tends to resonate with public opinion. Without this pre-existing disposition to construe nontraditional religions negatively, the anti-cult movement would have little or no social influence. However, even this influence is limited, in the sense that the stereotype the anti-cult movement has helped to shape has taken on a life of its own, independent of organized anti-cultism.

In their role as moral entrepreneurs, anti-cult spokespersons have effectively marketed their negative stereotype of minority religions to the general public. Because of the pre-existing fit between this negative image and the persistent social anxieties outlined in this section, our society has overwhelmingly bought into the stereotype (or purchased the *moral commodity,* to continue the entrepreneurial metaphor). Because of widespread acceptance of the stereotype, the anti-cult movement could disappear tomorrow and anti-cult discourse would still continue to shape public perceptions of minority religions.

SELF-FULFILLING STEREOTYPES

Once a stereotype is in place, a variety of different kinds of studies have shown that it becomes self-fulfilling and self-reinforcing. Thus in a study by Snyder, for example, students were asked to read a short biography about "Betty K," a fictitious woman. Her life story was constructed so that it would fulfill certain stereotypes of both heterosexuals and lesbians. In Snyder's words, "Betty, we wrote, never had a steady boyfriend in high school, but did go out on dates. And although we gave her a steady boyfriend in college, we specified that he was more of a close friend than anything else" (1988, 266). A week later, they told some of the students that Betty was currently living with her husband and another group of students that she was living with another woman in a lesbian relationship. When subsequently requested to answer a series of questions about Betty, they found a marked tendency on the part of students to reconstruct her biography so as to conform to stereotypes about either heterosexuality or homosexuality, depending on the information they had received: "Those who believed that Betty was a lesbian remembered that Betty had never had a steady boyfriend in high school, but tended to neglect the fact that she had gone out on many dates in college. Those who believed that Betty was now a heterosexual, tended to remember that she had formed a steady relationship with a man in college, but tended to ignore the fact that this relationship was more of a friendship than a romance" (1988, 266–267).

More directly relevant to the case at hand is an important article by Jeffrey E. Pfeifer reporting the results of a similar study which compared responses to a biography in which a fictitious student, Bill, dropped out of college to enter a Catholic seminary, join the marines, or join the Moonies. The short biography incorporated elements of indoctrination often attributed to cults: "While at the facility, Bill is not allowed very much contact with his friends or family and he notices that he is seldom left alone. He also notices that he never seems to be able to talk to the other four people who signed up for the program and that he is continually surrounded by [Moonies, marines, priests] who make him feel guilty if he questions any of their actions or beliefs" (1992, 535). When given a choice of describing Bill's indoctrination experience, subjects who thought Bill had joined the Catholic priesthood most often labeled his indoctrination "resocialization"; those who were told that he had joined the marines most frequently labeled the process "conversion"; and those who were under the impression that he had become a Moonie applied the label "brainwashing." On various other questions regarding the desirability and fairness of the indoctrination process, subjects who were told that Bill had joined the Moonies consistently evaluated his experience more negatively than subjects who were under the impression that Bill had joined either the marines or a priestly order.

The implication of this analysis is that minority religions lose their chance for a fair hearing as soon as the label "cult" is successfully applied to them. After that, the news media selectively seek out and present information that fits the stereotype. It is then only a matter of time before the group in question is completely "demonized."

THE CULT STEREOTYPE AS AN IDEOLOGICAL RESOURCE

Though the cult stereotype has come to dominate public discourse about minority religions, and though groups like the Unification Church and People's Temple seem to have become integral parts of that stereotype, there is enough ambiguity in the "cult" label to make its application in particular cases a matter of negotiation. Occasions for such negotiation arise in the context of social conflicts. For individuals or groups locked in certain kinds of struggles with members of minority religions, the cult stereotype represents a potent ideological resource which—if they are successful in swaying their immediate audience to reclassify a particular religion as a cult—marshals opinion against their opponent, potentially tipping the balance of power in their favor.

Situations in which this strategy can work are not restricted to the kinds of conflicts that are picked up by the national news media. For example, the stigma of the cult stereotype has been effectively deployed in child custody cases, in which one parent's membership in a minority religion is portrayed as indicative of her or his unworthiness as a parent. For such limited-domain legal conflicts, however, it is difficult to deploy the stereotype unless there is some larger, earlier conflict that led to press coverage in which the particular minority religion in question was labeled a cult. Lacking earlier bad press, the cult label can still sometimes be made to stick on the basis of testimony by disgruntled former members.

For the most part, individuals involved in such relatively limited conflicts do not become full-time anti-cult crusaders. Although they may enter into a relationship with the anti-cult movement, they normally drift away from this involvement within a short time after the termination of their particular struggle. To refer back to the entrepreneurial model, these people are not so much moral entrepreneurs as they are consumers of a moral commodity—they have "purchased" a pre-packaged cult stereotype and brought it to bear as one tool in the array of resources they have assembled to legitimate their cause. They may, of course, still have to exercise persuasive skills in getting the public or the court to accept the applicability of the stereotype, but otherwise they are not invested in the product per se. If anti-cult rhetoric fails to accomplish their end, but some other tool works in their particular conflict, they are usually quite ready to dispose of the cult stereotype and adopt an entirely different angle of attack.

As a low-intensity group that does not make excessive demands upon either the time or the resources of most participants, MSIA was largely overlooked by the anti-cult movement until the late 1980s. In 1988, the *Los Angeles Times* published a highly critical article on MSIA. A similar article then appeared in *People* magazine. Both pieces dwelt on charges by ex-staff members that MSIA's founder, John-Roger Hinkins, had sexually exploited them. Depending significantly upon the testimony of disgruntled ex-staff and drawing heavily on the cult stereotype, MSIA was portrayed as an organization that was created for no other purpose than to serve the financial, sexual, and ego needs of John-Roger Hinkins. After a brief moment in the spotlight, reporters turned their attention to other stories, and MSIA disappeared from the pages of the mass media.

Two events occurred in 1994 that once again brought MSIA to the attention of the media circus. First was Michael Huffington's campaign to become a California senator. Arianna Huffington, Michael Huffington's wife, was a personal friend of John-Roger, as well as a participant in MSIA. When someone in the media discovered this fact, the link became the focus of a number of sensationalistic articles in which all of the earlier accusations against John-Roger and MSIA were dragged out and uncritically repeated. In the same year as the campaign, Peter McWilliams, an ex-MSIA minister who had co-authored a series of popular books with John-Roger, dropped out of the movement and authored a bitter anti-MSIA book, *Life 102: What to Do When Your Guru Sues You* (1994), which attracted moderate media attention. As a result of this publicity, MSIA became a regular staple of anti-cult movement fare, frequently mentioned in any general discussion of the cult menace.

This relatively mild background of controversy set the stage for some of the conflicts in which MSIA has been involved. For example, in the mountains overlooking Santa Barbara, California, the Institute for the Study of the Individual and World Peace (IIWP, an organization inspired by John-Roger Hinkins, the founder of MSIA) purchased some property—later named Windermere—for the purpose of building a retreat facility. Bordered on one side by a national forest, their property is also directly adjacent to a semi-rural neighborhood populated by individuals who moved away from the city for the purpose of enjoying country living. These people viewed their new neighbor with concern. When they heard about plans to build a facility that, they imagined, would attract large numbers of outsiders from the Los Angeles area, people who would disturb their peaceful rural setting, they were upset. Eventually they organized the Cielo Preservation Organization (named after the primary road in the area, Camino Cielo) to oppose the construction of the retreat—construction which cannot proceed without approval from the county.

Not long after the negative *Los Angeles Times* piece mentioned earlier (Sipchen and Johnston 1988) appeared, almost everyone in the neighborhood received a copy. This slanted article immediately became a centerpiece legitimating the neighbors' opposition to the IIWP's retreat plans. By 1994, the *Times* report had been superseded by the considerable publicity that Arianna Huffington's MSIA connections were generating in the southern California media. Thus in a 1994 article in the local paper reporting on the conflict between Windermere and the neighborhood, Huffington and her cult connections were brought up and discussed near the beginning of the article: "His [John-Roger's] teachings drew national attention during this year's California Senate race between incumbent Diane Feinstein and Rep. Michael Huffington because the Montecito congressman's wife, Arianna, had ties to the John-Roger organization, which some critics claim is a cult. Arianna Huffington has said it is not a cult, and described her past connection with MSIA as a casual one" (Schultz 1994, 1B). Despite the cautious wording of this passage, the net effect of mentioning such accusations was that otherwise uninformed readers concluded that the cult label was probably appropriate for MSIA, influencing them to side with the ranch's neighbors.

This labeling enterprise was highly successful in generating anti-IIWP–anti-MSIA sentiment in Santa Barbara County. The point here, however, is that the Cielo Preservation Organization was less concerned about the ranch owners' religious persuasion than about preventing, in the words of a local organizer, hordes of "LA cowboys" from invading the area, thus spoiling their rural privacy. The claim that the Windermere Ranch was populated by weird cultists is what we have referred to as an ideological resource or a moral commodity—simply one among many accusations hurled at the IIWP in an all-out effort to short circuit their retreat plans.

The mention of the Huffingtons in the Santa Barbara paper alludes to an entirely different type of struggle that provides yet another example of the marshaling of the cult stereotype for deployment in a conflict not directly involving the anti-cult movement. The Feinstein-Huffington campaign for the U.S. Senate was a particularly bitter fight, with both camps relying heavily on expensive, negative TV ads. For a number of reasons, however, the media

seemed to take more offense at Michael Huffington's bid for senator than at Diane Feinstein's efforts to defend her seat in Congress.
For one thing, and this may have been his biggest sin in the eyes of
reporters, he consistently refused to be interviewed by what he felt
to be a biased liberal media. Instead, Huffington attempted to
bypass the news media altogether, appealing directly to voters
through television advertisements. Rebuffed by the Huffington
camp, the news media responded by characterizing Michael Huffington as a wealthy outsider attempting to buy a Senate seat and,
more generally, sought out and reported whatever negative bits of
information they could find on this Republican challenger.

When Arianna Huffington's connection with MSIA was discovered, the mass media in southern California immediately jumped on
the information. Uncritically repeating accusations from the 1988
Los Angeles Times piece and from McWilliams's *Life 102*, reporters
quickly reclassified Michael Huffington's senatorial bid from that
of an outsider trying to buy his way into the United States Senate
into the machinations of an evil cult leader working behind the
scenes through the candidate's wife to gain political influence for
himself and his cult agenda. This absurd accusation was repeated
(though sometimes more subtly and by implication) in a number
of articles published in major magazines (e.g., Carlson 1994). Not
a single reporter bothered to look more deeply into John-Roger
and MSIA, much less question the appropriateness of the cult
stereotype. Instead, as one might have anticipated, reporters' pre-
existing disposition to perceive Huffington negatively led them to
accept accusations of his cult connection without further reflection. It was then almost inevitable that, as prior research into the
self-fulfilling nature of stereotypes would have predicted, any new
information gathered on MSIA would be filtered through the cult
image.

The mass media are not, of course, motivated primarily by the
quest for truth. Instead, the mainstream news media are driven by
market forces and by the necessity of competing with other news-
papers, other TV news shows, and so forth. This is not to say that
reporters necessarily fabricate their stories from whole cloth.
Rather, in the case of minority religions, news people tend to ac-
centuate those facets of such groups that seem to be strange, dangerous, sensational, and the like because such portrayals titillate

consumers of news. This kind of reporting contributes to the perpetuation of the cult stereotype. However, while the news media are not particularly interested in uncovering the truth about minority religions, neither are they particularly interested in joining with the anti-cult movement to undertake a protracted campaign to destroy minority religions. Ultimately, all the mass media are concerned about is making a profit and, to the extent that the cult image helps them to accomplish this end, the media buy into— and, in turn, propagate—the stereotype as a moral commodity (Lewis 1994b).

The media may have been tipped off to the Huffingtons' MSIA link by Peter McWilliams, the disgruntled former MSIA minister who wrote *Life 102* (Sipchen 1995). McWilliams, who had co-authored a series of popular books (the Life 101 Series) with John-Roger, left MSIA in early 1994. At the time of his exit, he owed MSIA, as an employee for hire of John-Roger, hundreds of thousands of dollars in royalties. When McWilliams indicated that he had no intention of honoring his debt, MSIA sued him. McWilliams responded by writing *Life 102* (as he had previously threatened to do unless MSIA dropped pursuit of royalties owed), attempting to avoid his earlier financial commitment by conducting a campaign of defamation against John-Roger and MSIA. As part of this campaign, McWilliams mouthed the standard anti-cult line about self-serving evil gurus brainwashing helpless devotees, asserting that he was manipulated into listing John-Roger as co-author of books that he alone had written (thus relieving himself of responsibility for the royalty debt to the church founded by his former spiritual teacher). As in the other instances we have examined, McWilliams was not particularly interested in aligning himself with CAN's campaign against all minority religions. Rather, he was deploying the cult stereotype as part of an effort to marshal public opinion against MSIA, hoping thereby to tip the balance of power in his favor so that he would not be required to honor his bad debt.

To conclude this overview of MSIA-related conflicts with one final example, it has already been mentioned that the cult stereotype has been effectively deployed in some child custody cases. In the words of Michael Homer, an expert in legal cases involving minority religions, "Religious practices and beliefs have also become the subject of child custody cases where nonmembers attempt to highlight nontraditional aspects of a spouse's or ex-spouse's religion to obtain custody of a minor child. Nonmembers seek to show that the religion deviates from social normalcy and, therefore, adversely affects the child's behavior. It is argued that the church's influence is mentally, physically, and emotionally detrimental to the child's well-being. Nonmembers have been successful when the court determines that the practices complained of are not merely religious but are detrimental practices that harm the child" (1994, 129–130). In at least one case, a parent's association with MSIA was effectively used against her by the other parent in a dispute involving their mutual offspring. In this particular case, a divorced mother petitioned the court to permit her to relocate in order to take a position in an MSIA-inspired organization offering human potentials seminars. As his primary strategy for delegitimating his wife's position, the ex-husband argued that he did not want his son involved in a cult. To support his contention, he dragged up all of the old rumors about John-Roger and MSIA in an effort to prevent his ex-wife from leaving the state. Perceiving that not only would she have a difficult time winning, but also that her husband might undertake further actions that could result in her son being taken from her, she dropped her petition.

What is especially ironic about this case is that for several decades the father was deeply involved in EST—a human potentials group that has *very* frequently (*far more* frequently than MSIA) been labeled a cult. As someone whose participation in EST has likely sensitized him to the cult controversy, the ex-husband's utilization of the stereotype was clearly little more than a tactic intended to win support for his side of the case, rather than a reflection of deeply held views about the dangers of sinister cults. As the mother stated in a telephone interview, she felt that her former spouse was advised, "Shoot her where you think you can hurt her," and that her involvement in a MSIA-related organization was simply a convenient target.

The chances of this man becoming a full-time anti-cult crusader are practically nil. Here, as in the other instances we have examined, it is clear that the cult stereotype is an ideological resource, deployed without a deep investment in the stereotype per se. This way of understanding the cult image's role in particular struggles represents a variation on earlier theorizing. As has already been indicated, most recent theorizing has focused on the anti-cult movement's campaign to win acceptance of both its ideology and its agenda by the greater society. By shifting the point of focus from this broad level to more particular struggles, we are able to see that, in the context of grassroots conflicts, the cult stereotype becomes a moral commodity—an ideological resource that can easily be set aside if it is not persuasive or if some other tactic better suits the situation.

CONCLUDING REMARKS

As has been argued throughout the present chapter and the preceding two chapters, conflicts over the legitimacy or illegitimacy of religious groups can be understood as an argument over *classification*. In the context of such controversies, the authority of governmental agencies and courts that potentially threaten new religions is taken for granted. What is at issue is whether a particular group is a legitimate religion or a dangerous pseudo-religion, commonly referred to as a cult. If a given religion is successfully reclassified as a cult, then this classification is sufficient reason for legitimating its repression. Typically, however, it is only within the context of specific conflicts such as those examined above that the repressive powers of the state are actually invoked against a religious group or the members of that group.

11

SCHOLARSHIP AND THE DELEGITIMATION OF RELIGION

Although traditional ethnocentric analyses of other people's religions have been rejected by present-day academia, older patterns of prejudicial scholarship have tended to persist in the subfield of new religious movements. As a consequence, researchers have articulated judgmental points of view that, in effect, call into question the legitimacy of certain new religions. The present chapter analyzes this issue through an examination of select scholarship on a prominent Japanese new religion, Soka Gakkai International.

Analyses of the proper role of religious studies in the university—a key issue in recent discussions of religious studies as a discipline (for example, Wiebe 1999; McCutcheon 2001)—rarely mention new religious movements (NRMs). The unconscious value judgment here as elsewhere in the academy appears to be that the field is peripheral and therefore able to offer little insight into the broader concerns of religious studies. Perhaps the thorny issues raised by NRM studies are too raw and immediate, and hence get swept under the rug. In contrast to researchers who study the mating habits of earthworms or the chemical composition of meteorites—and even in contrast to colleagues who specialize in less controversial religions—new religion specialists are forced to work in a highly politicized atmosphere. Articles on controversial religious groups published in specialized academic journals can directly impact people's lives, particularly when they are cited in legal briefs and judicial decisions.

Because mainstream new religion scholars have generally been critical of the cult stereotype (particularly the notion of cult mind control; e.g., Barker 1984; Bromley and Richardson 1983; Bromley and Shupe 1981; Melton and Moore 1982), they have, in turn, been criticized by those interested in perpetuating this stereotype. One *de*legitimation strategy commonly utilized by such interest groups is to refer to academicians whose research tends to undermine anti-cult ideology as "cult apologists," implying that they are in a conspiracy with—and perhaps even covertly accept money from—malevolent religious groups. The cult apologist accusation is a handy tool because, in the hands of most anti-cultists, it is wielded as a tautology, immune to empirical disconfirmation. In other words, if a cult apologist is defined (implicitly or explicitly) as any researcher producing scholarship critical of the cult stereotype, then anyone whose scholarship is critical of the cult stereotype is ipso facto a cult apologist. This strategy allows anti-cultists to reject any scholarship with which they disagree a priori.

Anti-cultists adhering to this rhetorical strategy sometimes make it appear that sinister groups regularly seek out scholars to legitimate them and attack their critics. One of the more absurd examples of this delegitimation strategy can be found in the introduction to Michael Newton's *Raising Hell* (1993). Newton takes to task "liberal" academics who criticize the notion of occult crime— referring to them as cult apologists as if they were somehow on the payroll of the Church of Satan or, no less implausibly, as if their souls had been purchased by the Prince of Darkness himself. (For another example of this same approach, refer to Raschke 1990).

In point of fact, only a few groups—such as the Unification Church, which for many years courted academicians, presumably because of its Confucian-derived view of the importance of scholars in society—have believed that academicians wielded this kind of power. The leaders of most other new religions have been less naive about the social influence of scholars. Perhaps the only area where academic researchers have played a significant role in the cult controversy is in the discrediting of mind control notions and other aspects of the cult stereotype, making this the one area where academic specialists have entered the fray in support of new religions. The fact that some of the more prominent scholars in the field have testified against the brainwashing thesis in relevant legislative hearings and legal cases has evoked the ire of anti-cultists and is the principal evidence for their contention that such academicians have become apologists.

Of course, the primary target of anti-cultists is not scholars, but intensive religious groups. Implicitly or explicitly, the principal criticism leveled against such groups is that they are not real (that is, not *legitimate*) religions at all, but are instead elaborate con games. This line of analysis was examined in earlier chapters. A significant component of the anti-cult critique has been that intensive religious groups are illegitimate because they reject certain aspects of secular society. Alternately, among conservative Christian anti-cultists—sometimes referred to as "counter-cultists" to distinguish them from secular anti-cultists—this point is replaced by the accusation that new religions are illegitimate because they are doctrinally flawed.

Although the majority of specialists take a neutral approach, some mainstream scholars have leveled similar sorts of criticisms against controversial religious groups. Such evaluative approaches, however, run counter to the dominant consensus of contemporary religious studies. In the later half of the twentieth century, many different academic disciplines undertook critical reexaminations of earlier periods of scholarship, particularly the scholarship that was carried out by colonialist researchers. As one might anticipate, this scholarship was thoroughly (though often subtly) shaped by imperialist ideology and concerns. Such bias is particularly clear in the area of religious scholarship, where earlier writers all too often compared the religions of other peoples with Christianity, to the detriment of the former. (In this regard, refer, for example, to Whaling 1983; Sharpe, 1986).

Reacting to the excesses of the past, contemporary academic disciplines—especially religious studies—engage in a sustained effort to avoid expressing judgmental opinions about the customs and beliefs of others. Instead, the thrust of modern religious scholarship is on *understanding* rather than *judging* religious communities. Even scholars who proffer the most reductionistic kinds of explanations of religions typically refrain from making overt value judgments. This attitude is the current norm for academia. When this norm is violated, we assume that writers are expressing either personal opinion or the attitude of the faith community to which they belong. For example, when a conservative Christian undertakes a polemic against another religion, we all recognize that he or she is engaged in a partisan theological exercise and *not* doing objective scholarship.

Given this situation, no contemporary, mainstream scholar would seriously consider criticizing a traditional religion as wrong or deluded, particularly in an academic publication. However, although this may be taken for granted with respect to traditions that have persisted for centuries, it seems that the point is less obvious with respect to more recent new religions, particularly when such religions have been the subject of public controversy.

For over half a century, one of the most controversial new religions in Japan has been Soka Gakkai. Although this group has matured into a responsible member of society, its ongoing connection with reformist political activity served to keep it in the public eye. Until relatively recently, it also had a high profile as the result of sensationalist and often irresponsible media coverage. Apparently as a direct consequence of the social consensus against this religion, some scholars have felt free to pen harsh critiques of Soka Gakkai—critiques in which the goal of promoting understanding has been eclipsed by efforts to delegitimate Soka Gakkai by portraying it as deluded, wrong, and/or socially dangerous. This body of "scholarship" presents a useful case study for the paradigmatic manner in which it exemplifies inappropriate approaches to the study of religious bodies.

After briefly surveying Soka Gakkai and articulating a humanistic perspective on emergent religions, the present chapter will undertake to analyze a selection of such publications, discussing the various ways in which these writings reveal more about the polemical agendas of the authors than about the phenomena they purport to examine.

OVERVIEW OF SOKA GAKKAI INTERNATIONAL

Soka Gakkai International (SGI) is a Japanese Buddhist group with a comparatively large following in the United States and other

Western countries. Founded in the 1930s, Soka Gakkai has grown to become Japan's largest and—until the AUM Shinrikyo incident—most controversial new religion. Although classified as a new religion, SGI's roots lie in thirteenth century. (Relatively recent studies of Soka Gakkai in the West include Wilson and Dobbelaere 1994; Hammond and Machacek 1999.)

Like most other Japanese Buddhist groups, SGI belongs to the Mahayana school. One characteristic of many Mahayana Buddhist texts is that they extol the merit gained by reading, copying, and otherwise propagating that particular scripture. Reading these claims, later generations of Buddhists were led to ask the question, Which text is the most potent? This question was the subject of debate in thirteenth-century Japan, when the Buddhist reformer Nichiren concluded that the *Saddharmapundarika*—the Lotus of the True Law, better known simply as the Lotus Sutra—was the most important of all Buddhist books. In fact, the Lotus Sutra was so powerful that all one had to do was to chant *Nam-myoho-renge-kyo* (which can be translated in various ways, including "I bow to the Lotus Sutra") to gain the merit promised in its pages.

Nichiren and his teachings gave rise to a monastic movement, which eventually splintered into different sects. Soka Gakkai began as a movement of lay practitioners attached to the Nichiren Shoshu (Orthodox Nichiren Sect). By the early 1990s, Soka Gakkai had become an independent movement. The founder, Tsunesaburo Makiguchi (1871–1944), was an educator who died in prison during the Second World War. After the war, Josei Toda (1900–1958) took over as president and built Soka Gakkai into a major religion. This period of rapid growth was accompanied by negative media attention. The group matured under the presidency of Daisaku Ikeda, who became the third president of Soka Gakkai after the passing of Toda.

Soka Gakkai also spread to the United States and Europe, where it aroused controversy as a result of its intensive proselytizing activities. Although never as controversial as groups like the Hare Krishna Movement or the Unification Church, Soka Gakkai—which in the United States went under the name Nichiren Shoshu of America until after Soka Gakkai broke with Nichiren Shoshu—was not infrequently stereotyped as a brainwashing cult, particularly by anti-cult authors.

Throughout the latter half of the twentieth century, Soka Gakkai was attacked in Japan because of its support of political activity that challenged the ruling coalition. Exploiting the distrust of organized religion, distrust that characterized the public reaction to AUM Shinrikyo—the Japanese religious group responsible for the 1995 poison gas attack in the Tokyo subway system—the LDP (the Liberal Democratic Party, which was the dominant party in the ruling coalition) attempted to weaken its principal political rival, which Soka Gakkai supported. In particular, the LDP engaged in a campaign to portray religion in general, and Soka Gakkai in particular, as being incompatible with the principles of democracy. In 1999, however, the LDP underwent a sudden change of opinion and allied itself with the New Komeito Party, the party supported by Soka Gakkai. Unsurprisingly, the media assault on Soka Gakkai subsequently evaporated.

A HUMANISTIC ATTITUDE TOWARD NEW RELIGIONS

One generally accepted observation about new religions is that periods of renewed spiritual activity emerge in the wake of disruptive social and economic changes: The established vision of "how things work" no longer seems to apply, and people begin searching for new visions. Our modern world seems particularly prone to social and economic disruptions. More fundamentally, thinkers such as Jurgen Habermas have analyzed contemporary society and concluded that we are suffering from a broad-ranging "legitimation crisis" that calls into question our very foundations (Habermas 1975).

Most ordinary citizens do not, however, feel that the modern world has lost its legitimacy. As a consequence, those of us happily adjusted to the social-cultural mainstream often have a difficult time understanding intense religiosity. Academics have not been immune to this tendency. As mentioned in prior chapters, an earlier generation of sociologists of religion, seemingly obsessed with the issue of conversion to nonmainstream "sect" groups, gave excessive attention to explaining why individuals could become involved in such bizarre churches.

If, however, rather than dwelling on strange externals, we change our point of focus and attempt to really look at what might attract someone to an alternative religion, such involvement is not really difficult to understand. We live in a society that would have been an alien world to our ancestors. Surrounded by masses of people, we rarely know the names of our closest neighbors. In traditional societies, by way of contrast, everyone in a particular village knew everyone else and took care of everyone else. Most alternative religions recreate this kind of community—a community comparable to an extended family.

The family metaphor is particularly appropriate. In modern society, our families are not the close emotional units they were in traditional societies. A small religious group many times recreates the sense of belonging to a family. If one has never experienced the closeness of a traditional family, it is easy to understand how the sense of belonging to such a unit would be attractive, even healing.

Much the same can be said about worldviews. In a traditional society, beliefs about the ultimate nature of the universe are largely taken for granted. In contemporary society, by way of contrast, nothing can be taken for granted except death and taxes. We are taught to be "nice" by the educational system, but this moral teaching is not grounded in an ultimate source of value. We are also instructed in the basic skills necessary to operate in society, but public school teachers are quiet about the greater questions of death, purpose, and the meaning of life.

We may place a positive or a negative evaluation on this relativistic education, but in either case we have to acknowledge that modern culture's ambiguous approach to socialization departs radically from the socialization strategies of earlier societies. Our choices are always varying shades of gray, rather than black and white/good and bad. The results of this ambiguity may be liberating to some people, but to others it is confusing. Without some kind of ultimate grounding, this is necessarily the case.

Nontraditional religions are often criticized for offering their followers the "easy" answers that come with black-and-white thinking. However, to many of the people who belong to these religions, the seeming narrowness of such thinking can be a liberating experience: Once one has stable criteria for what is good and true, this clarity and stability can then free one to go about the business of working, loving, and living life without debilitating anxieties about meaning and value. This is not, of course, to advocate a rigid belief system, but rather to point out why such a system is attractive without depreciating adherents as being somehow weak or defective.

To advocate a humanistic approach to new religions may seem to run against the grain of recent discussions that have been sharply critical of any approach to religion not adhering to the ideal of the quest for "objective knowledge" (Wiebe 1999, xi). In the words of Donald Wiebe, "A study of religion directed toward spiritual liberation of the individual or of the human race as a whole, toward the moral welfare of the human race, or toward any ulterior end than that of knowledge itself, should not find a home in the university" (xiii). Wiebe's primary concern is that any and all *religious* agendas be systematically excluded from the discipline of religious studies. With respect to this specific concern, his argument has much merit; this same concern informs some of the criticisms that will be articulated later in this chapter. However, Wiebe's excessive focus on exorcising religion from religious studies has caused him to miss the fact that the contemporary university does *not* "exclude all values from scientific deliberation except the value called 'objective knowledge'" (xi). Instead, to take a prominent example, academics in all disciplines that conduct direct research on human subjects are compelled to adhere to strict ethical guidelines.

The Belmont Report, issued by the U.S. Department of Health, Education, and Welfare (1979), for instance, articulates three basic ethical principles that researchers should take into account—respect for persons, beneficence, and justice. To cite selectively from different sections of this report

1. Respect for Persons—To respect autonomy is to give weight to autonomous persons' considered opinions and choices while refraining from obstructing their actions unless they are clearly detrimental to others. To show lack of respect for an autonomous agent is to repudiate that person's considered judgments . . .

2. Beneficence—The term "beneficence" is often understood to cover acts of kindness or charity that go beyond strict obligation. In this document, beneficence is understood in a stronger sense, as an obligation. Two general rules have been formulated as complementary expression of beneficent actions in this sense: (1) do not harm and (2) maximize possible benefits and minimize possible harms . . .

3. Justice—Questions of justice have long been associated with social practices such as punishment, taxation and political representation. Until recently these questions have not generally been associated with scientific research [, however,] it can be seen how conceptions of justice are relevant to research involving human subjects.

Although scholars of religion rarely engage in the types of research directly addressed by these kinds of guidelines, it would be rather odd to argue that the ideals of respect, beneficence, and justice should not therefore be extended religious studies. Religion embodies many of the core beliefs and values informing the lives of the majority of the human race. Thus to analyze religion disrespectfully without concern for the possible social impact of one's research—a very real concern for scholars of NRMs, as was noted earlier—is to violate the ethos of the contemporary university. It is with reference to these values that a humanistic approach to new religions can "legitimately" be undertaken within the university environment. We will now turn to a critique of select scholarship.

SECULARIST CRITIQUES

A 1976 article, "Rise and Decline of Sokagakkai Japan and the United States," by Hideo Hashimoto and William McPherson, examines the slowdown in growth Soka Gakkai was beginning to experience by the 1970s. This is a mixed piece: The authors are clearly interested in documenting and understanding an empirical phenomenon. At the same time, it is evident that they find the group distasteful, as reflected in a number of judgmental statements found at various junctures in their discussion. These statements contribute nothing to the authors' overall analysis and only serve to make Soka Gakkai members appear defective and Soka Gakkai itself as socially undesirable.

We can capture the flavor of their discourse by isolating a series of adjectives and other characterizations that they apply to the group. In Hashimoto and McPherson's view, Soka Gakkai is simplistic, a crutch, escapist, one among many religious fads, and willing to "take advantage of the dislocations and inequities of post-war Japan" in order to gain new converts. Taken together, these items of superfluous rhetoric allow us to infer that—whatever their personal faith commitments may or may not be—the authors are judging Soka Gakkai as "bad" in terms of a marked secularist bias, making this a useful piece to examine in terms of how secularist value-judgments interfere with the task of understanding others.

The appropriate question to begin with is, Is secularism the appropriate criterion with which to judge the world of a religious community? Further, is it really so evident that secularism's offspring, modern mass society, should be regarded as the paragon of human possibilities, and any other social arrangement defective? To the contrary, for the great majority of people the advent of the modern world has not been an unmixed blessing. In fact, with the exception of the benefits conferred by technology, humanity as a whole was probably happier in traditional, premodern societies.

Prior generations of scholars used adaptation to modern, secular society as the standard for judging rationality and mental health because of an implicit evolutionary paradigm that caused them to view contemporary society as an evolutionary stage beyond traditional societies and secularism as a step above religion. It was assumed that traditional society and religion represented an earlier, childlike stage of development and that the secular social order embodied humanity's emergence into mature adulthood. (In this regard, refer to Fabian 1983). Any movement contrary to the evolutionary current, such as an individual's conversion from a secular to a religious worldview, was thus judged as regressive—a retreat from maturity to childhood. As the twenty-first century begins, these assumptions of our "academic ancestors" now strike us as quaint and naive, though their formulations continue to influence us in subtle or in not-so-subtle ways.

As was discussed earlier, new religions partially reestablish the world of traditional communities—arguably the "natural" environment for human beings. What this means for the present discussion is that, far from being symptomatic of social pathology, perhaps the emergence of new religious movements represent a *healthy*—or at least a health-seeking—response to the dislocations and inequities of modern secular society. From this more humanistic perspective, let us reexamine a few items from Hashimoto and McPherson's rhetorical dismissal of Soka Gakkai.

To begin with a citation from the latter part of the "Rise and Decline of Sokagakkai," the authors quote, with apparent disdain, a passage, from a Soka Gakkai publication, which asserts that religion will "rescue [them] from the complexities of the world" (91). It is clear Hashimoto and McPherson view this assertion as advice to retreat from mature engagement with modernity. However, to people confused by a complex, rapidly changing social environment, forced to make morally ambiguous choices in a world without ultimate meaning, it is not so self-evident that becoming an alienated cog in mass society is the most life-affirming option. Rather, the simplification introduced by conversion to a new religious movement can provide a stable context for individuals to engage in moral self-affirmation—a self-affirmation that might otherwise be stymied by the "complexities of the world."

The authors also stigmatize Soka Gakkai as "escapist." This particular characterization is interesting because of the manner in which the evaluative freight being carried by the term "escape" can be inverted when viewed from the perspective of a tale found in Soka Gakkai's primary scripture, the Lotus of the True Law. The relevant image is that of a burning house. The lesson of the parable revolves around the dilemma of an adult who must determine a way of helping a group of children *escape* from the house before they are killed in the fire. The burning building, the Lotus Sutra suggests, is like the world—it will destroy you unless you withdraw from it. From this perspective, escape is a positive act that preserves the integrity of the individual from an impossible situation. Perhaps, then, "escaping" into a religion like Soka Gakkai could also be viewed as a positive, life-affirming act.

Escapism is also one of the charges leveled (in a less dismissive way) in H. Neill McFarland's *The Rush Hour of the Gods* (1967), one of the first English-language books on Japanese new religions. *Rush Hour* was composed during the latter part of the middle period of Soka Gakkai's institutional life when it was still expanding rapidly and, in the eyes of some observers, appeared on the verge of taking over Japan. During that period, a number of different authors penned books that raised the specter of a country run by Soka Gakkai (for example, Brannen 1968; Dator 1969). These ranged from hysterical to more balanced treatments, frequently motivated by the desire to warn people that this movement was a political threat, particularly dangerous to the survival of democracy. Most of these works have long since been forgotten.

Rush Hour, however, has continued to be a useful volume be-cause it deals with a number of religions other than Soka Gakkai. *Rush Hour* has also persisted as a standard reference on the subject for lack of more adequate and up-to-date substitutes. Though in many ways McFarland echoes the concerns of other writers from the late 1950s and early 1960s, he also makes a concerted effort to balance his critical remarks with a more humane attempt to under-stand Soka Gakkai and to understand the world of Soka Gakkai members. Despite this effort, McFarland falls back on certain stereotyped, judgmental characterizations of mass movements and their participants, as expressed by such analysts as Eric Hoffer.

Hoffer (1951) describes the traits of members of social move-ments—including religious movements—with such terms and ex-pressions as "a facility for make-believe," "a proneness to hate," "credulity," and so on. These are presented as if they were objective characteristics rather than disparaging value judgments. If one ac-cepts this kind of discourse as normative, any participant in a mass movement must, by definition, be a defective, weak human being. Though personally far less prejudiced, McFarland's dependence on Hoffer as his theoretical touchstone causes him to attribute the suc-cess of Soka Gakkai to "its ability to reach a person who feels that he is nobody and to impart to him new hope and purpose by showing him a fellowship and a cause within which he can find both accep-tance and refuge" (212). Hence, what the convert is offered is this: "Not real freedom but fraternity and uniformity, signifying deliver-ance from the frustrations of independent, individual existence, are the goals" (213). This kind of rhetoric may have been tolerable when McFarland wrote *Rush Hour,* but is clearly inappropriate to the contemporary academic norm of viewing social-movement partici-pants humanely rather than as defective sociopaths.

Elsewhere, and without fully realizing the extent of his in-sight, McFarland notes that what many converts find in Soka Gakkai is a validation for "the rather primitive reliance upon magic and relic worship that is part of their folk-religious heritage" (1967, 204). This is essentially the same point—though expressed in a par-tial and prejudiced manner—that was advanced in the preceding section of this chapter, namely, that modern new religions repre-sent an attempt to reestablish the traditional world that has been the natural environment of the human species for millennia.

Let us consider finally one more item from Hashimoto and McPherson's rhetorical arsenal, namely, the notion that religion is a "crutch." This particular characterization has often been leveled against religions, and religionists have sometimes heatedly denied the accusation. Let us, however, let go of the connotations of this criticism and instead ask, What does a crutch actually do? Are crutches really so bad? To the contrary, crutches are devices that enable a person who cannot otherwise walk to exercise the power of movement. Correspondingly, many religions portray the human condition as being primarily a state of brokenness. To use the terminology of Buddha's day, human existence is *dukkha*—Pali for "out of joint." Thus the human condition is one of crippledness, and religion is the *crutch* that allows us to walk through life.

The point being made here is not that religion is good while secularism is bad (or vice versa, for that matter), but, rather, that it is not self-evident that secularism should be the standard by which religion is evaluated. Hence, instead of dismissing religion as defective because it does not live up to secularist criteria of health and well-being, a humanistic methodology—one that tries to *understand* rather than *judge* the religions of others (for example, Muesse 1999)—should attempt to describe religionists as acting out of reasonable motives rather than from errors of judgment or psychopathology. Though we may still disagree with their religion, the goal should be to avoid portraying others as weird or defective.

CRYPTO-THEOLOGICAL CRITIQUES

Another kind of critique that academics have leveled against Soka Gakkai is that some aspect of its ideology is wrong or self-contradictory. Ted Solomon's "Soka Gakkai on the Alleged Compatibility between Nichiren Buddhism and Modern Science," for instance, examines Soka Gakkai's claims that Buddhism is scientific and that Buddhist cosmology and metaphysics are compatible with modern physics. These views are expressed in Daisaku Ikeda's writings on science and religion (1968) as well as in Ikeda's conversations with the late Arnold Toynbee (Ikeda 1977). The goal of Solomon's critique is to demonstrate that Ikeda, the third president of Soka Gakkai, is *wrong*. In other words, not only is Buddhism not scientific, but also Ikeda is mistaken about the parallels to physics.

On the face of it, the thrust of this article may not strike one as being unusual or as outside the pale of academic norms. There is, however, something very peculiar about a scholar—while acting in the role of a mainstream academic—putting forward what is basically a *theological* critique of a religious leader. The highly unusual nature of this approach might be more evident if we changed the context and examined a few comparable examples of this kind of argument.

Yogis sometimes claim, for instance, that the physical body is interpenetrated by a subtle energy body or "sheath" (Sanskrit *kosha*) and that the principal structures in this paraphysical body are seven centers (chakras) lying along the spine. This subtle anatomy is the basis for certain yoga techniques, and most yogis would assert that the subtle energy sheath is "real" in a literal, non-figurative sense. Imagine, then, if a scholar of religion wrote an article contesting this claim because science is unable to demonstrate the existence of the energy body?

Or, to refer to another example, take the hypothetical situation of someone who has researched Jewish and Christian eschatology—particularly the notion of the resurrection. The same scholar has a background in the biological sciences. What if they authored an academic publication in which they critiqued eschatological notions on the basis that resurrection was scientifically impossible, hence both Jews and Christians are deluded?

In both cases, colleagues would *severely* question the appropriateness of such criticisms. The aim of mainstream religious scholarship is simply *not* to dispute the truth of other people's religious claims, even when participants in a particular religious tradition believe such claims to be true in a literal, scientific sense. Rather, the goal of mainstream academic analyses with respect to religious belief systems is to determine what others believe, why they believe what they do, and what consequences holding such beliefs have for participants.[1]

In the case at hand, it would have been more appropriate for Solomon to have questioned what led Ikeda to explore this topic and what advantages are gained for Soka Gakkai if he can convincingly demonstrate a strong compatibility between Buddhism and modern science. Instead, Solomon apparently fears that letting Ikeda's argument stand might give Soka Gakkai some actual legitimacy, and so feels compelled to dispute it. Such concerns are, however, *theological,* and hence inappropriate for a mainstream scholar.

One finds similar problems with Christina Naylor's "Nichiren, Imperialism, and the Peace Movement" (1991). This article is a strident polemic denouncing Soka Gakkai's involvement in the world peace movement as hypocritical. The primary basis for Naylor's denunciation is the "unpeaceful" sentiments expressed in the writings of Nichiren, the thirteenth-century prophet to whom Soka Gakkai looks as the inspiration for its movement. Stripped of the apparatus of scholarly discourse, footnotes and citations, her heavy-handed critique is little more than an overheated warning to her readers that Soka Gakkai is a wolf in sheep's clothing—a message more appropriate for a journalistic venue than for an academic journal.

One wonders what could possibly have motivated Naylor to have invested such passion into her article. Could it be that she is an adherent of some form of Christianity on a crusade against pagans? This seems like a reasonable assumption, given the two biblical allusions she makes in order to contrast the justice and peacefulness of Western religion with Nichiren Buddhism: "There is no call for justice, mercy, love for enemies and neighbors, honest work, or a simple lifestyle such as we find in Biblical writers" (70). "By contrast, the ideal of *shalom*—a just peace in which people's needs are so adequately and fairly met that they dance for joy—has inspired untold number of people motivated by the love of God, to pioneer or cooperate in peace programs" (75). Whether or not Naylor's theological diatribe arises out of a personal faith commitment, her mention of the Bible provides us with a perfect example with which to compare and contrast her analysis of Nichiren. Specifically, one does not have to be a student of scripture to be aware that many biblical books are not exactly blueprints for a society based on peace and love. To the contrary, the God of the Judeo-Christian scriptures is often a violent divinity who hates his enemies to the extent that he either orders his followers to destroy them or else destroys them directly with his own power.

On the basis of these parts of the Bible, would we be justified in saying that any Jews or Christians participating in the peace movement were therefore insincere and cynical? The answer here would have to be "Yes" if we subjected Western religions to the same criteria to which Naylor subjects Soka Gakkai. To drive home this point, we can take one of her statements and make the appropriate substitutions so that it applies to her own religious tradition. For instance, the last sentence in Naylor's article reads: "The claim that the inspiration for Soka Gakkai's peace programs comes from Nichiren is hard to justify" (75). Substituting Christianity for Soka Gakkai and the Bible for Nichiren, we get the following statement: The claim that the inspiration for Christianity's peace programs comes from the Bible is hard to justify. With these substitutions, the statement is at least as accurate as—and perhaps more accurate than—the original.

The point here, of course, is neither to criticize Christianity nor to defend Soka Gakkai, but, rather, to demonstrate the inappropriateness of Naylor's critique: We easily recognize the unscholarly nature of such an attack when leveled against a traditional religion, but are blind-sided when the religious group in question is a highly stigmatized organization like Soka Gakkai. Yet academics must resist allowing themselves to be swayed by popular prejudice and resist lowering the standards of what passes the test of sound scholarship. In the case at hand, the concerns expressed in "Nichiren, Imperialism, and the Peace Movement" are primarily *theological,* and hence—to agree emphatically with Wiebe (1999) on this point—inappropriate for mainstream scholarship.

CONCLUDING REMARKS

We began by noting that, although certain kinds of analyses of religion have been rejected by the academic mainstream, older patterns of prejudicial scholarship have tended to persist in the subfield of new religious movements. Although there is no sound reason for continuing to permit writers to articulate judgmental points of view that call into question the legitimacy of minority religions, popular prejudice against such religions has served to make us "tone-deaf" to a scholar's biases against such groups.

It was also noted that NRM researchers are forced to work in a highly politicized atmosphere. One result of this situation is that, unlike most other academic specialties, NRM scholarship can have ramifications outside the university for the groups we study. Thus, by producing scholarship that reinforces popular stereotypes, NRM specialists can unwittingly supply ammunition for critics seeking to destroy minority religions by challenging their legitimacy.

The present chapter analyzed select scholarship on Soka Gakkai International, an organization chosen because it has been highly controversial and because a reasonable quantity of articles and books has been composed on the group. It was also argued that the scholar's first goal should always be to articulate a humanly meaningful *understanding* of a given religion—both an understanding of the world of the participants as well as an understanding of what such religions mean for society as a whole.

CONCLUSION

One of the reasons scholars of new religious movements have not bothered to analyze the notion of legitimation is that, for the purpose of understanding the groups they study, it appears to be a simple concept. However, like many other taken-for-granted ideas, there are nuances in legitimacy that easily escape the casual observer.

Weber made it clear that he was discussing ideal types, meaning that in the empirical world one would never be able to find a pure example of charismatic authority. However, no later discussions of charisma have taken the further step of explicitly examining how the other sources of legitimacy analyzed by Weber might be deployed in modified ways by charismatic leaders.

The contribution of the present study was to advance the understanding of legitimacy by discussing a variety of ways in which new religions draw on the authority of charisma, tradition, and rationality. This was accomplished by introducing the notion of *legitimation strategies*. In the introductory chapter, a provisional list of specific strategies was drawn up. A selection of these strategies was then explicated via a series of case studies in chapters 1 through 7.

The complementary idea of delegitimation was introduced in chapter 8 and constituted the central theme of the balance of the study. The specific contribution of this later discussion to the notion of legitimacy was the simple but nevertheless important observation that conflicts over the legitimacy or illegitimacy of religious groups can be understood as an argument over *classification*. In the context of such controversies, the authority of governmental agencies and courts that potentially threaten new religions is taken for granted. What is at issue is whether the group in question should be classified as a legitimate religion and left alone or classified as a harmful pseudo-religion and repressed.

In the course of analyzing the dynamics of legitimation, the present study also addressed a number of other theoretical issues. In chapters 1 and 2, the contribution of religious experience to the generation of new religious movements was explored. Such experiences are especially important for legitimating new religions in the minds of their founders. The centrality of religious experiences for understanding the origins of religion has been a major theme in the approach of such important religious studies theorists as Otto, Wach, and Eliade. It is thus surprising that no one has brought these analytic categories to bear on contemporary new religions.

Some of the reasons for this were discussed. One factor examined was the discipline of religious studies' own quest for legitimacy, which influenced religious studies academicians to leave the field of new religions to social scientists. Another related factor was the perception of new religious movements as a trivial phenomenon. Drawing on the audience cult–client cult–cult movement distinction articulated by Stark and Bainbridge, it was argued that if audience cults and client cults are set aside, many of the remaining movements are serious *religious* movements for which traditional religious studies categories are more relevant.

However, other kinds of problems emerge when we attempt to apply these categories to new religions arising within Protestant Christianity. Emphasizing the importance of religious experience in the formation of new religions in this tradition is problematic because hierophanic and/or theophanic religious experiences are often not relevant to the founding of new Protestant sects and denominational bodies. Even after we delete from consideration the new organizations formed in response to internal political disputes, organizations that do not actually constitute new *religions*, there are still a host of new groups that emerge out of significant doctrinal disagreements. Though these conflicts rarely generate completely new religious *traditions,* the sects thus formed *are* technically new *religions.* And although a doctrinal dispute can have its roots in a deep religious experience, this is just as often not the case. Similar exceptions can be found in the formation of new sects in other religious traditions. This category of exceptions seems never to have been addressed in discussions of the origins of religion within the discipline of religious studies.

In chapters 2 and 6, the commonsense view of new religious movements as unstable and ephemeral was discussed. The conventional wisdom that views the death of the founding prophet as a crisis leading to the death of the prophet's movement has almost no empirical foundation. A factor that has sometimes led academics to attribute ephemerality to new religions is a mistaken theoretical perspective that portrays the personal charisma of the founder as the glue holding together alternate views of reality. Such a perspective misconstrues the role of charisma.

On the one hand, no matter how much personal charisma a prophet might have, his or her message must always address the concerns of the community in a satisfactory manner. On the other hand, though the prophet's charisma may be a key initial factor, the adoption of a new religion by a group of followers recruits the forces of social consensus to the side of the new revelation—forces that tend to maintain the alternate vision of reality independently of the founder. As a consequence, as long as a new religion continues satisfactorily to address the concerns of followers, even things like a failed prophecy or a leader's blatant hypocrisy will not necessarily induce a crisis of faith.

This point was amplified by noting that, in contrast to ideal-type prophets, empirical prophets do not rely upon personal charisma as their sole source of legitimation. Instead, they plant their new visions on the familiar foundations of a pre-existing cultural-religious matrix, which helps their new teachings to appear plausible (that is, "legitimate") to potential recruits. In other words, despite what critics of new religions sometimes allege, founders of new movements do not simply invent their religious systems out of their fertile imaginations with no reference to the surrounding cultural milieu.

Beyond showing that the issue of legitimacy in the cult controversy is a classification issue, most of the discussion in part 2 did not contribute new theoretical insights. The one possible exception to this was chapter 10, which called attention to an area missed in previous analyses. As indicated in that chapter, most older theorizing focused on individual conversions (what we might refer to as the micro level) while recent scholarship has focused on the larger social dynamics of new religious movements and on the anti-cult movement's campaign to win acceptance of its viewpoint by society (the macro level). By shifting the point of focus to specific struggles, it was found that there is an intermediate level at which the cult stereotype has become a moral commodity. In other words, this stereotype has become an ideological resource that individuals with no investment in the larger anti-cult cause deploy for winning support for their side of a particular conflict.

The bulk of the discussion in part 1 attempted to clarify the notion of legitimation strategies by examining a handful of specific strategies in the context of different case studies. For instance, through the legend of Jesus' journey to India, chapter 3 analyzed the phenomenon of the fabrication of a pseudo-tradition as a legitimation strategy. The larger significance of this particular discussion for religious studies is that the history of religions contains innumerable examples of forged scriptures—including documents in the scriptural canons of major world religions like Christianity and Buddhism. This legitimation strategy is thus a concrete example of how the study of contemporary new religions potentially sheds light on our understanding of older religious traditions, if only because such an approach compels us to view familiar phenomena against the backdrop of unfamiliar comparisons.

More generally, it is hoped that efforts like the present book will contribute to the desegregation of NRM studies from the larger discipline of religious studies. On the one hand, as has been argued in these pages, approaches to religion formulated by religious studies theorists should be explored more thoroughly for potential insights into the dynamics of NRMs. On the other hand, as noted with respect to the issue of the forging of scriptures, studies of current new religions can deepen our the understanding of more established religions. In view of the potential for mutual benefit, it is only a matter of time before the field of NRMs breaks out of its ghetto and joins the mainstream of religious studies.

Appendix A: Satanist Survey

The data for the research in Chapter 5 was gathered from an internet survey conducted in 2000–2001. In order to attract a significant sample, I constructed a simple, twenty-item questionnaire that could be answered in five or ten minutes. I also included a few open-ended items which allowed respondents to expound their thoughts at greater length, if they felt so inclined. Through email addresses posted on Satanist web sites, I began sending out questionnaires in early August 2000. Also, several of the people I contacted for information on their *organizations* agreed to post the questionnaire on their respective web sites. By the end of February 2001, I had received 140 responses, which I felt was adequate to use as the basis for constructing a preliminary profile. I also sent out a more ambitious follow-up questionnaire to respondents who had expressed interest in participating in further research. I received several dozen thoughtful responses to the second mailing.

I should finally note that I sent earlier versions of the present report to some of my Satanist contacts. A number of these individuals provided me with useful feedback and critical commentary. The most obvious criticism was that I might have missed a significant subgroup of Satanists who do not surf the web and who therefore would not have an opportunity to respond to the questionnaire. Although this criticism has merit, it would be difficult to address adequately, given that there exists no national directory of Satanists to utilize as a basis for mailing questionnaires to individuals not on line. On the other hand, most of my contacts noted that the great majority of modern Satanists *are* plugged into the internet and, furthermore, asserted that at the present time the primary arena for Satanist activity is the world wide web. This input gives me confidence that the individuals who responded to the questionnaire constitute as good a sample as one might reasonably hope to obtain, given the problems inherent in the task of contacting members of a decentralized subculture.

Another, related issue is the problem of where to draw the line between religious Satanists and Satanic "dabblers." This distinction was stressed to me by the web master of the Satanic Media Watch in a series of email communications. She notes, for instance,

> For every serious Satanist you can find online I would guess you could find at least two teens who are into Heavy Metal music, who never read anything on Satanism, and who have problems in their personal lives. Heavy Metal teens who are into vandalism form local groups and do not go online. It would also be very hard to make them take part in any survey. As you know there are many kinds of Satanists. A lot of teens fit [popular] stereotypes rather well. If you do not take this into account and show the public a false picture of Satanism, you will make the public accuse serious Satanists for the actions of teens. I think you need to explain the difference between at least these two groups, and that your survey does not cover both groups.

Though I question the two-to-one ratio, I would agree that there are some adolescents who dabble in Satanism and who have no interest in Satanism as a religion. Also, anyone who has read *The Satanic Bible* knows that Anton LaVey explicitly and strongly rejects unlawful activity, which places senseless vandalism beyond the pale of modern religious Satanism. At the same time, it should also be noted that some serious Satanists start out as Satanic dabblers, which means that there are some hazy areas in the line dividing genuine Satanists from those who merely adopt Satanic trappings.

STATISTICAL FINDINGS

The average Satanist is twenty-six years old (ranging from fourteen to fifty-six) and has been a Satanist for eight years (ranging from less than a year to forty-four years for an individual who claimed to have been raised in a Satanist household). This means that the average Satanist became involved at age eighteen. The youthfulness of this average is not surprising, but the length of involvement is. Even when the respondents who claimed to have been Satanists all their lives are excluded, the average age only drops to twenty-five and the length of involvement to seven years. This means the average age at which someone becomes involved is still eighteen.

Most Satanists are male. One hundred and one survey respondents were male, thirty-six were female, and two marked the item "not applicable." The heavy predominance of males sets Satanism apart from the active memberships of most other religious bodies, old or new.

Most Satanists are single (see table A.1). Ninety-six respondents—a full two-thirds of the sample—were single (though a few noted they were in long-term relationships and a few others that they were engaged), thirty-two were married, and twelve were divorced or separated. Thirty-one had children (eleven with one child, twelve with two children, seven with three children, and one with four children). This is not an unsurprising pattern, given the relative youth of Satanists.

Most Satanists are Caucasian. Two respondents were Asian-American, three Black, nine Hispanic, and eleven noted that at least one of their ancestors was Native American. Two other respondents indicated that they were "multi-racial," one was Turkish, and one was Indian (South Asian). Everyone else was "pure" Caucasian. This is also not surprising. Demographic studies of other alternative religions have found the predominance of participants to be White.

Table A.1. Marital Status

STATUS	COUNT	PERCENTAGE*
Single	96	69
Married	32	23
Divorced/separated	12	9

*Because percentages are rounded off throughout this report, they will sometimes total more, and sometimes less, than 100%.

Table A.2. Geographical Distribution

STATE/COUNTRY	COUNT	PERCENTAGE
Canada	9	6
United Kingdom	6	4
Netherlands	5	4
Australia	5	4
Denmark	3	2
Other countries*	11	8
California	13	9
Texas	9	6
Wisconsin	7	5
Virginia	7	5
Colorado	6	7
New York	6	7
Massachusetts	5	4
North Carolina	5	4
Pennsylvania	4	3
Oklahoma	3	2
Other U.S. states	56	40

*One respondent each from Germany, South Africa, Poland, Czech Republic, Sweden, New Zealand, India, Estonia, Russia, and the Philippines. One respondent also indicated South America without specifying a country.

Thirty-nine respondents (28 percent) lived outside of the United States. Nine were Canadian. Six lived in the United Kingdom, five in Australia, five in the Netherlands, and three in Denmark. U.S. respondents were spread across the country. The top Satanist states were California (13), Texas (9), Wisconsin (7), Virginia (7), Colorado (6), New York (6), Massachusetts (5), and North Carolina (5). While one might have expected to find more Satanists in California, thirteen respondents represent only 9 percent of the total, making this predominance less marked than anticipated (see table A.2).

The average Satanist has between one and a half and two years of college. Among respondents, twenty-five were college graduates and nine of these held advanced degrees. Forty respondents indicated they were currently in school. As the questionnaire did not explicitly ask about student status, more than these forty were likely students (see table A.3).

Satanists are employed in diverse occupations. Eighteen respondents were involved with computers and/or the internet. Forty were students. And eleven were writers or artists (fourteen, if

Table A.3. Education

YEARS/HIGHEST DEGREE	COUNT	PERCENTAGE
No college or nonresponse	55	39
1 year of college	19	14
2 years	28	20
3 years	11	8
Bachelor's	16	11
Master's	9	6

web writers are included). Otherwise, they ran the gamut from stripper to clinical psychologist and from salesman to engineer (see table A.4). With respect to the writer–artist category, one of my contacts, the web master of the Satanic Media Watch, offered the criticism that "'Satanic writers and artists' only do work on Web-Pages or in satanic magazines. In Satanism many people view the artist as an ideal and that makes a lot of Satanists want to view themselves as writers and artist. But the truth is, that most of them do not earn any money from their art." Although this observation is accurate with respect to some respondents, at least six—and maybe more—of these eleven respondents actually do make their livings as graphic artists and professional writers.

Satanists are politically diverse. Fourteen respondents were Democrats, nine Republicans, sixty-three nonpolitical, and forty-one Independent or Third Party. The significant number of Independent or Third Party respondents markedly sets Satanists apart from the larger population. This finding is congruent with what one might anticipate from people following an individualistic philosophy (see table A.5).

Table A.4. Employment

OCCUPATION	COUNT	PERCENTAGE
Student	40	29
Computers/internet	18	13
Writer/artist	11	8
Sales/retail clerk	11	8
Restaurant worker	9	6
Healthcare	7	5
Police/security	5	4

Table A.5. *Political Affiliation*

PARTY	COUNT	PERCENTAGE
Democrat	14	10
Republican	9	6
Libertarian	15	11
Green	8	6
Socialist	2	1
Communist	1	1
Anarchist	5	4
Independent	20	14
None	63	45

The traditions in which Satanists are raised reflect the general pattern of the larger society. Two respondents were raised as secular Jews, twenty-eight were raised Catholic, seventy-seven were raised Protestant (sixteen explicitly mentioned Baptist and nine mentioned Lutheran), and twenty-three put nothing or no response. Many respondents indicated that their Christian upbringing was nominal, though several were the children of ministers. The only unusual responses were two respondents who were raised Neopagan and two raised as Satanists (see table A.6).

People become involved in Satanism in diverse ways, though more often through reading and personal study: Sixty-four said they became involved through personal study/books (thirty explicitly mentioned the *Satanic Bible*), twenty-four through other people, seventeen through the internet, and two through music (one specifically mentioned Marilyn Manson). Other responses were harder to classify: One respondent, for instance, said he became interested in Satanism as the result of a Geraldo Rivera program; another, that he became interested as a result of taking a

Table A.6. *Religious Heritage*

RELIGION	NUMBER	PERCENTAGE
Protestant	77	55
Catholic	28	20
Jewish	2	1
Neopagan	2	1
Satanist	2	1
None or no response	23	16

Table A.7. Introduction to Satanism

MEDIUM	COUNT	PERCENTAGE
Friend/acquaintance	24	17
The Satanic Bible	30	21
Other reading/study	34	24
Internet	17	12
Music	2	1
Other	28	20

religious studies class. If the seventeen internet responses are added to the sixty-four personal study/book responses, we can assert that the majority of Satanists become involved through reading (see table A.7).

Most Satanists have been involved in other religions, usually Neopaganism or some other magical group: Forty-five respondents (slightly less than a third of the sample) indicated that, beyond the religion in which they were raised, they had not been involved in any other form of spirituality before coming to Satanism. Forty-eight mentioned Neopaganism, twenty-two some other "left-hand path" (e.g., Thelemic Magic, Chaos Magic), twenty-one an Eastern religion (fifteen Buddhism), and fourteen some form of Christianity (not counting the religion in which they were raised). These add up to more than the total number of respondents because twenty-two people had been involved in more than one other religion (see table A.8).

There is no typical pattern to involvement in Satanist groups. Sixty-seven respondents had never been involved in such a group, thirty-five are or have been involved in only one group, and thirty-eight have been or are involved in more than one group (see table A.9).

Table A.8. Other Religions

RELIGIONS	COUNT	PERCENTAGE
Neopagan/Wicca	48	34
Left-hand path	22	16
Eastern	21	15
Christianity	14	10
None	45	32

Table A.9. Satanist Group Involvement

NUMBER OF GROUPS	COUNT	PERCENTAGE
None	67	48
One	35	25
Two–three	21	15
Four–five	11	8
More than five	6	4

Most Satanists are humanistic (atheistic and/or agnostic) Satanists, reflecting the dominant influence of Anton LaVey's thought. Sixty percent of respondents (eighty-four) said that Satan was a symbol, an archetype, myself, nature, or some other anti-theistic understanding of Satan. Twenty-five indicated that Satan was an impersonal force. (Though not regarded as "supernatural," this force is something not adequately understood by current science.) Nineteen were theistic Satanists, although even most of these respondents did not have what one would call a traditional view of Satan/God/demons. Twelve respondents did not answer this item.

Satanists believe in the efficacy of magic. Only fourteen respondents stated that they did not believe in magic. Fifteen others did not respond to this item. The balance did answer this question, though they often noted that magic was not supernatural. This again reflects the influence of LaVey on this issue.

Eight-five respondents never meet with other co-religionists for religious–ritual purposes, thirty-one rarely, and everyone else ran the gamut from one or two times a year to every week. In other words, more than 80 percent of all respondents rarely or never meet with co-religionists for religious–ritual purposes.

Finally, the Satanist community is an internet community. While more than half of all Satanists do not meet with their co-religionists face-to-face, fifty-eight communicate with others in talk rooms or via email on a *daily* basis and another thirty-one communicate frequently. This finding is congruent with the scattered geographical distribution of Satanists.

SATANIST PROFILE

With a limited sample such as this, it is difficult to draw hard-and-fast conclusions. The representativeness of the sample partially depends on the size of the population from which the sample is drawn. Some of my Satanist contacts "guestimate" the total number of practicing, self-identified Satanists in North America to be no more than seven hundred to eight hundred. If this is the case, then the number of respondents represents a good sample.

To construct a statistical caricature, we could say that the average Satanist is an unmarried, white male in his mid-twenties with a few years of college. He became involved in Satanism through something he read in high school, and has been a self-identified Satanist for seven or eight years. Raised Christian, he explored one non-Satanist religious group beyond the one in which he was raised before settling into Satanism. His view of Satan is some variety of non-theistic humanism and he practices magic. His primary interaction with his co-religionists is via email and internet chat rooms.

Although this profile is statistically accurate with respect to the sample, there are obvious problems with regarding it as a static datum. Specifically, the relative youth of Satanists indicates that, if a similar questionnaire was sent to this same set of respondents five or ten years from now, a significantly higher percentage would be married college graduates with children. The occupational aspect of the profile would also likely be somewhat different. In other words, the survey's finding that a majority of questionnaire respondents are single and have not finished college does not mean that one can therefore conclude that most Satanists are "socially challenged" dropouts.

Appendix B: Ex-member Survey

The data for the research mentioned in chapters 8 and 9 were gathered by means of a mail survey conducted in 1984. The sample consisted of 154 ex-members of groups often labeled cults: the Unification Church (26 percent), Yogi Bhajan's 3HO (23 percent), the Hare Krishna Movement (20 percent), the Way International (16 percent), the Divine Light Mission (8 percent), the Church of Scientology (1 percent), and miscellaneous groups (5 percent). Anti-cult groups put me in touch with 72 ex-members, 72 percent of whom responded, plus 37 snowballs (contacted on reference of other respondents). I was directly or indirectly acquainted with 25 ex-members, 68 percent of whom responded (plus 4 snowballs). The Unification Church gave me a list of 16 former Unificationists, 62 percent of whom responded. The lists of former followers/devotees which the Way International and the Hare Krishna Movement passed on to me contained many partial and out-of-date addresses, so it is difficult to estimate response rates for these sample sources. As well as could be determined, there was no evidence of intentional bias in the lists of ex-members that the anti-cult groups and the new religions passed on to me. The strongest evidence for non-bias was the similarity of the two subsamples. For example, 21 percent of the former members in the sample from the new religions were coercively deprogrammed, while 26 percent of the ex-members in the anti-cult sample were coercively deprogrammed. Of greater importance for indicating the non-presence of intentional bias, the patterns of responses relative to mode of exit were comparable.

Forty-five percent of the respondents were females and 55 percent were males. Median age at recruitment was twenty-one, with a broad range of fourteen to forty-five. Average length of involvement was four and one-fourth years with a range of several weeks to thirteen years. Consistent with previous studies (for example, Solomon 1981; Wright 1984), the great majority of respondents were Caucasian (all but three Blacks). In terms of religious upbringing there were, again consistent with previous research, a disproportionately greater number of subjects from Jewish and Catholic backgrounds: 18 percent Jewish, 34 percent Catholic, 39 percent Protestant, and 10 percent who either had no religious affiliation or who did not respond to the item. At the time they joined, 4 percent had some kind of advanced degree, 26 percent had completed college, 41 percent had at least some college, 23 percent had completed high school, and 6 percent had not completed high school. Fifty-eight percent of the respondents left voluntarily and were not exposed to any form of anti-cult counseling, 19 percent voluntarily experienced some form of anti-cult counseling, and 23 percent were coercively deprogrammed.

As noted in the acknowledgments, this research was supported by grants from the Society for the Scientific Study of Religion and Syracuse University. Data from the survey formed the basis for three papers (Lewis 1986; Lewis and Bromley 1987; Lewis 1990).

Notes

INTRODUCTION

1. Various observers, including critics like Russell T. McCutcheon, have perceived these three theorists as the primary thinkers in a specific religious studies "tradition" (McCutcheon 1999, 69).

Chapter 4: SCIENCE, TECHNOLOGY, AND THE SPACE BROTHERS

1. Reprinted in 1998 as the first part of *The True Face of God*, by Rael.

Chapter 5: ANTON LAVEY, *THE SATANIC BIBLE*, AND THE SATANIST TRADITION

The basis for the current chapter is a paper on *The Satanic Bible,* presented at the International CESNUR Conference, "Minority Religions, Social Change, and Freedom of Conscience," Salt Lake City and Provo, June 20–23, 2002. Also, certain parts of this chapter have been adapted from sections of my articles "Who Serves Satan?" (Lewis 2001) and "Diabolical Authority" (Lewis 2002a). A special word of thanks to Satanists who provided me with thoughtful feedback on earlier drafts of this paper, particularly feedback from several members of the Obsidian Enlightenment and the Temple of Lylyth. One comment of particular note was that the social organization (or, perhaps more appropriately, *dis*organization) of modern Satanism cannot accurately be characterized as a "movement," "community," or "subculture." I have nevertheless used these terms throughout for lack of more adequate terminology. Another comment was that "conversion" is not appropriate in the context of Satanism. Again, however, I left this term in the chapter for lack of a better word. Finally, I was informed that Satanists prefer to refer to their community as the *Satanic* community (movement, subculture, etc.) rather than the *Satanist* community; I have tried to adhere to this convention throughout the present chapter.

1. Information on foreign-language editions is courtesy of Peter H. Gilmore, high priest of the Church of Satan.

2. Of my respondents, 110 (almost 80%) were North American. Because European Satanism is a somewhat different phenomenon, one should therefore be cautious about making inferences to European Satanism based on my survey findings.

Chapter 10: THE CULT STEREOTYPE AS AN IDEOLOGICAL RESOURCE

1. I have also discussed the anti-cult movement and the social psychology of stereotyping in my "Self-Fulfilling Stereotypes, the Anticult Movement, and the Waco Confrontation" (Lewis 1995b).
2. Secular anti-cult organizations such as the Cult Awareness Network should be clearly distinguished from Evangelical Christian anti-cult groups. The Christian anti-cult movement stands in marked contrast to the secular anti-cult movement by its focus on theological issues. While the religions criticized by Christian anti-cultists may be accused of exploiting and brainwashing their members, the more important accusation is their theological divergence from Evangelical Christianity. The Christian anti-cult movement, unlike the secular anti-cult movement, has also distanced itself from the practice of deprogramming (Melton 1992).

Chapter 11: SCHOLARSHIP AND THE DELEGITIMATION OF RELIGION

1. To the extent that McCutcheon's scholar-as-culture-critic (2001) would actively challenge the validity of religion—which, to my way of thinking, would resurrect the worst aspect of traditional comparative religion in secular guise—I would have to disagree that this should be the role of religious studies.

References

Aberle, David F. 1956. "The Prophet Dance and Reactions to White Contact." *Journal of Anthropological Research* 15.

Abhedananda, Swami. 1929. *Parivrajaka Swami Abhedananda*. Rev. 2nd ed. under editorship of Swami Prajnananda. Calcutta: Ramakrishna Vedanta Math.

———. 1954. *Kashmir O Tibbate* (In Kashmir and Tibet). Calcutta: Ramakrishna Vedanta Math.

About MSIA: The Movement of Spiritual Inner Awareness. n.d. MSIA brochure. Los Angeles: Church of the Movement of Spiritual Inner Awareness.

Adamski, George. 1955. *Inside the Space Ships*. New York: Abelard-Schuman.

Adamski, George, and Desmond Leslie. 1953. *Flying Saucers Have Landed*. New York: British Book Centre.

Alfred, Randall H. 1976. In *The New Religious Consciousness*, ed. Charles Y. Glock and Robert N. Bellak. Berkley: University of California Press.

Andre, Judith. 1988. "Stereotypes: Conceptual and Normative Considerations." In *Racism and Sexism*, ed. Paula Rothenberg. New York: St. Martins.

Anthony, Dick, Thomas Robbins, and Jim McCarthy. 1980. "Legitimating Repression." *Society* 17:3 (March/April).

Aquino, Michael A. 1999. *The Church of Satan*. 4th ed. Self-published.

Arnold, Thomas. 1806. *Observations on the Nature, Kinds, Causes, and Prevention of Insanity*. 2nd ed. London: Richard Phillips.

Arrington, Leonard J., and David Bitton. 1979. *The Mormon Experience*. New York: Alfred A. Knopf.

Arrington, Leonard J., and John Haupt. 1968. "Intolerable Zion: The Image of Mormonism in Nineteenth-Century American Literature." *Western Humanities Review* 22:3.

Baddeley, Gavin. 1999. *Lucifer Rising: Sin, Devil Worship, and Rock 'n' Roll*. London: Plexus.

Bailey, Paul. 1957. *Wovoka: The Indian Messiah*. Los Angeles: Westernlore Press.

Bainbridge, William Sims. 1984. "Religious Insanity in America: The Official Nineteenth-Century Theory." *Sociological Analysis* 45:3.

Bainbridge, William Sims, and Rodney Stark. 1979. "Cult Formation: Three Compatible Models." *Sociological Analysis* 40.

―――. 1980. "Client and Audience Cults in America." *Sociological Analysis* 41.

Balch, Robert W. 1995. "Waiting for the Ships: Disillusionment and the Revitalization of Faith in Bo and Peep's UFO Cult." In *The Gods Have Landed: New Religions from Other Worlds*, by James R. Lewis. Albany: State University of New York Press.

Ballard, Guy W. 1982. *Unveiled Mysteries*. 4th ed. 1935. Reprint, Chicago: St. Germain Press.

Barker, Eileen. 1984. *The Making of a Moonie: Choice or Brainwashing?* Oxford: Blackwell.

Barnett, H. G. 1972. *Indian Shakers*. 1957. Reprint, London: Feffer & Simons.

Barton, Blanche. 1990. *The Secret Life of a Satanist: The Authorized Biography of Anton LaVey*. Los Angeles, Calif.: Feral House.

―――. n.d. "Sycophants Unite!" http://www.churchofsatan.com/home.html.

Beach, Marery Ann. 1985. "The Waptashi Prophet and the Feather Religion: Derivative of the Washani." *American Indian Quarterly* 9.

Becker, Carl L. 1932. *The Heavenly City of the Eighteenth-Century Philosophers*. New Haven: Yale University Press.

Bednarowski, Mary Farrell. 1989. *New Religions and the Theological Imagination in America*. Bloomington: Indiana University Press.

Belisle, Orvilla A. 1855. *The Prophets; or, Mormonism Unveiled*. Philadelphia: W. M. White Smith.

Bell, Alfreda Eva. 1855. *Boadicea: The Mormon Wife*. Baltimore: Arthur R. Orion.

Berger, Peter L., and Thomas Luckmann. 1966. *The Social Construction of Reality*. Garden City, N.Y.: Anchor Books.

Bergesen, Albert. 1984. *The Sacred and the Subversive: Political Witch-Hunts as National Rituals*. Storrs, Conn.: SSSR Monograph Series.

Bethurum, Truman. 1954. *Aboard a Flying Saucer*. Los Angeles: DeVorss.

Bock, Janet. 1980. *The Jesus Mystery: Of Lost Years and Unknown Travels*. Los Angeles: Aura Books.

Brannen, Noah S. 1968. *Soka Gakkai: Japan's Militant Buddhists*. Richmond: John Knox Press.

Brigham, Amariah. 1835. *Observations on the Influence of Religion upon the Health and Physical Welfare of Mankind*. Boston: March, Capen & Lyon.

"Brinton: The Religious Sentiment." 1876. *Journal of Nervous and Mental Disease* 3.

Bromley, David G., and Anson D. Shupe. 1981. *Strange Gods: The Great American Cult Scare*. Boston: Beacon.

Bromley, David G., and James T. Richardson, eds. 1983. *The Brainwashing/Deprogramming Controversy: Sociological, Psychological, Legal, and Historical Perspectives*. New York: Edwin Mellen.

Bromley, David G., Anson Shupe, and J. C. Ventimiglia. 1979. "Atrocity Tales, the Unification Church, and the Social Construction of Evil." *Journal of Communication* 29:3.

Brown, Leslie. 1982. *The Indian Christians of St. Thomas: An Account of the Ancient Syrian Church of Malabar*. Cambridge, U.K.: Cambridge University Press.

Bunker, Gary L., and David Bitton. 1975. "Mesmerism and Mormonism." *BYU Studies* 15:2 (winter).

―――. 1983. *The Mormon Graphic Image, 1834–1914: Cartoons, Caricatures, and Illustrations*. Salt Lake City: University of Utah Press.

Burrows, George Man. 1828. *Commentaries on the Causes, Forms, Symptoms, and Treatment, Moral and Medical, of Insanity*. London: Thomas and George Underwood.

Campbell, Colin. 1972. "The Cult, the Cultic Milieu and Secularization." In *A Sociological Yearbook of Religion in Britain*, ed. M. Hill, vol. 5. London: SCM Press.

Cardno, J. A. 1968. "The Aetiology of Insanity: Some Early American Views." *Journal of the History of the Behavioral Sciences* 4:2 (April).

Carlson, Margaret. 1994. "Should the Huffingtons Be Stopped?" *Time Magazine*, October 3.

Cartwright, Samuel A. 1851. "Report on the Disease and Physical Peculiarities of the Negro Race." *New Orleans Medical and Surgical Journal* 7 (May).

Cayce, Hugh Lynn. 1980. *Earth Changes Update*. Virginia Beach: A.R.E. Press.

Chorover, Stephen. 1980. "Mental Health as a Social Weapon." In *New Religions and Mental Health*, ed. Herbert Richardson. New York: Edwin Mellen.

Chryssides, George D. 1999. *Exploring New Religions*. London: Cassell.

"The Church of Satan Information Pack." n.d. http://www.churchofsatan.com/ Pages/cosinfopack.pdf.

"Church of Satan Youth Communique." n.d. http://www.churchofsatan.com/ home.html.

Clark [channeled by Katar]. 1988. "Back to School—Earth Revisited." *Open Channel: A Journal with Spirit* 2 (November/December).

Clark, Jerome. 1998. *The UFO Encyclopedia: The Phenomenon from the Beginning.* 2nd ed. Detroit: Omnigraphics.

Clark, John G., Jr., Michael D. Langone, Robert E. Schecter, and Roger C. G. Daily. 1981. *Destructive Cult Conversion: Theory, Research, and Treatment.* Weston, Mass.: American Family Foundation.

Cohen, Daniel. 1977. *Myths of the Space Age.* New York: Dodd, Mead.

Conolly, D. 1848. "The Good and Evil of Religious Observances in Relation to Insanity." *American Journal of Insanity* 4 (January).

Conrad, Peter, and Joseph W. Schneider. 1980. *Deviance and Medicalization: From Badness to Sickness.* St. Louis: C. V. Mosby.

Conway, Flo, and Jim Siegelman. 1979. *Snapping: America's Epidemic of Sudden Personality Change.* New York: Lippencott.

———. 1982. "Information Disease: Have Cults Created a New Mental Illness?" *Science Digest* (January).

Conway, Flo, James H. Siegelman, Carl W. Carmichael, and John Coggins. 1986. "Information Disease: Effects of Covert Induction and Deprogramming." *Update* 10:2 (June).

Cox, Harvey. 1978. "Deep Structures in the Study of New Religions." In *Understanding the New Religions,* ed. Jacob Needleman and George Baker. New York: Crossroad.

———. 1983. "Interview with Harvey Cox." In *Hare Krishna, Hare Krishna,* ed. Steven J. Gelberg. New York: Grove.

Crawford, S. Cromwell. 1987. *Ram Mohan Roy.* New York: Paragon.

Cult Observer. 1986. "IRS Seeks Information from Ex-Members on Way International's Political Involvement." *Cult Observer* 3:3.

Curran, Douglas. 1985. *In Advance of the Landing: Folk Concepts of Outer Space.* New York: Abbeville Press.

Dain, Norman. 1964. *Concepts of Insanity in the United States, 1789–1865.* New Brunswick: Rutgers University Press.

Das, Sisir Kumar. 1974. "Religious Thought." In *Rammohun Roy: Bi-Centenary Tribute,* ed. Niharranjan Ray. New Delhi: National Book Trust.

Dator, James Allen. 1969. *Soka Gakkai: Builders of the Third Civilization, American and Japanese Members.* Seattle: University of Washington Press.

Davis, David Brion. 1960. "Some Themes of Counter-Subversion: An Analysis of Anti-Masonic, Anti-Catholic, and Anti-Mormon Literature." *Mississippi Valley Historical Review* 47:2 (September).

Dewey, Richard. 1899. "Remarks on Mental Contagion and Infection Inherited or Acquired; With Consideration of Some Measures of Prevention of Insanity and Degeneracy." *American Journal of Insanity* 54 (October).

Diagnostic and Statistical Manual of Mental Disorders. 1980. 3rd ed. Washington, D.C.: American Psychiatric Association.

Diem, Andrea Grace. 1995. "Shabdism in North America: The Influence of Radhasoami on Guru Movements." Ph.D. diss., University of California, Santa Barbara.

Douglas, J. Archibald. 1896. "The Chief Lama of Himis on the Alleged 'Unknown Life of Christ.'"*Nineteenth Century* (April).

Dowling, Levi H. 1916. *The Aquarian Gospel of Jesus the Christ: The Philosophic and Practical Basis of the Religion of the Aquarian Age of the World and of the Church Universal, Transcribed from the Book of God's Remembrances, Known as the Akashic Records.* 4th ed. [1911] Reprint, London: L. N. Fowler.

Driscoll, Neil. 1983. "Can't Follow the Way." *Syracuse Herald-Journal,* October 7.

Dubrow-Eichel, Steve K., Linda Dubrow-Eichel, and Roberta Cobrin Eisenberg. 1984. "Mental Health Interventions in Cult Related Cases: Preliminary Investigation of Outcomes." *Cultic Studies Journal* 1:2. (fall/winter).

Durkheim, Emile. 1960. *The Division of Labor in Society.* Trans. George Simpson. Glencoe, Ill.: Free Press.

Earle, Pliny. 1848. "On the Causes of Insanity." *American Journal of Insanity* 4 (January).

Eck Satsang Discourses. n.d. 3rd series, #3. N.p.

Edmunds, R. David. 1983. *The Shawnee Prophet.* Lincoln: University of Nebraska Press.

Edwards, Christopher. 1979. *Crazy for God.* Englewood Cliffs, N.J.: Prentice-Hall.

Eliade, Mircea. 1954. *The Myth of the Eternal Return, or: Cosmos and History.* New York: Bollingen.

———. 1959. *The Sacred and the Profane: The Nature of Religion.* New York: Harcourt Brace.

———. 1961. "History of Religions and a New Humanism." *History of Religions* 1.

———. 1972. *Shamanism.* [Transl. 1951] Princeton, N.J.: Princeton University Press.

Ellis, Bill. 2000. *Raising the Devil: Satanism, New Religions, and the Media.* Lexington: University Press of Kentucky.

Ellul, Jacques. 1975. *The New Demons.* New York: Seabury.

Ellwood, Robert. 1992. "How New Is the New Age?" In *Perspectives on the New Age,* ed. James R. Lewis and J. Gordon Melton. Albany: State University of New York Press.

Evans, Hilary. 1984. *Visions, Apparitions, Alien Visitors.* Wellingborough, U.K.: Aquarian.

———. 1987. *Gods, Spirits, and Cosmic Guardians: A Comparative Study of the Encounter Experience.* Wellingborough, U.K.: Aquarian.

Fabian, Johannes. 1983. *Time and the Other: How Anthropology Makes Its Object.* New York: Columbia University Press.

Festinger, Leon, Henry W. Riecken, and Stanley Schachter. 1956. *When Prophecy Fails.* New York: Harper & Row.

Fields, Rick. 1981. *How the Swans Came to the Lake.* Boulder: Shamballa.

Findhorn Foundation. 1986–1987. *Catalog* (autumn/winter).

Flowers, Stephen E. 1997. *Lords of the Left Hand Path.* Smithville, Tex.: Runa-Raven Press.

Freud, Sigmund. 1938. *The Basic Writings of Sigmund Freud.* Trans. A. A. Brill. New York: Modern Library.

Frothingham, Charles W. 1854. *The Convent's Doom: A Tale of Charleston in 1834.* Boston: Graves & Weston.

Gaines, M. Josephine, Mary Ann Wilson, Kerry J. Redican, and Charles R. Baffi. 1984. "The Effects of Cult Membership on the Health Status of Adults and Children." *Update* 8:3–4.

Gilman, Sander L. 1985. *Difference and Pathology.* Ithaca, N.Y.: Cornell.

Goodspeed, Edgar J. 1931. *Strange New Gospels.* Chicago: University of Chicago Press.

Goran, Morris. 1978. *The Modern Myth: Ancient Astronauts and UFOs.* New York: A. S. Barnes.

Grant, Francis R., Mary Siegrist, George Grebenstchikoff, Ivan Narodny, and Nicholas Roerich. 1926. *Himalaya: A Monograph.* New York: Brentanos.

Grim, John A. 1983. *The Shaman.* Norman: University of Oklahoma Press.

Grob, Gerald N. 1966. *The State and the Mentally Ill: A History of the Worcester State Hospital in Massachusetts, 1830–1920.* Chapel Hill: University of North Carolina Press.

Grönbold, Günter. 1985. *Jesus in Indien: Das Ende einer Legende.* München, Germany: Kösel.

Habermas, Jurgen. 1975. *Legitimation Crisis.* Boston: Beacon Press.

Hale, Edward Everett. 1894. "The Unknown Life of Christ." *North American Review* 159.

Hall, John R. 2000. *Apocalypse Observed: Religious Movements and Violence in North America, Europe, and Japan.* London: Routledge.

Haller, John S., and Robin M. Haller. 1977. *The Physician and Sexuality in Victorian America.* New York: Norton.

"Hamis Knows Not 'Issa': Clear Proof That Notovitch Is a Romancer." 1896. *New York Times,* April 19.

Hammond, Phillip E., and David W. Machacek. 1999. *Soka Gakkai in America: Accommodation and Conversion.* New York: Oxford University Press.

Hart, D. G. 1999. *The University Gets Religion.* Baltimore: Johns Hopkins University Press.

Harvey, Graham. 1995. "Satanism in Britain Today." *Journal of Contemporary Religion* 10:3.

Hashimoto, Hideo, and William McPherson. 1976. "Rise and Decline of Sokagakkai Japan and the United States." *Review of Religious Research* 17:2.

Hassan, Steven. 1988. *Combatting Mind Control*. Rochester, Vt.: Park Street Press.

Heaven's Gate. 1996. "Time to Die for God?—The Imminent 'Holy War'—Which Side Are You On?" Heaven's Gate internet statement, September 24.

Heckenwelder, John. 1876. *History, Manners, and Customs of the Indian Nations Who Once Inhabited Pennsylvania and the Neighbouring States*. In *Memoirs of the Historical Society of Pennsylvania*. Vol. 12. Philadelphia: Historical Society of Pennsylvania.

Herring, Joseph B. 1988. *Kenekuk, the Kickapoo Prophet*. Lawrence: University Press of Kansas.

Hicks, Robert. 1991. *In Pursuit of Satan*. Amherst, N.Y.: Prometheus Books.

Hillman, James. 1979. "A Note on Story." *Parabola* 4:4.

Hoffer, Eric. 1951. *The True Believer: Thoughts on the Nature of Mass Movements*. New York: Harper.

Holmes, Ernest. 1944. *The Science of Mind*. 1926. Reprint, New York: Dodd, Mead, and Company.

Homer, Michael W. 1994. "Freedom of Religion under the First Amendment: Church Universal and Triumphant." In *Church Universal and Triumphant in Scholarly Perspective*, ed. James R. Lewis and J. Gordon Melton, a special issue of *Syzygy: Journal of Alternative Religion and Culture* 4.

Hubbard, L. Ron. 1950. *Dianetics: The Modern Science of Mental Health*. New York: Hermitage House.

Hultkrantz, Ake. 1953. *Conceptions of the Soul among North American Indians*. Stockholm: Ethnographic Museum of Sweden.

———. 1987. *Native Religions of North America*. Prospect Heights, Ill.: Waveland Press.

Hutton, Ronald. 1999. *The Triumph of the Moon*. New York: Oxford University Press.

Huxley, Aldous. 1972. *Island*. New York: Harper & Row.

Hyppolytus. 1877. *Refutation Omnium Haeresium*. Trans. J. H. MacMahon. London: Hamilton & Co.

Ikeda, Daisaku. 1968. "Science and Religion." In *Complete Works of Daisaku Ikeda*. Vol. 1. Tokyo: Seikyo Press.

———. 1977. *Dialogue on Life*. 2 Vols. Tokyo: Nichiren Shoshu International Center.

Introvigne, Massimo. 1998. Interview with John-Roger and John Morton, January 28.

Jefferson, Thomas. 1961. "Letter of Thomas Jefferson to John Adams." April 20, 1812. In *Tecumseh: Fact and Fiction in Early Records*, ed. Carl F. Klinck. Englewood Cliffs, N.J.: Prentice-Hall.

Jenkins, J. Craig. 1983. "Resource Mobilization Theory and the Study of Social Movements." *Annual Review of Sociology* 9.

John-Roger [Hinkins]. 1980. *The Way Out Book*. Los Angeles: Baraka Press.

———. 1994. *The Christ Within and The Disciples of Christ*. Los Angeles: Mandeville.

———. 1998a. Interview, January 28.

———. 1998b. Personal communication to author, July 22.

———. n.d. "Christmas Eve with John-Roger." MSIA Audio Tape #1330.

———. n.d. "The Meditation of the Christ." MSIA Audio Tape #1329.

———. n.d. "What Is the Secret Center?" MSIA Audio Tape #1507.

Judah, J. Stillson. 1967. *The History and Philosophy of the Metaphysical Movements in America*. Philadelphia: Westminster Press.

Juergensmeyer, Mark. 1991. *Radhasoami Reality*. Princeton: Princeton University Press.

Jung, Carl Gustav. 1956. *Symbols of Transformation*. New York: Harper Torchbooks.

———. 1965. *Memories, Dreams, Reflections*. New York: Vintage.

———. 1978. *Flying Saucers: A Modern Myth of Things Seen Flying in the Sky*. Princeton, N.J.: Princeton University Press.

Jwnody. 1996. "Overview of Present Mission." Heaven's Gate internet statement, April.

Kehoe, Alice Beck. 1989. *The Ghost Dance: Ethnohistory and Revitalization*. New York: Holt, Rinehart and Winston.

Kelley, Dean. 1977. "Deprogramming and Religious Liberty." *Civil Liberties Review* 3 (July/August).

Kersten, Holger. 1986. *Jesus Lived in India*. Shaftesbury, Dorset: Longmead. Originally published as *Jesus lebte in Indien*, 1983.

Kilbourne, Brock K. 1983. "The Conway and Siegelman Claims against Religious Cults: An Assessment of Their Data." *Journal for the Scientific Study of Religion* 22:4.

Kim, Byong-Suh. 1979. "Religious Deprogramming and Subjective Reality." *Sociological Analysis* 40:3.

King, Godfre Ray [pseud. of Guy Ballard]. 1935. *Unveiled Mysteries*. Chicago: St. Germain Press.

Klinck, Carl F., ed. 1961. *Tecumseh: Fact and Fiction in Early Records*. Englewood Cliffs, N.J.: Prentice-Hall.

Kopf, David. 1970. "The Brahmo Samaj Intelligentsia and the Bengal Renaissance." In *Transition in South Asia*, ed. Robert I. Crane. Durham: Duke University Program in Comparative Studies in Southern Asia.

———. 1979. *The Brahmo Samaj and the Shaping of the Modern Indian Mind*. Princeton: Princeton University Press.

Kranenborg, Reender. 1997. "Jesus' Stay in India." *Syzygy: Journal of Alternative Religion and Culture* 6:2.

LaBarre, Weston. 1938. *The Peyote Cult*. New Haven, Conn.: Yale University Publications in Anthropology.

Lane, David Christopher. 1994. *Exposing Cults: When the Skeptical Mind Confronts the Mystical*. New York: Garland.

Langone, Michael D. 1993. *Recovery from Cults*. New York: Norton.

Lanternari, Vittorio. 1965. *The Religions of the Oppressed: A Study of Modern Messianic Cults*. New York: Mentor.

Lavan, Spencer. 1977. *Unitarians and India*. Boston: Beacon.

LaVey, Anton Szandor. 1969. *The Satanic Bible*. New York: Avon.

Lesser, Alexander. 1933. *The Pawnee Ghost Dance Hand Game: A Study of Cultural Change*. New York: Columbia University Press.

Levine, Saul. 1984. *Radical Departures: Desperate Detours to Growing Up*. New York: Harcourt, Brace, Jovanovich.

Lewis, James R. 1986. "Reconstructing the 'Cult' Experience: Post-Involvement Attitudes as a Function of Mode of Exit and Post-Involvement Socialization." *Sociological Analysis* 46:2.

———. 1990. "Apostates and the Legitimation of Repression: Some Historical and Empirical Perspectives on the Cult Controversy." *Sociological Analysis* 49:4.

———. 1991. "American Indian Prophets." In *When Prophets Die: The Postcharismatic Fate of New Religious Movements*, ed. Timothy Miller. Albany: SUNY Press.

———. 1992. "Approaches to the Study of the New Age." In *Perspectives on the New Age*, ed. James R. Lewis, and J. Gordon Melton. Albany: State University of New York Press.

———. 1994a. *Encyclopedia of Afterlife Beliefs and Phenomena*. Detroit, Mich.: Gale Research.

———, ed. 1994b. *From the Ashes: Making Sense of Waco*. Lanham, Md.: Rowman & Littlefield.

———. 1995a. *The Gods Have Landed: New Religions from Other Worlds*. Albany: State University of New York Press.

———. 1995b. "Self-Fulfilling Stereotypes, the Anticult Movement, and the Waco Confrontation." In *Armageddon at Waco*, ed. Stuart A. Wright. Chicago: University of Chicago Press.

———. 1997. *Seeking the Light*. Los Angeles: Mandeville Press.

———. 1998a. "Did Jesus Die for Our Karma? Christology and Atonement in a Contemporary Metaphysical Church." *Journal of the Society for the Study of Metaphysical Religion* 4 (fall).

———. 1998b. *The Encyclopedia of Cults, Sects, and New Religions*. Amherst, N.Y.: Prometheus Books.

———. 1999. *Witchcraft Today*. Santa Barbara, Calif.: ABC-Clio.

———. 2000. *UFOs and Popular Culture: An Encyclopedia of Contemporary Myth*. Santa Barbara, Calif.: ABC-Clio.

———. 2001. "Who Serves Satan? A Demographic and Ideological Profile." *Marburg Journal of Religious Studies* 6:2.

———. 2002a. "Diabolical Authority: Anton LaVey, *The Satanic Bible*, and the Satanist Tradition." *Marburg Journal of Religious Studies* 7:1.

———. 2003. *The Encyclopedic Sourcebook of UFO Religions*. Amherst, N.Y.: Prometheus Books.

Lewis, James R., and David G. Bromley. 1987. "The Cult Withdrawal Syndrome: A Case of Misattribution of Cause?" *Journal for the Scientific Study of Religion* 26:4 (December).

Lewis, James R., and Evelyn Dorothy Oliver. 1995. *Angels A to Z.* Detroit: Gale Research.

Lewis, James R., and J. Gordon Melton, eds. 1992. *Perspectives on the New Age.* Albany: State University of New York Press.

———, eds. 1994. *Church Universal and Triumphant in Scholarly Perspective.* Special issue of *Syzygy: Journal of Alternative Religion and Culture* 4.

Long, Charles H. 1963. *Alpha: The Myths of Creation.* New York: George Braziller.

Lowie, Robert H. 1982. *Indians of the Plains.* 1954. Reprint, Lincoln: University of Nebraska Press.

MacCormac, Henry. 1864. "Some Remarks on the Ulster Revival, so named, of 1859." *Journal of Mental Science* 10.

Majumdar, J. K. 1975. *Raja Rammohun Roy and the World.* Calcutta: Sadharan Brahmo Samaj.

———. 1983. *Raja Rammohun Roy and Progressive Movements in India.* 1941. Reprint, Calcutta: Brahmo Mission Press.

Mazzeo, Joseph Anthony. 1978. *Varieties of Interpretation.* Notre Dame: University of Notre Dame Press.

McCutcheon, Russell T. 1997. *Manufacturing Religion: The Discourse on Sui Generis Religion and the Politics of Nostalgia.* New York: Oxford University Press.

———, ed. 1999. *The Insider/Outsider Problem in the Study of Religion: A Reader.* London: Cassell.

———. 2001. *Critics Not Caretakers: Redescribing the Public Study of Religion.* State University of New York Press.

McFarland, H. Neill. 1967. *The Rush Hour of the Gods: A Study of New Religious Movements in Japan.* New York: Macmillan.

McIntoch, W. C. 1866. "On Some of the Varieties of Morbid Impulse and Perverted Instinct." *Journal of Mental Science* 11.

McWilliams, Peter. 1994. *Life 102: What to Do When Your Guru Sues You.* Los Angeles: Prelude Press.

Meighan, Clement W., and Francis A. Riddell. 1972. *The Maru Cult of the Pomo Indians: A California Ghost Dance Survival.* Los Angeles: Southwest Museum.

Melton, J. Gordon. 1989. *The Encyclopedia of American Religions.* 3rd ed. Detroit: Gale Research.

———. 1990. *New Age Encyclopedia.* Detroit: Gale Research.

———. 1992. *Encyclopedic Handbook of Cults in America.* 2nd ed. New York: Garland.

———. 1994. "Church Universal and Triumphant: Its Heritage and Thoughtworld." In *Church Universal and Triumphant in Scholarly Perspective,* ed. James R. Lewis and J. Gordon Melton, a special issue of *Syzygy: Journal of Alternative Religion and Culture* 4.

———. 1995. "The Contactees: A Survey." In *The Gods Have Landed: New Religions from Other Worlds,* James R. Lewis. Albany: State University of New York Press.

Melton, J. Gordon, and Robert L. Moore. 1982. *The Cult Experience: Responding to the New Religious Pluralism.* New York: Pilgrim Press.

Miller, Donald E. 1983. "Deprogramming in Historical Perspective." In *The Brainwashing/Deprogramming Controversy: Sociological, Psychological, Legal, and Historical Perspectives,* ed. David G. Bromley and James T. Richardson. New York: Edwin Mellen.

Monk. Maria. 1977. *Awful Disclosures of the Hotel Dieu Nunnery of Montreal.* 1836. Reprint, New York: Arno.

Montgomery, Ruth. 1979. *Strangers among Us: Enlightened Beings from a World to Come.* New York: Coward, McCann & Geoghegan.

———. 1983. *Threshold to Tomorrow.* New York: G. P. Putnam's Sons.

———. 1985. *Aliens among Us.* New York: Putnam's.

Moody, Edward J. 1974. "Magical Therapy: An Anthropological Investigation of Contemporary Satanism." In *Religious Movements in Contemporary America,* ed. Irving I. Zaretsky and Mark P. Leone. Princeton, N.J.: Princeton University Press.

Moody, Raymond A. 1976. *Life after Life.* New York: Bantam.

———. 1989. *The Light Beyond.* New York: Bantam.

Mooney, James. 1965. *The Ghost-Dance Religion and the Sioux Outbreak of 1890*. 1896. Abridged reprint, Chicago: University of Chicago Press.

Morton, John. 1998. Interview, June 9.

Moynihan, Michael, and Didrik Soderlind. 1998. *Lords of Chaos: The Bloody Rise of the Satanic Metal Underground*. Venice, Calif.: Feral House.

Muesse, Mark. 1999. "Religious Studies and 'Heaven's Gate': Making the Strange Familiar and the Familiar Strange." In *The Insider/Outsider Problem in the Study of Religion: A Reader*, ed. Russell T. McCutcheon. London: Cassell.

Müller. F. Max. 1894. "The Alleged Sojourn of Christ in India." *Nineteenth Century* (October).

Naylor, Christina. 1991. "Nichiren, Imperialism, and the Peace Movement." *Japanese Journal of Religious Studies* 18:1.

Necchi, Joe. 2000. "The Xloptuny Curse." http://www.churchofsatan.org/xloptuny.html.

Neihardt, John G. 1972. *Black Elk Speaks*. Lincoln: University of Nebraska Press.

Nemo. n.d. "Recognizing Pseudo-Satanism." http://www.churchofsatan.com/home.html.

———. n.d. "Satanism and Objectivism." http://www.churchofsatan.com/Pages/SatObj.html.

———. n.d. "Satanism Needs an Enema!" http://www.churchofsatan.com/home.html.

Newton, Michael. 1993. *Raising Hell: An Encyclopedia of Devil Worship and Satanic Crime*. New York: Avon Books.

Notovitch, Nicolas. 1907. *The Unknown Life of Jesus Christ*. Trans. Virchand R. Gandhi. Chicago: Progressive Thinker Publishing House. Originally Published as *La vie inconnue du Jesus Christ*, 1894.

O'Gorman, Edith. [1881.] *Convent Life Unveiled*. [1871.] Reprint, London: Lile & Fawcett.

Olson, Roger E. 1995. "ECKANKAR: From Ancient Science of Soul Travel to New Age Religion." In *America's Alternative Religions*, ed. Timothy Miller. Albany: State University of New York Press.

Otto, Rudolf. 1992. *The Idea of the Holy*. 2nd ed. 1950. Reprint, London: Oxford University Press.

Overholt, Thomas W. 1974. "The Ghost Dance of 1890 and the Nature of the Prophetic Process." *Ethnohistory* 21.

Paelian, Garabed. 1974. *Nicholas Roerich*. Agoura, Calif.: Aquarian Education Group.

Pagels, Elaine. 1989. *The Gnostic Gospels*. New York: Vintage.

Parekh, Manilal C. 1927. *Rajarshi Ram Mohun Roy*. Rajkot, Kathiawad, India: Oriental Christ House.

Patrick, Ted, and Tom Dulack. 1977. *Let Our Children Go!* New York: Ballantine.

Perfect, William. 1976. *Annals of Insanity, Comprising a Selection of Curious and Interesting Cases in the Different Species of Lunacy, Melancholy, or Madness, with the Modes of Practice in the Medical and Moral Treatment, as Adopted in the Cure of Each*. 1798. Facsimile reprint, New York: Arno Press.

Perkins, Rodney, and Forrest Jackson. 1997. *Cosmic Suicide: The Tragedy and Transcendence of Heaven's Gate*. Dallas, Tex.: Pentaradial Press.

Petersen, Jesper Aagard. 2002. "Binary Satanism: Being Dark and Secretive in a Prismatic Digital World." Unpublished paper.

Peterson, Scott. 1990. *Native American Prophecies*. New York: Paragon House.

Pfeifer, Jeffrey E. 1992. "The Psychological Framing of Cults: Schematic Representations and Cult Evaluations." *Journal of Applied Social Psychology* 22:7.

Prophet, Elizabeth Clare. 1984. *The Lost Years of Jesus: On the Discoveries of Notovitch, Abhedananda, Roerich, and Caspari*. Livingston, Mont.: Summit University Press.

Rael (Claude Vorilhon). 1975. *"Real" Space Aliens Took Me to Their Planet*. Waduz, Lichtenstein: Face.

———. 1986. *Let's Welcome Our Fathers from Space: They Created Humanity in Their Laboratories*. Tokyo: AOM Corporation.

———. 1998. *The True Face of God*. Geneva, Switzerland: Raelian Religion.

Rand, Ayn. 1957. *Atlas Shrugged*. New York: Random House.

Raschke, Carl A. 1990. *Painted Black*. San Francisco: Harper San Francisco.

Redbeard, Ragnar. 1910. *Might Is Right; or, The Survival of the Fittest*. 5th ed. 1896. Reprint, London: W. J. Robbins.

Reed, Rebecca Theresa. 1835. *Six Months in a Convent*. Boston: Russel, Odiorne & Metcalf.
"Religious Insanity." 1876. *American Journal of Insanity* 33 (July).
Richardson, James, Joel Best, and David G. Bromley. 1991. *The Satanism Scare*. New York: Aldine de Gruyter.
Ricoeur, Paul. 1981. "The Narrative Function." In *Hermeneutics and the Human Sciences*, ed. and trans. John B. Thomspon. Cambridge: Cambridge University Press.
Roerich, Nicholas. 1929a. *Altai-Himalaya: A Travel Diary*. New York: Frederick A. Stokes Co.
———. 1929b. *Heart of Asia*. New York: Roerich Museum Press.
Ross, Catherine, and Michael D. Langone. 1988. *Cults: What Parents Should Know*. Weston, Mass.: American Family Foundation.
Rothenberg, Paula. 1988. "The Prison of Race and Gender: Stereotypes, Ideology, Language, and Social Control." In *Racism and Sexism*, by Paula Rothenberg. New York: St. Martins.
Rothman, David J. 1971. *The Discovery of the Asylum*. Boston: Little, Brown & Co.
Said, Edward W. 1979. *Orientalism*. New York: Vintage.
Saliba, John A. 1998. Interview with John-Roger and John Morton, June 9.
———. 2000. "The Aetherius Society." In *UFOs and Popular Culture: An Encyclopedia of Contemporary Myth*, James R. Lewis. Santa Barbara, Calif.: ABC-Clio.
"Satanic Bunco Sheet." http://www.churchofsatan.com/home.html.
Schreck, Zeena. 2002. Email communication to author, August 25.
Schreck, Zeena, and Nikolas Schreck. 1998. "Anton LaVey: Legend and Reality." http://www.churchofsatan.org/aslv.html.
Schultz, Chuck. 1994. "Neighbors Vow War over Peace Retreat." *Santa Barbara News-Press*, December 27.
Schutz, Noel William, Jr. 1975. "The Study of Shawnee Myth in an Ethnographic and Ethnohistorical Perspective." Diss., Indiana University.
Sentes, Bryan, and Susan Palmer. 2000. "Presumed Immanent: The Raelians, UFO Religions, and the Postmodern Condition." *Novo Religio* 4:1 (October).
Sharpe, Eric J. 1986. *Comparative Religion: A History*. 2nd ed. La Salle, Ill.: Open Court.
Shivani, Sister (Mary LePage). 1947. *An Apostle of Monism: An Authentic Account of the Activities of Swami Abhedananda in America*. Calcutta, India: Ramakrishna Vedanta Math.
Shupe, Anson D., and David G. Bromley. 1980. *The New Vigilantes: Deprogrammers, Anti-Cultists, and the New Religions*. Beverly Hills, Calif.: Sage.
Simmons, J. L. 1990. *The Emerging New Age*. Santa Fe, N.M.: Bear and Co.
Singer, Margaret Thaler. 1979. "Coming out of the Cults." *Psychology Today* 12.
Singh, Iqbal. 1983. *Rammohun Roy*. 2nd ed. 1958. Reprint, Bombay: Asia Publishing House.
Singh, Kirpal. 1971. *The Crown of Life: A Study in Yoga*. Delhi: Ruhani Satsang.
Sipchen, Bob. 1995. "The Guru and the Gadfly." *Playboy Magazine* (March).
Sipchen, Bob, and David Johnston. 1988. "John-Roger" (Part I) and "Negativity Shakes the Movement" (Part II). *Los Angeles Times*, August 14 and 15.
Sitchin, Zecharia. 1976. *The Twelfth Planet*. New York: Avon.
———. 1995. *Divine Encounters: A Guide to Visions, Angels, and Other Emissaries*. New York: Avon.
Slotkin, Richard. 1973. *Regeneration through Violence: The Mythology of the American Frontier, 1600–1860*. Middletown, Conn.: Wesleyan.
Smith, George C. 1999. "The Hidden Source of the Satanic Philosophy" (Appendix 11). In *The Church of Satan*, by Michael A. Aquino. 4th ed. Self-published. Originally published in *The Scroll of Set*, June 1987.
Snyder, Mark. 1988. "Self-Fulfilling Stereotypes." In *Racism and Sexism*, Paula Rothenberg. New York: St. Martins.
Solomon, Ted J. 1980. "Soka Gakkai on the Alleged Compatibility between Nichiren Buddhism and Modern Science." *Japanese Journal of Religious Studies* 7:1.
Solomon, Trudy. 1981. "Integrating the 'Moonie' Experience: A Survey of Ex-Members of the Unification Church." In *In Gods We Trust*, ed. Thomas Robbins and Dick Anthony. New Brunswick: Transaction.
Soul Transcendence. 1995. Los Angeles: Peace Theological Seminary & College of Philosophy.

Sowards, Bruce A., Michael J. Walser, and Rick H. Hoyle. 1994. "Personality and Intelligence Measurement of the Church Universal and Triumphant." In *Church Universal and Triumphant in Scholarly Perspective,* ed. James R. Lewis and J. Gordon Melton, a special issue of *Syzygy: Journal of Alternative Religion and Culture* 4.

Spangler, David. 1977. "The Role of the Esoteric in Planetary Culture." In *Earth's Answer: Explorations of Planetary Culture at the Lindisfarne Conferences,* ed. Michael Katz, William P. Marsh, and Gail Gordon Thompson. New York: Harper & Row.

Spier, Leslie. 1935. *The Prophet Dance and Its Derivatives: The Source of the Ghost Dance.* General Series in Anthropology 1. Menasha, Wis.: George Banta Pub.

Stark, Rodney, and William Sims Bainbridge. 1979. "Of Churches, Sects, and Cults." *Journal for the Scientific Study of Religion* 18.

Steiger, Brad. 1968. *In My Soul I Am Free: The Incredible Paul Twitchell Story.* New York, Lancer Books.

Stevens, Anthony, and John Price. 2000. *Prophets, Cults, and Madness.* London: Duckworth.

Sweeney, John Myles, Jr. 1992. "Declaration of John Myles Sweeney, Jr." Maricopa County, Arizona: Affidavit, March 17.

Sweetser, William. 1850. *Mental Hygiene; or, An Examination of the Intellect and Passions.* New York: George P. Putnam.

Tanner, Adrian. 1979. *Bringing Home Animals.* New York: St. Martin's Press.

Terry, Robert J., and Catherine Manegold. 1984. "Krishna Complex Bombed." *The Philadelphia Inquirer,* June 18.

Thomas, Evan. 1997. "The Next Level." *Newsweek Magazine,* April 7.

Thompson, Keith. 1991. *Angels and Aliens: UFOs and the Mythic Imagination.* Reading, Mass.: Addison-Wesley.

Trafzer, Clifford E., and Marery Ann Beach. 1985. "Smohalla, the Washani, and Religion as a Factor in Northwestern Indian History." *American Indian Quarterly* 9.

Trafzer, Clifford E., ed. 1986. *American Indian Prophets.* Newcastle, Calif.: Sierra Oaks.

Trull, D. 1998. "Fortean Slips: Death of a Devil's Advocate." *SF Weekly.*

U.S. Department of Health, Education, and Welfare. 1979. *The Belmont Report: Ethical Principles and Guidelines for the Protection of Human Subjects of Research.* Produced by the National Commission for the Protection of Human Subjects of Biomedical and Behavioral Research. Washington, D.C.: Government Printing Office. April 18. http://ohrp.osophs.dhhs.gov/hmansubjects/guidance/belmont.htm.

Vallee, Jacques. 1979. *Messengers of Deception.* Berkeley, Calif: And/Or Press.

van der Leeuw, Gerardus. 1967. *Religion in Essence and Manifestation I and II.* Glouchester, Mass.: Peter Smith.

Voegelin, C. F., and John Yegerlehner. 1957. "Toward a Definition of Formal Style, with Examples from Shawnee." In *Studies in Folklore,* ed. W. E. Richmond. Bloomington: University of Indiana.

Voltaire. 1965. *The Philosophy of History.* Trans. Thomas Kierman. New York: Philosophical Library.

von Däniken, Erich. 1969. *Chariots of the Gods? Unsolved Mysteries of the Past.* New York: Berkley Publishing.

Wach, Joachim. 1944. *Sociology of Religion.* Chicago: University of Chicago Press.

———. 1958. *The Comparative Study of Religions.* New York: Columbia University Press.

Walker, Deward E. 1969. "New Light on the Prophet Dance Controversy." *Ethnohistory* 16.

Wallace, Anthony F. C. 1956. "Revitalization Movements." *American Anthropologist* 58.

———. 1966. *Religion: An Anthropological View.* New York: Random House.

———. 1972. *The Death and Rebirth of the Seneca.* New York: Vintage.

Walls, Andrew. 1987. "Primal Religious Traditions in Today's World." In *Religion in Today's World: The Religious Situation of the World from 1945 to the Present Day,* ed. Frank Whaling. Edinburgh: T & T Clark.

Ward, Maria. 1855. *Female Life among the Mormons.* New York: J. C. Derby.

Weber, Max. 1962. *Basic Concepts in Sociology.* Trans. H. P. Secher. New York: Philosophical Library.

———. 1968. *Economy and Society: An Outline of Interpretive Sociology.* Ed. Guenther Roth and Clau Wittich. Trans. Ephraim Fischoff et al. New York: Bedminster Press.

Wessinger, Catherine. 2000. *How the Millennium Comes Violently: From Jonestown to Heaven's Gate.* New York: Seven Bridges.

Whaling, Frank. 1983. *Contemporary Approaches to the Study of Religion.* Vol. 1. Berlin: Mouton.
Whitney, Louise Goddard. 1969. *The Burning of the Convent.* 1877. Reprint, New York: Arno Press.
Wiebe, Donald. 1999. *The Politics of Religious Studies.* New York: St. Martins Press.
Wiggins, James B. 1975. "Within and Without Stories." In *Religion as Story,* ed. James B. Wiggins. New York: Harper & Row.
Wilbur, Earl Morse. 1952. *A History of Unitarianism.* Vol. 2. Cambridge: Harvard University Press.
Williams, George Huntson. 1967. "The Attitudes of Liberals in New England toward Non-Christian Religions, 1784–1885." *Crane Review* 9 (winter).
Wilson, Bryan, and Karel Dobbelaere. 1994. *A Time to Chant: The Soka Gakkai Buddhists in Britain.* Oxford: Clarendon Press.
Wolfe, Burton H. 1974. *The Devil's Avenger: A Biography of Anton Szandor LaVey.* New York: Pyramid Books.
Workman, Joseph. 1869. "Insanity of the Religious-Emotional Type, and Its Occasional Physical Relations." *American Journal of Insanity* 24 (July).
Wright, Conrad. 1955. *The Beginnings of Unitarianism in America.* Boston: Starr King Press.
Wright, Lawrence. 1991. "Sympathy for the Devil." *Rolling Stone,* September 5.
———. 1993. *Saints and Sinners.* New York: Vintage.
Wright, Stuart A. 1983. *A Sociological Study of Defection from Controversial New Religious Movements.* Ann Arbor, Mich.: University Microfilms International.
———. 1984. "Post-involvement Attitudes of Voluntary Defectors from Controversial New Religious Movements." *Journal for the Scientific Study of Religions* 23:2.

Index

Abhedananda (Swami), 76, 82, 83, 84, 88

Abington Township School District v. Schempp (1963), 30

Adam, William, 148, 149

Adamski, George, 98

Advaita Vedanta philosophy, 77

Aetherius Society, 97, 127

Ahmad, Mirza Ghulam, 78

Alcohol use, 33, 55, 60, 64

Alfred, Randall H., 115

Algonquin, 62

Aliens among Us (Montgomery), 131

Altai-Himalaya (Roerich), 84–85

American Academy of Religion, 31

American Council of Learned Societies, 31

American Family Foundation, 162

Ancient astronauts, 132–134

Andre, Judith, 202

Andrews, Lynn, 32

Anthony, Dick, 187

Anti-Catholic narratives, 18, 156–160

Anti-cultists, 1, 4, 155; in "anti-cult cult," 167–168; atrocity tales and, 18, 155–174; attention to post-member-ship syndrome, 187; biased research by, 162, 163; blurring of distinctions among groups by, 168, 169; cult wars and, 19; delegitimation strategies, 19, 160–174, 198–213; deprogramming and, 200–201; dismissal of scholarly research by, 160–161; former cult members as, 160; government inter-vention and, 159, 160; parents as, 162, 186; reliance on pseudo-scientific theories, 159; secular, 216; use of negative stereotypes by, 199; use of reclassification of movements as delegitimization, 198–213

Anti-Mormon narratives, 18, 156–160

Apostasy, 162, 169, 170, 193

Apostate tales, 156–160

Applewhite, Marshall Herff, 123, 124, *124*, 125, 127–129, 130, 132, 133, 134, 138

Aquarian Gospel of Jesus Christ, The (Dowling), 77, 84, 85, 86

Aquino, Michael, 111, 112, 113, 114, 117, 121

Arapaho, 52, 69

Arnold, Kenneth, 97, 98

Arnold, Thomas, 181, 183

Ascended Masters, 3, 7

Ashtar Command, 127

Assassination, 130

Astral projection, 34

Atlas Shrugged (Rand), 114, 115

Madison, James, 131
Magic, 225, 241, 242
Maharaji, Guru, 37
Maharaj Ji, Guru, 168
Main Poc, 55
Majumdar, J.K., 148, 149, 150
Makiguchi, Tsunesaburo, 218
Making of a Moonie, The (Barker), 161
Mandalas, 97, 127
Manson, Marilyn, 240
Maru Cult, 70
Masih Hindustan Mein (Ahmad), 78
Master of Life, 57, 58, 61
Matriarchy, 27
Mayer, Peter, 112
Mazeway stress, 53
Mazzeo, Joseph A., 145
McCutcheon, Russell T., 26, 247*n1*,
    248*n1*
McFarland, H. Neill, 224, 225
McIntoch, W.C., 181
McWilliams, Peter, 208, 210, 211
Media: anti-cult activities and, 162; irre-
    sponsible reporting by, 162; market
    forces and, 210, 211; negative cover-
    age by, 4, 15; sensation-driven, 210,
    211
Meditation, 88, 137; sound current, 34,
    37, 38
Mediumship, 94
Meighan, Clement W., 70
Melton, J. Gordon, 8, 98, 186, 199, 215
Meng-ste, 85
Mesmerism, 158
Messengers of the Elohim, 100
Messiah Letter, 56
Metaphysical tradition, 35, 36, 106; an-
    cient astronauts and, 132–134; Christ
    in, 36; learning experiences and grad-
    uation, 134–138; mind investigation
    in, 95; role of scripture in, 43–45
Miami, 61
Might is Right (Desmond), 112, 113
Miller, Donald E., 203
Mind control, 4, 125, 158, 159, 215
Minorities, 168, 169, 186; seen as de-
    viant, 202
Miracles, 76, 148
Mistassini Cree, 52
Mohammed, 28
Mohawk, 65
Monk, Maria, 156, 157, 169
Montgomery, Ruth, 131, 134
Moody, Raymond, 139

Mooney, James, 49, 56, 69
Mormonism, 157–159
Morton, John, 34, *34*, 46
Moses, 131
Movement for Spiritual Inner Aware-
    ness, 16, 17, 19, 33–35, 199; cosmol-
    ogy of, 37; departure from tradition
    by, 44–45; emphasis on Christ in, 37;
    increasing "appeal" of, 40; initiations
    in, 34, *34*; legitimacy of, 45; levels of
    involvement in, 34, *34*; lineage of
    Christ in, 42; metaphysical subculture
    and, 35–38; role of scripture in,
    43–45; soul travel and, 34, 43, 44; use
    of stereotyping against, 207–213
Muhammad, 131
Müller, Max, 76, 83
Myths, 45; creation, 58; cultural, 53;
    earth-diver variety, 58; Great Serpent
    in, 59, 61, 62, 63; historical narratives
    as, 145; migration, 58–59; Native
    American, 58; of space aliens, 99; tra-
    ditional, 53; water symbolism in, 58

Nanak, Guru, 28
National Association of Biblical Instruc-
    tors, 31
National Spiritualist Association of
    Churches, 95
Native American Church, 70
Native American prophet religions, 17,
    47–72; adaptive, 56, 60, 64–67; com-
    munity ceremonials in, 55; conquest
    situation and, 54–57; destruction of
    Euro-Americans and, 67, 68; as
    ephemeral phenomena, 70; as flexible
    tradition, 54; hostile, 56; legitimating
    new visions in, 51–54; messianic
    movements, 70; near-death experi-
    ences in, 47, 48, 49; new cosmology
    of revelations, 53–54; persistence of,
    71; prophetic visions in, 51–52;
    prophets and, 48–51; religious visions
    in, 55; shamans and, 48–51; survival
    of, 57
Native Americans: assimilation and,
    54–55; Euro-American conquest of,
    54–57; lifestyle adjustment by, 56;
    messianic movements of, 56; mil-
    lenarian expectancy among, 70; pan-
    American Indian religious movement
    and, 57–63; post-conquest life of, 55;
    rejection of Euro-American culture,
    56, 57–63; religious alliances by, 58

ABOUT THE AUTHOR

James R. Lewis teaches religious studies at the University of Wisconsin, Stevens Point. In the new religions field, he has edited more than a half-dozen scholarly anthologies, authored a major reference book, *The Encyclopedia of Cults, Sects, and New Religions,* a textbook, *Odd Gods: New Religions and the Cult Controversy,* and a forthcoming overview of new religion scholarship, *The Oxford Handbook of New Religious Movements.* His book *Cults in America: A Reference Handbook* received Choice's Outstanding Academic Title Award in 1999.